Comrades and Sisters

Previous publications by the same author:

The Feminist Movement in Germany, 1894–1933 (1976, repr. 1978)

The Feminists (1977, repr. 1979, 1984, Spanish and Swedish eds. 1980)

Sozialdemokratie und Frauenemanzipation im deutschen Kaiserreich (1979)

Edited Books:

Society and Politics in Wilhelmine Germany (1978, repr. 1980, Japanese ed. 1987)

The German Family (1981, with W.R. Lee)

The German Working Class (1982)

The German Peasantry (1986, with W.R. Lee)

The German Unemployed (1987, with Dick Geary)

Comrades and Sisters

Feminism, Socialism and Pacifism in Europe 1870–1945

Richard J. Evans

Professor of European History
University of East Anglia, Norwich

WHEATSHEAF BOOKS · SUSSEX

ST. MARTIN'S PRESS · NEW YORK

First published in Great Britain in 1987 by
WHEATSHEAF BOOKS LTD
A MEMBER OF THE HARVESTER PRESS PUBLISHING GROUP
Publisher: John Spiers
16 Ship Street, Brighton, Sussex
and in the USA by
ST. MARTIN'S PRESS, INC.
175 Fifth Avenue, New York, NY 10010

© Richard J. Evans, 1987

British Library Cataloguing in Publication Data
Evans, Richard J.
    Comrades and sisters: Feminism, socialism
    and pacifism in Europe 1870–1945.
    1. Women and socialism   2. Feminism—
    Europe—History
    3. Socialism—Europe—History
    I. Title
    305.4′2′094   HX546
    ISBN 0-7450-0271-4

Library of Congress Cataloging-in-Publication Data
Evans, Richard J.
    Comrades and sisters.

    Bibliography: p.
    Includes index.
    1. Women's rights—Europe—History—20th century.
    2. Women and socialism—Europe—History—20th century.
    3. Women in politics—Europe—History—20th century.
    4. Pacifism—History—20th century.   I. Title.
    HQ1236.5.E85E82   1987   305.4′2′094   87-9475
    ISBN 0-312-00963-1

Typeset in Times 11/12 point by
Quality Phototypesetting Ltd, Bristol
Printed and bound in Great Britain
by Billings & Sons Limited, Worcester.

For the two Siggas

Contents

Acknowledgements

I am grateful, with the publishers, for permission to reproduce material which first appeared in the following: 'Theory and practice in German Social Democracy 1880–1914: Clara Zetkin and the socialist theory of women's emancipation', *History of Political Thought,* III (1982), pp. 285–304 (Imprint Academic, Exeter); 'Bourgeois feminists and women socialists in Germany 1894–1914: lost opportunity or inevitable conflict?', *Women's Studies International Quarterly*, 3 (1980), pp. 355–76 (Pergamon Press, Oxford); 'German Social Democracy and women's suffrage 1891–1918', *Journal of Contemporary History*, 15 (1980), pp. 533–57 (SAGE Publications Ltd, London); 'Politics and the family; Social Democracy and the working-class family in theory and practice before 1914', in Richard J. Evans and W.R. Lee (eds), *The German Family: Essays on the Social History of the Family in 18th and 19th Century Germany* (Croom Helm, London, 1981), pp. 256–88; 'German women and the triumph of Hitler', *Journal of Modern History* 48 (March, 1976), 1 (University Microfilms Inc./University of Chicago Press).

In putting this book together, I was fortunate enough to have the benefit of the tranquil and collegial atmosphere of the Humanities Research Centre at the Australian National University, Canberra, where I held a Visiting Fellowship from April to June 1986, and I am very glad of the opportunity to thank the Centre, its Director Ian Donaldson, its Deputy Director Graeme Clarke, my fellow Fellows and the Centre's calm and efficient staff for making the task of editing and writing such a pleasant one. I have been helped greatly by the

Acknowledgements

discussion of some of my ideas at a 'Work in Progress' seminar held at the Centre during its 'Feminism and the Humanities' year, and I was also fortunate enough to be able to present some of the chapters as papers or lectures in New Zealand, at the Universities of Auckland, Canterbury and Otago, at Massey University and Victoria University, Wellington, and in Australia at the Universities of Sydney, Queensland, New England, New South Wales, Tasmania, Melbourne and Adelaide, at Griffith University, Deakin University, La Trobe University, Flinders University, the Australian National University and the Conference of European Historians held in Canberra in May 1986. I am grateful to all the audiences, and especially the feminists in them, for helping to clarify my ideas and forcing me to think again on a number of issues. A special word of thanks is due to the British Council and the Goethe Institute in New Zealand for helping to fund my visit, and my gratitude also goes to the friends and colleagues who did so much to make the experience of academic tourism in the Antipodes such a pleasant one.

At the University of East Anglia, Norwich I would like to thank Elvi Dobie for typing the final draft; and I owe a great deal, probably more than they realize, to the students who have taken part in my class on feminist movements in modern Europe, which I have been teaching at UEA since 1984. The ideas and criticisms they have put forward, in essays and papers and in class discussion, have shaped this book in many ways, as much by persuading me that some ideas would not work as by encouraging me to believe that others would. To all of them my thanks.

List of Abbreviations

ABDF	Archiv des Bundes Deutscher Frauenvereine (Berlin–Dahlem)
BDF	Bund Deutscher Frauenvereine (Federation of German Women's Associations)
BGB	Bürgerliches Gesetzbuch (German Civil Law Code, 1900)
DDP	Deutsche Demokratische Partei (German Democratic Party)
DHV	Deutschnationaler Handlungsgehilfenverband (German-national Commercial Assistants' Union)
DNVP	Deutschnationale Volkspartei (German-national People's Party)
DVP	Deutsche Volkspartei (German People's Party)
FB	*Die Frauenbewegung*
FES/ASD	Freidrich-Ebert-Stiftung/Archiv der Sozialen Demokratie
GL	*Die Gleichheit*
GLA	Generallandesarchiv
Hbg	Hamburg
HC	*Hamburgischer Correspondent*
HE	*Hamburger Echo*
HN	*Hamburger Nachrichten*
HStA	*Hauptstaatsarchiv*
IML/ZPA	Institut für Marxismus-Leninismus beim ZK der SED/Zentrales Parteiarchiv (East Berlin)
IISG	Internationaal Instituut voor Sociale Geschiedenis

KPD	Kommunistische Partei Deutschlands (Communist Party of Germany)
LVZ	*Leipziger Volkszeitung*
NL	Nachlass
NPD	Nationaldemokratische Partei Deutschlands (National-Democratic Party of Germany)
NSDAP	Nationalsozialistische Deutsche Arbeiterpartei (National Socialist German Workers' Party)
PP	Politische Polizei
PTP	Parteitagsprotokoll der Sozialdemokratischen Partei Deutschlands
SMH	*Sozialistische Monatshefte*
SPD	Sozialdemokratische Partei Deutschlands (Social Democratic Party of Germany)
StA	Staatsarchiv
UB	Universitätsbibliothek
USPD	Unabhängige Sozialdemokratische Partei Deutschlands (Independent Social Democratic Party of Germany)
VW	*Vorwärts*

Introduction

I

This is a book about socialism, feminism and pacifism in late nineteenth- and early twentieth-century Europe, and about the complex and changing relationships between them. It looks at socialists who believed in women's emancipation, at feminists who fought for peace, at pacifists who considered female suffrage was the quickest way to bring war to an end: but it also sets these people against the wider background of the movements to which they belonged and the times in which they lived. The book takes the form of a series of linked essays. Most of these were written over the last decade or so in connection with a research project on women's emancipation movements in modern Germany, and were published in journals (some of them rather difficult to obtain) or collections of articles (now mostly out of print), though chapter 5 is new. Some of the chapters have been reduced and restructured in order to make the argument clearer, and comparative material added to set the German research in a broader context. A decided bias towards Germany remains, but it is justified by the numerical strength of German socialism and feminism, and particularly of the ideological hegemony of the Germans in the Socialist Women's International.

Women in late nineteenth- and early twentieth-century Europe were oppressed and discriminated against to a degree that is sometimes difficult to recall today. In most countries women were not able to vote before 1918, and in some—like France—not until the end of the Second World War. In large

1

parts of Central Europe it was illegal until shortly before the outbreak of the First World War for women to belong to political parties or form their own political organizations. Women were barred from most professions, such as (for example) the law, and in many countries they were not allowed to study at university until the turn of the century or shortly before. Women's right to sign contracts and act as persons legally independent of their husbands or fathers was severely circumscribed in most European law codes. Divorce was generally easier for men to obtain than for women, and the dice were loaded in favour of the man when it came to deciding custody of the children and control of the property. Married women were universally expected to do the housework and look after the children, even if they went out to work, as increasing numbers of them did in the burgeoning, industrializing economies of the period. The double standard of morality, in which women were expected to be chaste and faithful while men were allowed a degree of sexual freedom before marriage and even, as the extent of prostitution in the cities of the time indicates, during it, was generally accepted without question.[1]

The formality of social life, in which clothing, deportment, language, gestures were all regulated by rigid convention, assigned women their place in polite society, while the lives of the vastly greater number of women who eked out their existence in the proletarian quarters of the great industrial centres was ruled by poverty, toil and the need to maintain a life of strict frugality on the margins of existence. Women who worked for wages were assumed to be doing so for housekeeping money, an income secondary to that of the male head of the household, even if there was none. It was scarcely surprising that widows made up the bulk of the pauper population in many European cities at this time. Younger women generally worked in domestic service or factories until they married; after that, their working life was dominated by intermittent, casual, part-time employment in cleaning, washing, sewing and other forms of poorly-paid manual labour. The vast expansion of the service sector which so dominates women's work today was only just beginning at the turn of the century, and typists, secretaries, department store

assistants and the like were still few and far between. The birth
rate was still high, especially among the working classes, in
most European countries, and families of four, five or six
children were far from uncommon. Infant and perinatal
mortality was still widespread, though like the birth rate it too
was beginning to decline by 1900.[2]

Inequality, deprivation of rights and lack of personal
freedom were thus the lot of the vast majority of European
women around the turn of the century. The assumption of
women's inferiority to men was much more commonly and
openly expressed than it is today. Discrimination against
women was overt and widely accepted. By 1900, however,
increasing numbers of women were coming to challenge this
situation and seek a way out of it. All over Europe, from Tsarist
Russia and the Habsburg Monarchy through the Kaiser's
Germany to the Third Republic in France, women were
organizing in the struggle for equal rights and emancipation.
Some of them concentrated on single issues, like the right to
vote, the reform of the civil law or the improvement of
women's education. Others organized on a more general basis.
Many devoted their time to tireless propaganda on behalf of
their cause, to advancing the argument for women's
emancipation in novels, plays, newspaper articles, tracts,
pamphlets, books and speeches. The debate on women's
emancipation was an accepted, familiar feature of European
public life long before the First World War. On this, as on
other subjects, opinions were deeply divided. Most men
rejected the notion of female equality outright; some paid at
least lip-service to some aspects of it; a few supported it with
real conviction. Some women thought that formal, legal
equality was the key to emancipation; others argued that social
and economic factors lay at the root of their oppression.[3]

Of all the divisions within the camp of the many women (and
the few men) who actively supported the idea of women's
liberation, the deepest, the most obvious and the most long-
lasting was the division between feminists and socialists,
between those who argued that the way forward lay through
independent action by women to secure basic reforms affecting
all women, and those who argued that this would not affect
fundamental structures of oppression, that the way forward

lay through the overthrow of the capitalist system in a socialist revolution. Both feminist and socialist ideologies before the First World War, and even in the 1920s, differed in many ways from their counterparts today. Feminists were more concerned with formal, legal aspects of equality: socialists were more strongly Marxist in orientation, and the socialist movement was more firmly rooted in the industrial working class. Yet the debate over the relative merits of these two concepts of women's liberation has continued to the present day, as feminists deride the socialist revolutions of 1917 and after as irrelevant to women's cause, while socialists point out that the granting of female suffrage and other rights so dear to the feminists of the past has brought little improvement in the lives of the vast majority of women. In recent years the growth of women's history has led to an increasing interest in the historical dimensions of these controversies, and a great deal of important work has been published.[4] Inevitably, however, much of it has been polemical in character, as feminists and socialists of various shades of opinion have sought to obtain justification in the past for their own stance in the present.[5] Reading such polemics, in various political journals over the last few years, led to the conviction that it would be useful to bring together the essays printed below, since they have been written, often, from a different angle, and with different questions in mind.

II

The essays in this book concentrate on women's organizations in the public sphere. Such a concentration, some have objected, betrays a 'male-orientated approach' to women in the past. A feminist approach, it is suggested, would see the history of feminism instead in its relation to women's experience. There is no doubt that the essays in this book concentrate on women in political organizations and social movements. They focus on women as they entered the public sphere, and admittedly do little to render them visible for the greater part of their lives, when they remained outside it. Yet this concentration on 'women in public' is a feature of other historical work too. In the context of the 1970s, when these essays were written, their approach involved a widened notion of what the public sphere actually was: they formed part of a new wave of writing on pressure-groups, nationalist movements, voluntary associations, labour organizations and the like, which was challenging the previous historical concentration on foreign policy, formal ideology and high politics that had remained dominant, above all in Germany, for so long. Certainly no-one had previously paid much attention to women's involvement in the public sphere. Moreover, at that time no-one could surely deny that the history of feminist movements had been neglected and needed to be studied. Many feminist historians also researched and wrote on women in the public sphere, and most of them would probably angrily deny having adopted a 'male-oriented' approach.[6] And nineteenth-century feminism was in fact mainly (though not exclusively) about women's struggle to gain the right to enter the public sphere, if we define it to include the professions, universities and so on, as well as political life.[7] It is only because this struggle has largely been won—perhaps also in part because the gains it has brought have proved disappointing—that present-day feminism has come to concentrate on less immediately obvious, less formal modes of oppression.

Given the millions of women who were involved in this struggle, and whose efforts were so ignored until recently, it is surely reasonable to suggest that this subject is one worth studying in its own right. Naturally, the study of organized feminism, of the entry of women into the male-dominated public sphere, has its limitations; it deals with only one aspect of women's experience in the past, and other aspects of that experience urgently need to be studied. Nor is the approach represented in these essays the only one possible: of course women's organizations can be studied equally fruitfully by relating their concerns primarily to the lives of women who took part in them. Nevertheless, the work collected in the present volume is justifiable not only in its own terms, but also—as a number of the essays explicitly point out—as a corrective to other approaches which, like all historical work, have limitations and problems of their own.

Studying women's involvement in the public sphere, it has further been objected, is male-oriented because it imposes on their activities categories and criteria which may be appropriate for 'male' politics but are not appropriate for women. The questions asked in this book, whether socialist women were revolutionary or reformist, for example, or how far women supported the Nazis, are, it has been argued, invalid because they represent an assimilation of women—and feminism—to 'male' political categories. One critic has argued that such questions are the outcome of a 'pre-fabricated understanding of politics which fits the "correct" feminist movement into the SPD (i.e. socialist) pattern and disqualifies all other movements, especially feminist opinion and activities'.[8] But the following chapters are not intended to demonstrate that socialism in an unreconstructed form offers, or has offered in the past, the only road to women's emancipation. This dogma, of course, is still the orthodoxy in Eastern Europe, and it was at the root of much of the literature on European feminism before the feminist revival of recent years. What writing there was on the history of German feminism in the 1960s, for example, certainly tended to argue that only the SPD before 1914 had a correct theory of women's emancipation, that the party's theorist in this area, Clara Zetkin, was right and everyone else was wrong, and that the way ahead for women lay through adherence to revolutionary Marxism, not reformism or revisionism. This was the view put forward by Werner Thönnessen, Jutta Menschik, Gundula Bölke, Gisela Brandt and others, and it was characteristic of the kind of dogmatic and—in retrospect—often unrealistic Marxism current in the student movement of the 1960s. It was based not least on a belief that German feminism before 1914 was reactionary and conservative, a belief fostered by the suppression of the history of radical feminism by moderate feminist historians such as Agnes von Zahn-Harnack in the 1920s.[9]

The following chapters began as attempts to get beyond this crude and unhistorical view. They argue that Clara Zetkin, for example, was far from being the grandmother of orthodox Marxism–Leninism that she is often portrayed as, that the socialist movement's attitude to women's emancipation was complex and contradictory, and that revolutionary Marxists were often less interested in the subject than reformists and revisionists were. Not surprisingly, perhaps, some of these views have run into strong criticism from orthodox Marxist–Leninists in the Communist parties of both East and West.[10] The studies collected in this book, taken together, are intended to provide a more nuanced picture, which shows how difficult it is to categorize the socialist women's movement of the past in simple political terms.

Nevertheless, the conventional political categories of modern European history—socialism, liberalism, radicalism, revisionism and so on—are far from irrelevant to the history of women's liberation movements. Women in politics, whether they belonged to socialist or feminist organizations, did not remain aloof from factional struggles in other movements but aligned themselves willingly with left- or right-wing groups and conservative or radical strands of thought. It was well known that Clara Zetkin stood on the left wing of the German Social Democratic Party, and that up to the First World War her Russian equivalent Alexandra Kollontai belonged to the Mensheviks. Feminists thought it important to join political parties because they were often excluded from them by party statute or even, in some countries, by law. A few feminists, like Madeleine Pelletier in France, joined the party they thought most likely to support the feminist cause, and were only committed to it in so far as it responded to their efforts to persuade it to do so.[11] Most feminists, however, joined political parties out of conviction and stuck with them despite their often inadequate policies on feminist issues. Socialist women were no exception to this rule, faced as they were with the question of whether revolution or reform was the best way to achieve emancipation.

Splits and quarrels within the feminist movements frequently followed splits and quarrels in the political parties with which they were most closely associated. Thus the Danish Women's Associations' Suffrage Federation, founded in 1898, was associated with the moderate Liberal Party in Danish politics in the 1890s, while the breakaway Danish National League for Women's Suffrage, founded two years later in 1900, took a more radical line not only in feminist terms, fighting for full female suffrage, but also more generally, through its close ties with the Reform Liberal Party, the Venstre. Indeed such ties could be personal as well as political. The leaders of the moderate wing of the Hungarian feminist movement, for example, which campaigned for the admission of women to the universities (granted in 1895) and other educational reforms, were Countess Batthyány, Countess Appónyi and Countess Andrássy, all of them married to leading politicians on the more conservative wing of Magyar nationalism. What really mattered were the ideological connections; feminism did not simply exist in a vacuum unrelated to other political and social movements. Not least because it operated primarily in the public sphere, and was concerned above all to secure legislative reforms, it allied itself to male-dominated parties and organizations and shared many of their fundamental beliefs. Thus the Czech feminist movement, which was closely allied to Czech nationalism before 1914, blamed the subjection of Czech women mainly on the policies of the Habsburgs in Vienna, not on Czech men, and even went so far as to demand that Czech be made the fourth official language of the International Woman Suffrage Alliance along with English, French and German, a request that (not surprisingly) the Alliance refused to grant.[12]

Feminist movements never shirked from pronouncing on general political issues in the nineteenth century, any more than they do today. They did not regard war and peace, the secularization of education, the rivalries of ethnic groups, the self-determination of nations, the powers of the police, or the many other issues which they discussed, as merely 'men's politics'. Feminism's demands also had wider political implications. For example, in Prussia where there was a three-class manhood suffrage system based on income levels, feminists had to decide whether they merely wanted the participation of women in this system or whether they wanted a wholesale reform involving equal votes for all adults. In Hungary, extending the property-qualified franchise to women would increase the political power of the Magyar upper class, while universal adult suffrage—the enfranchisement of all women and men on equal terms—would mainly benefit the poorer ethnic groups such as the Romanians. Feminists could not escape such implications of their demands, and it is not surprising that they were often deeply and sometimes bitterly divided by them.[13]

Ideologies of women's emancipation inevitably shared many theoretical positions which applied to other social and political issues (and conversely political theorists from Fourier and Condorcet to Engels and Mill frequently took into consideration the implications of their philosophical stance for the rights of women). The demand for equal rights could be advanced on the basis of liberal individualism—that all human beings, including women, were endowed with fundamentally the same faculties of reason and intelligence, and that legal barriers to the free competition of all individuals against one another for the goods that society had to offer should therefore be torn down. Or it could be advanced on the basis of an essentialist assumption about the nature of the sexes—that women were naturally more humane, more just, more nurturing than men and that the extension of their influence would benefit society as a whole. Or it could be advanced on the basis of a religious argument, that every human soul had the right to work individually towards its own salvation, and that hindrances to this process should be removed. Or it could be advanced on the basis of a socialist position, according to which working-class women—potentially the majority of the female sex in industrialized countries—needed equal rights to help them overcome the exploitation under which they suffered in capitalist society. All these arguments committed those who held them to a whole series of further positions on the organization of human society in general, and political and social reforms in particular, even if they also took them on to a set of propositions about women's place in society which went beyond the conclusions which others had derived from these ideological premises previously.

Parliamentary elections (even under manhood suffrage), party-political conflicts, cabinet policies and other events and processes in the world of politics at large were seldom wholly irrelevant to women and often had the most direct bearing on their lives. For example, anti-clerical French governments of the Third Republic were certainly far from sympathetic to the feminist cause, but in order to strike a blow against the church, which they believed had a dangerously powerful hold over the female population of France, they implemented a number of important reforms which undoubtedly made it easier for women to exercise more control over their own lives.[14] Similarly, the Nazi seizure of power brought with it the victory of militarist and racist policies which, as Gisela Bock has recently shown, affected women in specifically sexist ways even though at first sight they did not have any explicit connection with what were thought of at the time as 'women's issues'.[15]

In European society of the late nineteenth and early twentieth centuries, class was a major determinant of political behaviour, in some ways much more so than it is today, or than it has customarily been in the United States. It is sometimes argued by modern feminists that it is illegitimate to apply the concept of class to women because their position in society is primarily defined by their sex. Particularly strong objections have been raised to the practice of defining a woman's class position according to that of her husband or father.[16] But while definitions of women's place in society to some extent cut across class boundaries, they were in many ways secondary to them in industrializing Europe, and the concept of class remains essential for the study of women's place in the European past. The strength of patriarchal attitudes and mores was far greater before the First World War than it is today, and ensured that women in general did indeed acquire their class position through their fathers or husbands; marriages across class lines were very rare and did little to alter this fundamental fact. This was, after all, a society in which many of the legal rights which women enjoy today were exercised through their fathers or husbands. Class lines were also drawn by income and employment, and this was a society in which already the majority of adult women worked for wages or salaries outside the home, although—and this was an important distinction in itself—the role of women of the upper class and *haute bourgeoisie* was defined precisely by the fact that they did not take any paid employment, indeed were not supposed to 'work' at all, not even in the home, when servants were there to do everything for them.[17] Class was also expressed in terms of language and dialect, accent, manners and deportment, dress and a thousand other distinctions, far sharper than those existing today. Unless we realize the sheer strength and depth of class divisions among women as well as among men in late nineteenth- and early twentieth-century Europe, it is impossible to understand why, as we shall see in chapter 2, socialist women and feminist activists found it so difficult to co-operate with one another.

III

The approach adopted in the following chapters is based on a set of questions about women and politics, about women as they crossed the sexual divide and entered the male-defined public sphere. The questions are important ones, and the approach which these essays represent can be seen as a possible, indeed a necessary complement to other, alternative approaches to women's history. An exclusively 'gender-oriented' approach to the past that ignores women as members of social classes, national or racial groups, religious congregations and so on, can lead to serious consequences not only for understanding the past but also for political action in the present. This is therefore a controversial book, with an argument running through it and binding the different parts together: but it is not an intemperate book; still less it is intended as an anti-feminist book: feminism today comes in many forms, and the arguments put forward here are only directed against a limited number of feminist views, though these are quite widely held.

The following Chapters seek, among other things, to illustrate these arguments by example. Chapter 1 examines the ideas of the leading socialist women theorist of female emancipation in the early twentieth century, Clara Zetkin, and argues that she cannot easily be categorized as an 'orthodox Marxist' or a 'reluctant feminist'. Chapter 2 enquires into the reasons behind the failure of the 'bourgeois' feminist and socialist women's movements to join forces in the struggle for equality and emancipation. Chapter 3 looks at the record of the European left on women's suffrage, and finds it better than that of other parties, but by no means as unblemished as many socialists might perhaps imagine. Chapter 4 discusses changing socialist attitudes to the family, in theory and practice, and touches on the more personal aspects of women's subjection. The last two Chapters move forward in time and broaden the focus once more to include 'bourgeois' feminists as well as socialist women. Chapter 5 takes the First World War as its subject and tries to discover whether feminism and pacifism have always been as closely associated as they seem to be now. Finally, Chapter 6 looks at the legend that 'it was the women's vote that brought Hitler to power', and asks what feminists did to counter the fascist menace.

All these studies attempt to show what can be learned from looking at the history of women and feminism in relation to its general political context, but also, perhaps, how the act of doing so changes our understanding of the context as well. European socialism, it will be seen, was a male-dominated movement based to a large extent on unreflected assumptions about the place of women both in capitalism and in the future socialist society. The notion of 'revolution' appears less comprehensive and all-embracing when it is considered how revolutionaries conceived of the relevance of their creed to women, or rather how they failed to do so. Conversely, 'reformism' looks rather more radical, at least in theory, while a consideration of the appeal of fascist ideology to women forces a reconsideration of its nature and meaning as a sexist creed. The extension of the right to vote, a central issue in European politics in an age dominated by restrictive property-qualified franchises, is usually seen mainly in terms of class, but everywhere in Europe before and during the First World War it also involved the issue of women's suffrage, and the implications of this fact for European political systems were not trivial. This is a book, therefore, that seeks not only to contribute to the study of women's history, but also to influence the writing of European history in a general sense.

NOTES

1. The literature on the general history of European women in this period is now very substantial. For introductory material, with further references,

see Renate Bridenthal and Claudia Koonz (eds), *Becoming Visible: Women in European History* (2nd edn, New York, 1987).
2. For a useful introduction, see Louise Tilly and Joan Scott, *Women, Work and Family* (New York, 1978), on France and England; Rose L. Glickman, *Russian Factory Women: Workplace and Society 1880–1914* (Berkeley, 1984), on Russia; and the second half of John C. Fout (ed.), *German Women in the 19th Century* (New York, 1984), on Germany.
3. For a comprehensive collection of documents with linking commentaries, see Susan Groag Bell and Karen M. Offen (eds), *Women, the Family, and Freedom: The Debate in Documents* (2 vols, Stanford, 1983). There is a general survey (now outdated in some respects) in my book *The Feminists: Women's Emancipation Movements in Europe, America and Australasia 1840–1920* (London, 1977).
4. I have discussed some of this in my article 'The history of European women: a critical survey of recent research', *Journal of Modern History* 52 (December, 1980), pp. 656–75.
5. See for example Gloria Steinem, *Outrageous Acts and Everyday Rebellions* (New York, 1985), pp. 305–26 on women and Nazi Germany, or Tony Cliff, 'Clara Zetkin', *International Socialism* 2 (1981).
6. See for example Jill R. Stephenson, *The Nazi Organisation of Women* (London, 1981), Linda Edmondson, *Feminism in Russia 1900–1917* (London, 1984), Jean H. Quataert, *Reluctant Feminists in German Social Democracy 1880–1917* (Princeton, 1979), and numerous other authors and works discussed or referred to below. See also Richard Stites, *The Women's Liberation Movement in Russia. Feminism, Nihilism and Bolshevism, 1860–1930* (Princeton, 1978); Charles Sowerwine, *Sisters or Citizens? Women and Socialism in France since 1876* (Cambridge, 1982); Charles Sowerwine, *Les femmes et le socialisme: Un siècle d'histoire* (Paris, 1978); James McMillan, *Housewife or Harlot: The Place of Women in French Society 1870–1940* (Brighton, 1981); Paul McHugh, *Prostitution and Victorian Social Reform* (London, 1979).
7. Cf. Patricia Hollis (ed.), *Women in Public. Documents on the Women's Movement in Britain 1850–1900* (London, 1979).
8. Ute Gerhard, 'A hidden and complex heritage: reflections on the history of Germany's women's movements', *Women's Studies International Quarterly*, vol. 5 (1982), 6, pp. 561–7. See also her book, *Verhältnisse und Verhinderungen* (Frankfurt, 1980).
9. Werner Thönnessen, *The Emancipation of Women. The Rise and Decline of the Women's Movement in German Social Democracy 1863–1933* (London, 1973); Jutta Menschik, *Gleichberechtigung oder Emanzipation? Die Frau im Erwerbsleben der Bundesrepublik* (Frankfurt, 1974); Gisela Brandt, Johanna Kootz, Gisela Steppke, *Zur Frauenfrage im Kapitalismus* (Frankfurt, 1973); Gundula Bölke, *Die Wandlung der Frauenemanzipationstheorie von Marx bis zur Rätebewegung* (Hamburg, 1971); and see below, pp. 72–81.
10. Florence Hervé, *Geschichte der deutschen Frauenbewegung* (Frankfurt, 1981); cf. her review of my book *The Feminist Movement in*

Germany 1894–1933 (London, 1976), in *Marxistische Blätter,* 6 (1980), pp. 122–3. This view was shared by the East German critique of the book in *Zeitschrift für Geschichtswissenschaft* (1980).

11. Stites, *op. cit.,* pp. 249–50; Sowerwine, *Sisters or Citizens?* pp. 113–22; and see also below, pp. 38–9.
12. Cf. Evans, *The Feminists* pp. 79, 97–9.
13. See ibid., for a fuller description of these points.
14. Patrick K. Bidelman, *Pariahs Stand Up! The Founding of the Liberal Feminist Movement in France, 1858–1889* (Westport, Conn., 1982); Theodore Zeldin, *France 1848–1945, Vol. I: Ambition, Love and Politics* (Oxford, 1975), Part II.
15. Gisela Bock, 'Racism and sexism in Nazi Germany: motherhood, compulsory sterlization and the state', in Renate Bridenthal, Atina Grossmann and Marion Kaplan (eds), *When Biology Became Destiny: Women in Weimar and Nazi Germany* (New York, 1984), pp. 271–96.
16. e.g. by Gerhard, 'A Hidden and Complex Heritage'.
17. Useful recent studies of women of the middle and upper-middle classes in France and Switzerland include Bonnie G. Smith, *Ladies of Leisure Class. The Bourgeoises of Northern France in the Nineteenth Century* (Princeton, 1981), and Ursi Blosser and Franziska Gerster, *Töchter der guten Gesellschaft. Frauenrolle und Mädchenerziehung im schweizerischen Grossbürgertum um 1900* (Zurich, 1985).

1 An Opposing Woman

I

Clara Zetkin (1857–1933) was the leading socialist theorist and activist in the field of women's emancipation in Europe before the First World War. Her friend and political ally Rosa Luxemburg has subsequently gained more widespread fame, but Luxemburg had little political interest in questions of women's rights or women's place in society; she wrote next to nothing on the subject and carefully avoided the socialist women's movement.[1] Zetkin, by contrast, devoted most of her energy before the First World War to working out a socialist theory of women's emancipation, getting it accepted by socialist men, and building up a socialist women's movement in accordance with the principles she believed in. Zetkin was always an international figure; she never confined her activities to Germany alone. She had close Russian connections, visited Russia frequently, was closely involved in the financial affairs of the Russian socialists, and indeed after the Nazi seizure of power she emigrated to Russia and died there in July 1933.[2] Much earlier in her life, she had lived in exile in Zurich and Paris for several years while the socialist movement was banned in her native Germany. She was a gifted linguist, and translated or interpreted into or out of French, German, Russian and English on a number of occasions.[3] Her first appearance on the political stage was at the founding Congress of the Second Socialist International, held in Paris in 1889; subsequently she became the Secretary of the International's women's section, founded in 1907.

Zetkin's influence extended across the whole of the international socialist movement, even after she returned to Germany in 1890. Not only did she effectively formulate the policy of the Socialist Women's International, but her ideas profoundly influenced socialist theorists of women's emancipation in other countries. Alexandra Kollontai, for example, was deeply indebted to her, and indeed Kollontai's major work, *The Social Bases of the Woman Question,* has been seen largely as an attempt to systematize Zetkin's ideas and adapt them to a Russian context.[4] Zetkin's intellectual dominance over the leading French woman socialist, Louise Saumoneau, has also been attested.[5] Zetkin was not only a socialist theorist and campaigner for women's emancipation on an international scale, she was also during the First World War a leading figure in the socialist movement to bring hostilities to an end. In her personal life she was unconventional, living with the Russian socialist Ossip Zetkin without being married to him, and later marrying an artist eighteen years her junior. Her selected works fill three stout volumes in German, and extracts have been translated into many languages.[6]

Yet curiously, perhaps, Zetkin's reputation has diminished rather than grown since her death. Despite her voluminous writings she never completed a major, book-length statement of her ideas, so that they have to be pieced together from scattered speeches, articles and pamphlets. However unconventional her lifestyle, she did not seek to develop any theory of sexual freedom and emancipation of the sort that has given the life and work of Kollontai such fascination for later generations. Nor did she meet the martyr's death that has lent a posthumous glow to the reputation of Rosa Luxemburg. Most of all however, Zetkin has suffered from her appropriation by orthodox Marxism–Leninism. As a passionate supporter of the Bolshevik Revolution, a friend of Lenin, and a committed communist who stayed in the party throughout the vagaries of the twenties and early thirties, she has been virtually canonized by subsequent historians in the Soviet Union and East Germany, where indeed she is regarded as one of the ancestral figures of the German Democratic Republic. Correspondingly the standard accounts of her life and the standard editions of her works all stress the unwavering orthodoxy of her views and their close adherence to the 'correct' party line, her opposition to reformism, her detestation of 'feminist' deviations from the revolutionary struggle, and so on. In turn, this image has led to contemporary feminists regarding Zetkin in very negative terms, as the one woman who more than any other, perhaps, managed to force the socialist theory and practice of women's emancipation into a rigid, dogmatic ideological straitjacket that left no room for the development of ideas more in tune with the feminist principles of today.[1]

Although she is conventionally portrayed either as a Marxist–Leninist heroine or an anti-feminist villainess, in reality Zetkin was neither. The available selections of her work carefully omit all the numerous resolutions, protests and speeches that marked Zetkin out as a persistently oppositional figure in the communist movement of the 1920s. Nor do the great majority of accounts of her life and work take account of the many complexities and ambivalences of her theoretical position before 1917. Most analyses of her ideas have either treated them as a unified and unchanging corpus of theory, and so have obscured the fact that they changed quite rapidly and in some aspects even quite radically over time, or they have, while recognizing the fact that they did change, failed to relate these changes to their political context, and so have not presented any convincing explanation of the reasons behind them. This is particularly true of a recent debate on Zetkin's ideas in the pages of *International Socialism,* an interesting example of the use—and distortion—of past ideas to justify present politics. Tony Cliff has attempted to argue that Zetkin consistently rejected 'bourgeois feminism' as divisive and diversionary, and that she was uninfluenced by the ideas of her bourgeois contemporaries in the feminist movement. He has used this to argue that women's place is in socialist rather than feminist organizations. His critics have denied the legitimacy of a rigid division between socialism and feminism. While they correctly point out that conditions in Britain in the 1980s are not the same as those obtaining in Germany a century or so ago, they also tend to dismiss some of Zetkin's ideas as 'playing to the gallery' in the male-dominated SPD. In a sense, both sides seem to want to claim Zetkin as a legitimate precursor, though Cliff is less critical of her ideas than are his opponents.[8] This is not the place for a detailed discussion of the arguments on both sides, but it is perhaps relevant to recall that Zetkin's ideas have to be seen in their totality, rather than selectively, and against their historical background, not just ripped out of their context to serve a political end, if they are to be properly appreciated. Finally it is particularly important to realize that her ideas changed over time more or less continuously, making it even more important to take account of the historical context. This chapter hopes to rectify these deficiencies through an analysis of Zetkin's thought against its political background, concentrating particularly on women's work, on marriage and the family, on civil rights for women and on the question of how far women's struggle could be conducted separately from the struggle of the working class as a whole. In order to understand these in their context, however, it is necessary first to begin with a brief account of Zetkin's personal background and early career.

II

Clara Zetkin was born on 5 July 1857 in Wiederau (Saxony), as Clara Eissner.[9] She moved with her father, a local school-teacher, and her mother, an unusually independent woman with strong feminist views, to Leipzig, the then headquarters of the bourgeois liberal feminist movement, in 1872. There in 1873 she entered a teacher-training college for girls *(Lehrerinnenseminar)* run by Auguste Schmidt, a leading figure in the General German Women's Association and later (1894–9) first President of the Federation of German Women's Associations (Bund Deutscher Frauenvereine, or BDF). In the 1870s Schmidt was already an influential figure in the bourgeois women's movement, and contact with her may well have aroused Clara's interest in feminist ideas, though it must be added that Auguste Schmidt was in many ways a conservative influence within the women's movement, with a strictly limited concept of female rights. In 1878, Clara fell under the influence of a circle of emigré Russian socialists living in Leipzig, which was a major centre of socialist activity in Germany. She struck up a close personal relationship with Ossip Zetkin, one of the leading members of this group. Though she had already acquired some familiarity with socialist ideas, it was these Russians who introduced her to the local SPD and encouraged her to attend its meetings. In 1879–80, too, she paid a prolonged visit to Russia. In Leipzig, she did secret work for the banned socialist movement. This led to a break with Auguste Schmidt and with her own family. Until 1880, she worked as a governess in the home of a landed gentleman in Wormsdorf, Saxony, but was dismissed for her radical views. A subsequent appointment of the same kind, with the family of a factory owner in Trauenstein, Austria, ended in the same way, in 1882. This was the end of her attempt to live the life of a young, educated, unmarried middle-class woman. Henceforth her whole existence was to be devoted to the cause of Social Democracy.

After the introduction of the Anti-Socialist Law in 1878, Ossip Zetkin was expelled from Saxony and went to live in Switzerland. On leaving Austria, Clara met him in Zurich, and here they lived amid the community of socialist exiles. Clara met many leading Social Democrats here, and began work for the clandestine Social Democratic press. In November 1882, the couple settled in Paris, where they remained until Ossip's death in 1889. Clara bore him two sons, in 1883 and 1885, though, because she did not wish to lose her German citizenship and thereby run the risk of being expelled as an undesirable alien—as happened to Gertrud Guillaume-Schack, the leading figure in the early socialist women's movement, in 1886—they were never married and lived together in a 'free marriage' without legal validity.[10] Despite this, from now on Clara assumed the surname of Zetkin. This was to cause her trouble later on. In 1894 she was charged by the Hamburg police with holding public meetings under a false name. She replied that 'Zetkin' was a *nom de plume* which, as a writer, she was entitled to use. This reasoning did not impress the Hamburg police, and she was fined for four separate 'offences' with the alternative of eight days in prison.[11] The incident was typical of the petty harassment which Social Democrats had to suffer at the hands of the police after the lapsing of the Anti-Socialist Law. In 1899, however, Clara did enter into a formal, legal marriage with the painter Georg Friedrich Zundel, who was eighteen years her junior. This caused some scandal among the party leaders, especially since the pair lived together before marrying. The marriage broke up during the First World War, and they were divorced in 1927, when Clara was seventy. Throughout this period, however, she was still generally known as Clara Zetkin, occasionally as Clara Zetkin-Zundel.

Clara's active participation in the Social Democratic movement began in earnest in the 1880s, when she began to take over many of Ossip Zetkin's literary and political activities during his illness. She helped organize the founding congress of the Second Socialist International in Paris in that year, acting as a translator during the sessions. Then, after staying for some time in Zurich, she settled in Stuttgart in 1890, following the lapsing of the Anti-Socialist Law, and worked in the Social Democratic publishing house of Dietz from 1890 until 1892. Thereafter she supported herself, her two children and to a degree also her second husband, as a writer, editor and speaker.[12]

Zetkin's background was thus that of a middle-class socialist intellectual with early contacts to the bourgeois feminist movement. Her early ideas owed more to utopian socialism than to Marxism. Her first important statement which showed a clear influence of Marxist thought was her address to the founding congress of the Socialist International in 1889, subsequently published separately as *Die Arbeiterinnen- und Frauenfrage der Gegenwart* (1891). This address, which with one bound brought Zetkin into the front rank of international socialism, and constituted the first important socialist statement on women since Engels' *Origin of the Family, Private Property and the State* (1884), has sometimes been regarded as laying the foundation for Zetkin's subsequent thought, and enunciating the principles upon which all her later career rested. In reality, however, it represented a relatively early, transitional development of her ideas. Between 1889 and 1896, when Zetkin delivered another major address on the subject, this time to the Gotha Congress of the SPD, her thought underwent a number of significant changes, as will become clear if we now turn to a detailed comparison of the two speeches in question.[13]

III

In both her speeches, Paris (1889) and Gotha (1896), Zetkin regarded labour as the most fundamental aspect of the 'woman question'. She began her 1889 speech by attacking the 'erroneous opinion' which, she said, was surprisingly still present in the socialist camp, according to which women's work should be abolished. 'The question of women's emancipation', she declared, was 'in the last instance the question of women's work'. It was an 'economic question'. It was not, she said, women's work in itself that depressed men's wages, but the exploitation of women's work by capitalists. Moreover, men who wrote the emancipation of the human race on their banner should not leave half the human race out of consideration. They should support women's work because the basis of freedom was economic independence. Women, she said, 'would remain in subjection as long as they are not economically independent'. But this process was already occurring with industrialization as women flocked into the factories and other kinds of paid employment outside the home: economic independence from the male head of household would inevitably bring social independence with it. Under capitalism, however, women were becoming independent from men only to be enslaved by the capitalist instead. Despite this, women were now at least economically equal with men.

Several consequences followed from this analysis. The first, as far as Zetkin was concerned, was that because economic independence—the right to earn one's own living—was so fundamental to the process of female emancipation, anything which hindered it should be removed. This included legal restrictions on women's work. 'We women', she declared, 'protest, on principle, most decidedly against a limitation of women's work. Because we do not at all want to separate our cause from that of the workers in general, we shall therefore devise no special formulas; we demand no other protection than that which labour demands in general against capital.'[14] Zetkin maintained that it was impossible to present a special report on the situation of women workers, since this was the same as that of men workers. By 1896, her views on these

matters had changed. She recognized that many branches of industry where women were active had their own peculiar problems; above all domestic production in the clothing industry, where the putting-out system created especially bad conditions for women workers;[15] and she supported 'the abolition of domestic industry, the introduction of a legally-determined working day, and the securing of higher wages' for women. She recognized that there were special reforms necessary to improve the position of working women, and no longer rejected the idea of 'special treatment'.[16]

In 1889, Zetkin believed that economic change was rapidly undermining the institution of the family and she presented this development in a relatively positive light. While the old form of production 'chained the woman to the family', the rise of mechanized industry had liberated her and made it possible for her to stand on her own feet. Zetkin seems to have regarded the family in 1889, and also in 1891, in very negative terms, seeing it as an institution which perhaps more than any other, prevented women from emancipating themselves. Consequently, when the socialist society was eventually established, she thought that teaching and childcare should be carried out by communal, publicly owned state institutions.[17] By 1896 her views were quite different:

It cannot be the task of socialist propaganda to alienate the proletarian woman from her duties as mother and wife; on the contrary, it must work towards a state in which she fulfils these tasks better than before, in the interests of the emancipation of the proletariat. The better the circumstances in the family . . . the more capable it will be of taking part in the struggle.[18]

Many mothers and wives who filled their children with class consciousness, she declared, were doing just as effective socialist work as the women who took part regularly in socialist meetings. Zetkin admitted in 1896 that her views on the family in 1891 had been 'one-sidedly negative', and that she had since become more positive in her assessment of the family as an institution.[19]

Zetkin had little to say in 1889 about civil rights for women, and what little she did have to say was dismissive of their importance:

We expect our full emancipation neither from the admittance of women to what are called the free professions, nor from an education equal to that of the male sex—although to demand these two rights is only natural and right—nor from the granting of political rights. The countries in which the allegedly general, free and direct suffrage exists, show us how little this is really worth. The right to vote, without economic freedom, is no more and no less than a currency without a rate of exchange.

In 1889, Zetkin emphasized the economic struggle of women workers almost to the exclusion of any general struggle for women's rights. In 1896, she repeated her warning that female suffrage would not alter the existing distribution of power in society. But she now saw civil rights for women in more positive terms, as essential preconditions for proletarian women's full and equal participation in the class struggle. It was necessary, she said, to erect new barriers against the exploitation of the proletarian woman, it was necessary to give her back her rights as wife and mother, and to make these secure. By gaining equal civil rights, proletarian women would be drawn into the class struggle through politicization. Thus by 1896 Zetkin had abandoned her exclusive emphasis on economic freedom as the basis for female emancipation and was stressing the importance of equal civil rights as well. Moreover, she ceased to refer to equal rights as 'natural' and was now basing the demand for them on the class interest of the proletariat.[20]

These arguments related closely to Zetkin's ideas on how far the struggle for women's emancipation could be regarded as something different from the struggle of the labour movement as a whole. In 1889 she was uncompromising on this issue. 'Women workers are completely convinced that the question of female emancipation is no isolated, self-enclosed question but a part of the great general social question.'[21] Women could only be emancipated through a general social revolution. In 1896, too, Zetkin continued to argue that an unbridgeable gulf divided proletarian women from their sisters in the middle class; but there had also been some subtle changes. 'The proletarian woman', she said, '. . . also agrees with the demands of the bourgeois women's movement. . . . The demands of the bourgeois supporters of women's rights are fully justified both in their economic and in their moral and intellectual aspects.'[22] Of course, she added, proletarian women saw the conquest of equal rights as a means to the end of achieving socialism: it was important for them to gain civil equality in order to go into battle on an equal footing with proletarian men. Nevertheless, Zetkin devoted a good part of her 1896 speech to analysing the 'woman question' in the middle classes and as we have seen, she explicitly regarded the demand for equal rights as both justified and useful. Thus by the mid-1890s, Zetkin was advancing arguments which clearly indicated that she now recognized that some aspects of women's struggle were in fact unique. Moreover, she also argued in 1896 that proletarian women had to organize themselves separately from proletarian men, and that special efforts should be made to develop propaganda and recruitment campaigns directed specifically at women.[23]

IV

In these four major respects, therefore—women's work, the family, civil rights and the legitimacy of a separate struggle for female equality—Zetkin's thought underwent major changes between 1889 and 1896. When we take both Zetkin's speech of 1889, made after several years of exile in Paris away from the realities of the German labour movement, and her speech of 1896, delivered after half a decade of involvement with the working-class struggle inside Germany itself, and compare them with what it is possible to discover of the views of rank-and-file members in the SPD during this period, it quickly becomes clear that the changes that took place in Zetkin's thought between 1889 and 1896 owed a great deal to her coming to terms with the realities of the situation in Germany. Already in September 1893, indeed, she wrote:

We must keep our feet firmly on the ground of the facts, and deal with the situation as it really is. So we have to come to terms at the moment with the fact that women are socially weaker than men. . . . Women are more docile, and less capable of resistance than men; obedience, subjection and complaisance have become second nature to them.

With these words, which betrayed, perhaps, a certain disappointment at the inadequacies of the socialist women's movement and of the trade unions in Germany, Zetkin was almost precisely echoing Wilhelm Liebknecht's reference in the party congress of 1890 to 'the greater tenderness of the female organism, the weakness of the woman'. And indeed in 1893 Zetkin herself argued that the fact that women bore children was enough to entitle them to special protection. Even as she had uttered them, in fact, her arguments against special legislation to protect women workers had been attacked on all sides. Engels himself supported special legislation to protect women workers, and demands along these lines were incorporated into the 1891 Erfurt Programme of the SPD. Zetkin's demands for the same treatment for women as for men were also rejected by the 1889 congress, which voted once more for special protective laws.[24] So whatever Zetkin herself had originally thought on the basis of a reading of the classical Marxist texts, in fact the pressures in favour of restrictions on women's work were overwhelming both in the Socialist International and within the SPD itself. Her amended views, as presented in her speech of 1896, constituted a recognition of this fact, and indeed they may also have owed a good deal to a reading of the lengthy investigations of women's work in various branches of industry that appeared in almost every issue of *Die Gleichheit*, the SPD women's magazine, edited by Zetkin.

Similarly, Zetkin's critique of the family ran up against a strong commitment to familial values within the SPD and in the German working class as a whole. Already in the 1880s such SPD women's organizations as there were consisted mainly of wives of men already active in the party, a pattern that was not to change until the First World War; so that the growth of female membership in the SPD was a sign of the strengthening, rather than of the weakening of family ties in the working class, or at least in those sectors of it that supported the SPD. SPD women saw themselves not least as supporting the political beliefs of their husbands and communicating them to their children.[25] In 1887 one SPD women's organization in Hamburg looked forward to a time 'when our men will earn

more, so that we don't need to work any more and can devote
ourselves more to bringing up our children'.[26] Zetkin herself
recognized this aspect of women's commitment to the labour
movement in 1898 when she described the ideal socialist
woman in the following terms:

Rooted and active in the world and in the family she is able to make the
husband completely at home in the house again. From her own rich, wide
circle of influence there flows in her an untroubled understanding of his
struggles and his work. She stands by his side no longer as a faithful and
solicitous handmaid, but rather as a convinced, warm guardian of his
struggles, as a comrade in his efforts and his exertions, giving and receiving
intellectual and moral support. . . . The more she can be the educator and
the moulder of her children, the more she can enlighten them and ensure that
they carry out in rank and file the struggle for the emancipation of the
proletariat with the same enthusiasm and spirit of self-sacrifice as we do.
When the proletarian then says 'my wife', he adds to this in his mind: 'the
comrade of my ideals, the companion of my exertions, the educator of my
children for the future struggle'.[27]

It was on this basis that women were in reality committed to the
SPD and not, as Zetkin had wrongly believed in 1889, as a
result of their separation from family ties. Zetkin's increasing
tendency to appeal to proletarian women as wives and mothers
rather than as workers was no more than a gradual recognition
that this was what, in their own consciousness and that of their
husbands, they mainly were.

Nor did Zetkin's belief of the early 1890s in the identity of
the women's struggle with that of the socialist movement as a
whole survive the test of practical experience. In 1892 Zetkin
and her followers, in particular the leading Berlin activist
Ottilie Baader, tried to give practical expression to the idea that
a separate struggle for women's emancipation did not exist, by
persuading the SPD Party Congress to delete the clause in its
statute which allowed women in local party branches to elect a
delegate to the party congress from their own ranks, in cases
where the local party organization failed to include a woman
among the delegates it elected itself. The reason for this change
was, as Baader explained, that the original clause prevented
women from playing an active role in the general political work
of the branches. Thus in 1892 four of the six Berlin party
branches had refused from the start to elect a female delegate

to the congress and told the women instead to hold their own women's assemblies to go ahead with their own elections. Baader and Zetkin regarded this as a form of compulsory separatism, and beyond this said that the clause was unnecessary in any case because the inseparability of the women's cause and that of the working class as a whole would ensure of itself that women obtained proper representation at the party congress. Two years later, however, Zetkin and Baader returned, disillusioned, with the request to reinstate the original statute. All that had happened had been that the men had continued to elect men to the congress, so that the women's representation had become seriously threatened.[28] Men in the SPD were indeed always opposed to women in positions of responsibility. As one woman complained at the party congress in 1896,

> many male comrades treat the women's question as such a joke, so that one must really ask, 'are these Party comrades, who, support equal rights?' In many places the men don't even let the women play a role in the movement at all, they don't even educate the women, they just say: 'that doesn't concern you, you don't understand any of that'. And that's that as far as our male comrades are concerned.[29]

The inescapable consequence of this attitude was that the women were forced to form their own organization within the party, with its own congresses (from 1900) and its own agents (from 1901). This tendency was compounded by legal constraints. Until 1908 women in most parts of Germany were legally barred from joining political parties, so that socialist women had at the very least to present themselves as a separate and to a large degree 'non-political' organization; until 1900 the illegality of political parties organized on a national basis was the only factor preventing an earlier development of this separate movement for socialist women.[30]

In 1889, Zetkin had regarded the bourgeois feminist cause as fundamentally opposed to that of the women of the proletariat, or, at best, irrelevant to the real cause of women's emancipation. By the mid-1890s, renewed contact with the bourgeois feminist movement in Germany had caused her to change her mind on this question too. 'The equality of the sexes', as Zetkin remarked at the Social Democratic Party

Congress the previous year, 1895, 'is not a specifically Social Democratic demand, but merely a consequence of bourgeois liberalism'.[31] In Germany, however, bourgeois liberalism was, Zetkin argued, so weak that it failed to pursue the demands for the equality of the sexes raised by liberals elsewhere. This weakness extended to the bourgeois feminist movement, which clearly failed to advance the demands for female suffrage, legal equality within marriage, the abolition of state-regulated prostitution and the double standard of sexual morality, the admission of women to the universities and the professions, and the granting of equality to women in other spheres of social and political life which were advanced by feminists in other countries. In this situation, the Social Democratic Party felt that it had a duty to carry out the historic tasks which the German liberals had clearly failed to perform. 'While representatives of the most varied political parties in other countries support equal rights for women', continued Zetkin in her speech at the 1895 party congress, 'this task has not been solved by our cowardly bourgeoisie and so it falls to the lot of the proletariat to carry it out.' Zetkin wrote in the same year:

> In Germany the cause of the bourgeois woman has also become the cause of Social Democracy. The German bourgeoisie enjoys the undisputed honour of being among the most backward and narrow-minded of all bourgeoisies. . . . In Germany, therefore, among other things that do not immediately lie in the class interest of the proletariat, the task of solving the question of female emancipation in the bourgeois sense has also fallen to the working class.[32]

Zetkin, however, did not calculate in this way that it might win over the women of the bourgeoisie to its ranks; she continued to insist—with occasional exceptions—that the class interests of bourgeois and proletarian women remained irreconcilable. On the other hand Zetkin and other members of the SPD attempted to argue that rights which were useful to bourgeois women might also be serviceable, though in a rather different way, to the women of the working class. These attitudes found their most paradoxical expression in the policies advocated by the SPD Reichstag members in the debates on the Civil Code in 1895–6. In every relevant clause, the party leader August Bebel and his followers attempted to amend the partriarchal stipulations of the Code so as to give the wife complete equality with her husband in every respect. Bebel proposed to insert a clause declaring that 'both parties in the marriage have equal rights in all matters concerning their common life', and to delete the clause which gave the right of final decision in such matters to the husband. He also proposed a whole series of amendments dealing with the control over property within marriage—control which the original proposals gave to the husband. In the SPD version, the property of husband and wife was to be separate within the marriage. These proposals were rejected even by the left-wing liberals, who strongly criticized the original draft as too patriarchal. The original clauses however were carried, with the support of the National Liberals and the Catholic Centre.

In other countries, for example England, Married Women's Property Acts or their equivalent had long since given women control over the property they brought into marriage. It was easy to see why the left-liberals supported the introduction of a similar measure in Germany. It was not so easy, however, to see what the Social Democrats had to gain from such a proposal. The granting of equal rights to women over the income and property belonging to a marriage could only bring a minimal direct advantage to a political party which represented those whose income was small and whose property was negligible. Clara Zetkin attempted to argue however, that 'the legal regulation of property relations' would benefit the working-class woman because it would provide a safeguard against 'the danger that poverty will deliver the husband to the devil drink, and that the wife will be condemned to suffer because of this'.[33] This was less than convincing, for while a rich and educated bourgeois wife might perfectly well be able to file a suit in civil law against a husband who was appropriating for his own ends the property she had brought into the marriage, and to pursue that suit through all the wearisome and costly process of law to its conclusion, a working-class woman was in no position to do so; neither her financial resources, nor her social position, nor her educational deficiencies and general outlook on life would really admit of such a possibility, and the SPD and other labour organizations made no move to rectify this situation in terms of practical help.

Zetkin added that there was another reason why the SPD supported equal rights for women in the Civil Code debates. 'The equality of women in private law', she said, 'is the first step towards the equality of women in public life. If their chains are loosened in this respect, then the political equality of women is only a matter of time.'[34] It was surprising to find Zetkin taking this gradualist line. The truth was that neither the equality of women in Civil Law nor their equality in public life was possible in Imperial Germany without a fundamental change in the distribution of political power; and the Reichstag's rejection both of Bebel's proposals and of the proposals of the left-liberals showed how remote a possibility even the first of these developments was. Nor did the experience of 1908, when the greatest single step forward in the legal position of women in the Imperial German political system, the new *Reichsvereinsgesetz*, allowing them for the first time full rights of assembly and association, came into effect, provide any confirmation of the theory that the granting of more legal rights to women, even in the public sphere, would automatically lead to the granting of the ultimate political right, the right to vote.

Zetkin's changed stance on the issue of civil rights for women, and her rather strained attempt to argue that these would benefit the women of the working class as well as those of the bourgeoisie, again were developed in response to the views of the party. The fact that women's rights were increasingly the subject of debates in the Reichstag meant that the SPD Reichstag delegation had to develop a policy on them. Already there were far-reaching demands for women's rights, including the vote, in the Erfurt Programme of 1891. But the party also had to respond on a more detailed level when complex issues such as women's rights in civil law were being debated. In addition, the conservatism of the bourgeois women's movement on such issues made it seem like a good opportunity for the Social Democrats to present themselves as the only convinced supporters of equal women's rights. In fact, this move caused serious problems for the theory which Zetkin had been developing, and cast serious doubt on the argument, fundamental to her theory, that there was an irreconcilable conflict of interest between the women of the proletariat and the women of the bourgeoisie.

But these developments in Zetkin's ideology also have to be seen against the background of Zetkin's own activities within the party and the women's movement at this time. She saw her task as essentially twofold. First, she had to purge the existing SPD women's movement of bourgeois ideas. As she wrote to Kautsky in 1901,

Our women's movement up to the time of my return was internally infested throughout with really vulgar bourgeois feminism and also threatened internally at any moment to form an alliance with the bourgeois feminist movement and had by no means cut all ties between itself and the latter.[35]

The campaign which Zetkin waged in the 1890s in numerous speeches and in the pages of the SPD women's magazine *Die Gleichheit* to purge the socialist women's organizations of 'bourgeois feminism' was also designed to convince the party leadership of the women's complete loyalty to the socialist cause. Only through a constant emphasis on the identity of the women's struggle with that of the labour movement as a whole could the party in general be persuaded that the women's cause was worth supporting; and indeed in 1902 the party took over the financial burden of publishing *Die Gleichheit*,[36] which continued for a few years more to make a loss; while increasing sums of money were poured by the party into *Frauen-Agitation*, the effort to recruit women to its ranks. At the same time, however, the experiences of the early 1890s led Zetkin to try and preserve some autonomy and freedom of action for the socialist women, who otherwise would have been denied any independent voice in party affairs, or indeed in their own affairs. It was the attempt to reconcile these two aims that underlay the tension in Zetkin's mature theory between the special nature and special interests of women on the one hand, and the identity of their cause with that of the proletariat on the other.

V

Though her Gotha speech remained the fullest and elaborate exposition of Zetkin's views on the 'wo question', it was far from being her last word on the subject. In several respects her views continued to change and develop. To begin with, the rapid emergence of a radical wing of bourgeois feminism from about the turn of the century, and the successful imposition of many of its views upon the bourgeois women's movement as a whole, quickly invalidated Zetkin's earlier strictures about the inadequacy of German feminism. By 1902, when the bourgeois feminists were demanding the vote and advocating a wide series of reforms in many areas of public life, Zetkin could no longer claim that it was the task of the Social Democratic women to take up the causes which the bourgeois feminists had so shamefully neglected. Secondly, Zetkin's own position within the SPD as a whole began to undergo a far-reaching transformation. Up to 1901 she was in general orthodox in her views, and depended intellectually to a large degree on the party's chief theorist Karl Kautsky. In 1901, however, she quarrelled with Kautsky and transferred her intellectual allegiance to the far more radical Rosa Luxemburg. Zetkin's leftward move was accelerated by the Russian Revolution of 1905–6. Ever since her association with Ossip Zetkin and her visit to Russia in 1879–80 she had been passionately committed to the overthrow of tsarism. After 1905–6 a new note of urgency entered her commitment to the cause of revolution.

While these influences were driving Zetkin to the left, the SPD as a whole was falling more and more under the influence of reformists. Zetkin began to stress the revolutionary potential of women's commitment to socialism, and to try to convert the SPD women's movement into a bastion of revolutionary socialism within the increasingly reformist German labour movement. By 1907, in her pamphlet *Zur Frage des Frauenwahlrechts*, Zetkin, far from presenting votes for women as nothing more than a demand of bourgeois feminism, was arguing that female suffrage would help the political education and mobilization of proletarian women, and bring the socialist revolution nearer by adding further to the strength of the SPD. In this way she was able to present female suffrage as a measure hostile to the interests of the bourgeoisie. To an increasing degree after 1905, Zetkin began to use the SPD women's magazine *Die Gleichheit* to present articles on general political questions written from the point of view of the party's extreme left wing. By 1914, *Die Gleichheit* was the only party journal in which the left could still be sure of being able to express its own viewpoint. Here too, and in the SPD women's movement as a whole, Zetkin thought the threat of reformism was growing. By 1913, she was calling for the creation of a 'socialist women's movement' free from reformist influences. Its 'driving and executive forces will be predominantly women', she declared, and if 'the male comrades are not insightful enough to guarantee it this necessity of life, independence and freedom of manoeuvre, then it will have to be fought for'. Thus, ironically, the more Zetkin moved to the left, the more she came to stress the belief that the women's movement should be independent and separate from the main party, a view she had condemned in the early 1890s as bourgeois.[37] Indeed, when she eventually joined the Communist Party in 1919, Zetkin's insistence on the need for communist women to control their own affairs led within a short time to her effective exclusion from any real power in the women's organizations of the Communist International and its German branch.[38]

The changes that took place in Zetkin's views after the turn of the century can in most instances—above all, the growing insistence on the need for the increasing independence of the socialist women's movement and the increasing emphasis on woman's role as wife and mother—be seen as a further development of the views she had reached by the time of her Gotha speech. Between 1889 and 1896 Zetkin came into contact with the views of ordinary party members, above all of the men in the party, and adapted her own theoretical position accordingly. Despite her gradual loss of power within the party and indeed within the woman's movement itself from the early 1900s onwards, this fundamental fact did not really change, and the basic tenets of the Social Democratic theory of the emancipation of women remained basically unaltered: a testimony to the fact that they represented, not the imposition of an abstract and alien theory on a pragmatic and empirically oriented organization, but rather an amalgam of socialist theory and the everyday attitudes and values of the men and women on whose support the socialist movement rested.

As far as Zetkin's overall position is concerned, it seems incorrect to portray her either as a socialist who rejected all feminist ideas, or as a feminist who used socialism as the most appropriate vehicle for the struggle for female emancipation. Her fundamental commitment to the cause of socialism and revolution cannot be doubted; it never wavered, no matter how much the cause of women suffered at the hands of male chauvinists within the SPD. Zetkin was first and foremost a socialist. But within the socialist movement, once she had become familiar with conditions in Germany after her long period of exile, she devoted herself principally to the cause of female politicization, female equality and female emancipation. This inevitably brought her into contact with bourgeois feminism, and indeed the pages of *Die Gleichheit* show a constant awareness of what was going on in liberal feminism, while Zetkin was on personal terms with many liberal feminist leaders, and often tried to encourage the more radical of them. She was demonstrably influenced by feminist ideas, and by the eve of the First World War her growing despair at the increasing reformism of the SPD leadership was leading her in organizational terms to something akin to a feminist position. There was always a tension in Zetkin between a fundamental loyalty to the movement to which she belonged, and a consistent independence which expressed itself in constant criticism of the way it was going. This was perhaps at its weakest when she was at the height of her influence within the SPD, in the late 1890s and around the turn of the century; but well before the First World War, Zetkin had become what she was to remain, with varying accentuations, through 1914–18 and into the communist movement of the 1920s: an opposing woman.[39]

NOTES

This chapter is a revised version of 'Theory and practice in German Social Democracy 1880–1914, Clara Zetkin and the socialist theory of women's emancipation', *History of Political Thought III* (1982), pp. 289–304.

1. J. P. Nettl, *Rosa Luxemburg* (London, 1966), p. 136.
2. The standard work is the quasi-official East German biography by Luise Dornemann, *Clara Zetkin. Leben und Wirken* (5th edn, East Berlin, 1973).
3. For example, she acted as an interpreter at the 1889 Congress of the Second International, and later published a German translation of Edward Bellamy's *Looking Backward.*
4. Cf. Richard Stites, *The Women's Liberation Movement in Russia. Feminism, Nihilism and Bolshevism 1860–1930* (Princeton, 1978).
5. Charles Sowerwine, *Sisters or Citizens? Women and Socialism in France since 1876* (Cambridge, 1982)
6. Clara Zetkin, *Ausgewählte Reden und Schriften* (3 vols, East Berlin, 1953).
7. See for example the contrasting interpretations of Philip Foner (ed.), *Clara Zetkin. Selected Writings. With an Introduction by Angela Y. Davis* (New York, 1984); Jean H. Quataert, *Reluctant Feminists in German Social Democracy 1885–1917* (Princeton, 1979); and Alfred G. Meyer, *The Feminism and Socialism of Lily Braun* (Bloomington, Indiana, 1985). For allegations of the 'dogmatism' of Marxist theorists such as Zetkin, and that their adherence to Marxist theory prevented them from gaining a proper insight into the problem of women's emancipation, see in particular Marilyn Boxer, Jean Quataert (eds), *Socialist Women: European Socialist Feminism in the Nineteenth and Early Twentieth Centuries* (New York, 1978).
8. See for example Quataert, *op. cit.,* or Karen Honeycutt, 'Clara Zetkin: A Left-Wing Socialist and Feminist in Wilhelmian Germany' (Ph.D., Columbia, 1975); and Tony Cliff, 'Clara Zetkin' in *International Socialism,* 2 (1981), 13, with replies by his critics in no. 2 (1981), 14, pp. 105–24 of the same journal.
9. The following details of Zetkin's early life are taken from Maxim Zetkin, 'Biochronik', in IML/ZPA, NL 5/3; Honeycutt, 'Clara Zetkin', pp. 23–94; and Dornemann, *Clara Zetkin.*
10. For Guillaume-Schack, see Margrit Twellmann, *Die deutsche Frauenbewegung im Spiegel repräsentativer Frauenzeitschriften. Ihre Anfänge und erste Entwicklung 1843–1889* (Marburger Abhandlungen zur politischen Wissenschaft, ed. W. Abendroth, vol. 17, Meisenheim-am-Glan, 1972), 2 vols, esp. vol. I, pp. 166–72, 178–93; vol. II, pp. 529–34.
11. Staatsarchiv Hamburg (StA Hbg), Politische Polizei (PP), S1909: Zetkin to Hamburg police (3 April 1894), clipping of *Hamburger Fremdenblatt* (16 April 1894).
12. cf. the sources cited above, note 9.
13. These speeches are available in Clara Zetkin, *Ausgewählte Reden und Schriften,* vol. I (East Berlin, 1953), pp. 3–11, 95–111.
14. cf. Clara Zetkin, *Zur Geschichte der proletarischen Frauenbewegung Deutschlands* (Frankfurt-am-Main, 1969), p. 143.
15. cf. Robyn Dasey, 'Women's work and the family: women garment

workers in Berlin and Hamburg before the First World War', in *The German Family*, ed. Richard J. Evans and W. R. Lee (London, 1981), pp. 221–55.

16. Zetkin, *Ausgewählte Reden und Schriften*, vol. I, pp. 105–6.
17. Honeycutt, 'Clara Zetkin', pp. 76–7, note 99.
18. Zetkin, *Ausgewählte Reden und Schriften*, vol. I, p. 108.
19. Zetkin, *Die Gleichheit*, vol. VI, no. 25 (9 December 1896), and no. 26 (23 December 1896), pp. 197–200, 203–7.
20. Zetkin, *Ausgewählte Reden und Schriften*, vol. I, pp. 102–4.
21. *ibid.*, p. 4.
22. *ibid.*, pp. 103, 101.
23. *ibid.*, pp. 107–8.
24. *Marx-Engels Werke*, vol. 36, (East Berlin, 1959–71) p. 341; Honeycutt, 'Clara Zetkin', p. 93; Zetkin, *Die Gleichheit*, vol. III, no. 19 (20 September 1893), p. 100.
25. See Chapter 4 below.
26. StA Hbg, PP, V 581: Versammlungsbericht, 23 February 1887.
27. Zetkin, *Die Gleichheit*, vol. VIII, no. 2 (19 January 1898), pp. 9–10.
28. *Protokoll des Parteitags der Sozialdemokratischen Partei Deutschlands* (hereinafter, PTP) (1892), pp. 144–5; *ibid.* (1894), pp. 174, 178–9.
29. *ibid.* (1896), p. 170.
30. Dieter Fricke, *Die deutsche Arbeiterbewegung 1896–1914. Ein Handbuch über ihre Organisation und ihre Tätigkeit im Klassenkampf* (Berlin, 1976), pp. 299–330.
31. PTP (1895), p. 90.
32. Zetkin, *Die Gleichheit*, vol. V, no. 1 (9 January 1895), p. 1.
33. PTP (1895), p. 90. For a full discussion of this whole problem see Wolfgang Plat, 'Die Stellung der deutschen Sozialdemokratie zum Grundsatz der Gleichberechtigung der Frau auf dem Gebiet des Familienrechts bei der Schaffung des Bürgerlichen Gesetzbuchs des Deutschen Reichs' (Ph.D. Humboldt University, East Berlin, 1966). For the Reichstag debates on the subject, see *Stenographische Berichte über die Verhandlungen des deutschen Reichstags*, 9. Leg. Per., 4. Sess., vol. 4 (25 June 1896), 2910–38.
34. PTP (1895), p. 90.
35. Quoted in Honeycutt, 'Clara Zetkin', p. 168.
36. *ibid.*, p. 126.
37. Zetkin to Heleen Ankersmit (7 September 1913), in W. Eildermann (ed.), 'Unveröffentlichte Briefe Clara Zetkins an Heleen Ankersmit', *Beiträge zur Geschichte der deutschen Arbeiterbewegung*, 9 (1967), 4, pp. 665–6.
38. Honeycutt, 'Clara Zetkin', 'Conclusion'.
39. The phrase is taken from the autobiography of the unconventional Austrian communist, Ernst Fischer, *An Opposing Man* (London, 1974).

2   The Impossible Alliance

All over Europe, before 1914, women were mobilizing in their thousands, even in their millions, in the battle for equality and emancipation; but they were mobilizing in two different camps. Feminist and female suffrage movements found themselves confronted by mass movements of socialist women which pursued many of the same aims, including the reform of the civil law and the granting of political rights to women, but the two movements failed to join forces and conducted the struggle separately from one another. More than that, as we shall see, each regarded the other with distrust, even hostility, and little love was lost between the two. This division between socialists and feminists in pre-First World War Europe undoubtedly weakened the struggle for women's rights. It also had longer-term effects, and its legacy indeed has continued to affect the women's movement to the present day. It is important, therefore, to understand its origins, to ask why the two movements were so bitterly divided, and why attempts to reconcile them failed.

I

Feminism was one of the great social and political causes of the late nineteenth and early twentieth centuries. By 1900 almost every European country had its feminist movement, often thousands strong. The great majority of these movements campaigned actively for a wide range of reforms, from married women's property rights and the right of women to study at

37

university and join the professions, to the abolition of the state regulation of prostitution and major changes in the civil law. Increasingly, and above all after the turn of the century, they came to concentrate on the vote. By 1914 this had become feminism's central issue. Only in Norway and Finland had female suffrage actually been won: elsewhere it was still being fought for, by violent means in the case of the English suffragettes, by more modest but on the whole no less determined efforts elsewhere. In most countries the only political parties to support votes for women were socialist ones.[1] Socialists were in general far more favourably disposed to women's emancipation than liberal parties were. So it seemed obvious that feminists should consider joining forces with them.

This in fact is precisely what a number of feminists did. A good example was the French feminist Madeleine Pelletier (1874–1939), who came from an impoverished background, but trained and practised as a doctor, and became active in the feminist movement in the early 1900s. Pelletier once declared: 'A woman cannot sacrifice feminism to any masculine political party whatsoever, without betraying her own cause.'[2] Pelletier was famous as a militant, and took part in overturning a ballot box and smashing the windows of a polling station during the elections of 1906. However, she did join the French socialist party and became a speaker for its Marxist faction, the Guesdists. On this basis she got to the Party Congress in 1906 and persuaded it to endorse votes for women. But despite further pressure she never managed to push the party into taking action on this resolution. Pelletier concluded that the party needed special sections for women. But they never materialized, partly because they were seen as a diversion, and partly because she had become absorbed in the meantime in the far-left, 'insurrectionist' faction of the party, led by Gustave Hervé. Pelletier became a leading member of this faction despite its belief that women's rights were useless without a revolution. When Hervé began to move to the right again she left his faction. Beyond using the party to conduct feminist election campaigns in 1910 and 1912, she had little to do with it again, and indeed was soon involved with the anarchists, who were outside the party altogether.[3]

As Charles Sowerwine has remarked, Pelletier became disillusioned with the French socialist party not because it was anti-feminist but because it was reformist.[4] Despite her initial intention of using the party for feminist ends, she soon discovered that she had a real commitment to socialism, and this took precedence over her feminist beliefs; indeed, this was probably why she never pushed for the creation of special women's sections in the party, since her own career in it suggested that they were not needed. Other French feminists associated with Pelletier, such as Caroline Kauffmann, also joined the party but with far less conviction or commitment. The French socialist party never had a strong female membership. In 1914 there were fewer than 1,000 women in the party, or not much more than 1 per cent of the total, as compared with 16 per cent in the German SPD and 23 per cent in the Finnish socialist party. The male party leadership was indifferent to the recruitment of women, not least because it focused on elections and parliamentary politics, where women did not have a role to play. The lack of a separate women's section deterred women from joining. Petty-bourgeois Proudhonian traditions in the French labour movement, and the lack of a broadly based assimilation of Marx's and Engels' fundamentally positive attitude towards women's work and the political mobilization of women, allowed the party leadership to remain indifferent to the entry of women into politics. Indeed the leader of the Marxist wing of French socialism, Jules Guesde, accepted a rather simplified version of Marxism in which he regarded the fight for women's rights as a diversion from the class struggle, while other French Marxists such as Lafargue thought that socialism would return women to the home, away from the horrors of factory exploitation.[5] None of this offered very fruitful ground for feminists to cultivate, even if it was less barren than that occupied by the other parties such as the Radicals, who opposed votes for women on the grounds that women would undermine the Republic by voting Catholic.

Figures like Pelletier and Kauffmann, it must also be said, were very much a minority in French feminism as a whole. They were among a small group on its left wing who favoured militant tactics and wanted quick results. The estimated membership of this group, Women's Solidarity, founded in 1891, was under 100 in 1900 and only 25 in 1910–14, compared to the mainstream women's suffrage movements, the French League for Women's Rights, which had between 500 and 1,000 members in 1910–14, and the French Union for Women's Suffrage, which had 12,000 members at the same time, not to mention the French National Council of Women, a moderate feminist organization, whose membership topped 100,000 by the outbreak of the First World War.[6] There was very little co-operation between this majority and socialist parties or women's groups. Most feminists, as Stephen Hause and Anne Kenney remark, were from a middle-class background, especially from the liberal professions, and with a strongly bourgeois character. The feminist movement often showed little understanding for the problems and aspirations of the working-class women to whom the socialist movement appealed.[7] Characteristically, when socialist women did attend a feminist conference in 1900, they clashed with the feminists over domestic servants (which most of the feminists, as bourgeois women, employed). While socialists sought to improve servants' conditions or unionize them, the feminists attacked even the idea of giving them a day off every week, on the grounds that this would allow them to drift into prostitution, and hostile exchanges took place over this issue. The feminists thought workers, both male and female, had to be disciplined; socialist women bitterly resented this point of view. The leading moderate feminist Maria Pognon attacked socialism as preaching class hatred: 'I do not accept class struggle,' she said, 'I accept class harmony'.[8] But it was class harmony without many concessions to the workers. Even a radical feminist like Hubertine Auclert denied the legitimacy of a separate socialist women's movement: 'There cannot be a bourgeois feminism and a socialist feminism', she wrote, 'because there are not two female sexes.'[9] With views such as these, it is not surprising that co-operation between the two movements was rare.

The gulf between feminism and socialism was, if anything, reinforced by the attitudes of the socialist women. In France, the fact that the socialist party was a relatively established and accepted feature of political life made it easier than in most other European countries for feminists like Pelletier to cross the divide and work within it. Conversely, when the group of socialist women was formed in 1913, a number of its members could be described as feminists and were also active in feminist groups. One of these, Hélène Brion, tried to commit the group to co-operating with the feminists, arguing that 'there can be no question of class struggle between bourgeois feminists and women who work'.[10] The fact was, she declared, women of all classes were oppressed by men and should join together. Another prominent member of the group, Marguérite Martin, thought that a socialist–feminist alliance would increase the chance of obtaining worthwhile reforms, and suggested that it might well help convert many feminists to the socialist point of view. But such women as Brion and Martin were outmanoeuvred by the hard-line socialist faction led by the seamstress Louise Saumoneau (1875–1950), who within a short space of time had pushed the feminists out of the group and established a rejection even of co-operation, let alone an alliance. Saumoneau argued that feminism was a relic of a past age, an attempt to defend the class privileges of the bourgeoisie. The idea of feminine solidarity was a myth designed to divide the working class: 'There can be no antagonism between the men and women of the proletarian class'.[11]

Saumoneau was violently opposed to what she called 'that amalgam of intriguing, naive, deranged and hysterical women which is bourgeois feminism'.[12] Bourgeois feminists, she said, wanted to maintain the economic interests and class privilege of bourgeois women, and thus to perpetuate the misery of the proletariat, however much they might claim to want to alleviate it. Saumoneau asserted the primacy of class struggle and warned socialist women against the 'danger' of listening to 'that lying phrase, "women's emancipation"'.[13] Thus she opposed the formation of a separate women's movement and continually insisted that women had to join the party as individuals. There was to be no special recruiting of women, by women. Under Saumoneau's leadership, the group of socialist women even rejected the idea of appearing separately at socialist rallies, telling its members to go with their local party branches instead. The celebrations she organized on

International Proletarian Women's Day[14] included men from the start. The irony was that the socialist women did little to further their own cause within the party by these impressive demonstrations of solidarity with the men. Despite some expansion under Saumoneau's leadership, the group was still pitifully small on the eve of the First World War. It was not surprising that the group had been shunned from the start by Madeleine Pelletier, whose prediction on its foundation ('I fear that the socialist women's group will only be the kindergarten of the socialist party and that it will leave feminism behind to please the men in the party') had proved only too true.[15]

II

Conditions in Germany were very different from all this. There was a successful socialist women's movement, reaching the substantial membership of 175,000 by 1914, led by Clara Zetkin and (later) Luise Zietz. It was largely autonomous, even when the legal restrictions which made this necessary were removed in 1908. The commitment of the German Social Democrats, the SPD, to women's rights in general, had been obvious at least since the early 1890s. The bourgeois feminists for their part also had a large movement, incorporated in the Federation of German Women's Associations (Bund Deutscher Frauenvereine, or BDF), founded in 1914; it numbered perhaps 250,000 women by the eve of World War I. From the start the BDF was divided into self-styled 'moderate' and 'radical' wings, with the moderates wanting to go slowly and the radicals pushing for an all-out feminist campaign, especially on subjects such as votes for women, which the moderates had so far shrunk from demanding.

On the foundation of the BDF in 1894, it was clear that the bourgeois feminists were divided over the issue of co-operation with the SPD. Under the Anti-Socialist Law of 1878–90, there had been no question of any bourgeois organization inviting co-operation from the SPD if it wanted to stay in existence. But by the time of the foundation of the BDF in 1894, the SPD was a legal party-political organization once more. Since the BDF claimed to represent all German women, it had to decide at the outset whether it was to join forces with the Social Democrats, or to co-operate with them in certain limited fields, or to ignore them altogether, as far as it was able. According to the 'radical' feminist Minna Cauer, quoting a copy of the minutes of the founding meeting of the BDF, there had been a heated debate on the subject. Minna Cauer and her supporter Lily Braun, backed by other, less radical figures, such as Hanna Bieber-Böhm and Jeannette Schwerin, had spoken in favour of admitting SPD organizations, but had been overruled by the conservative old guard of long-serving 'moderate' leaders from older organizations in the BDF, including Auguste Schmidt, Helene von Forster, Betty Naue and Ottilie Hoffmann.[16] The reason given by the old guard for their refusal to admit SPD organizations into the BDF was that the SPD organizations were political associations, and their presence would open the BDF to prosecution under the Law of Association; and, indeed, in 1895 these SPD organizations were in fact dissolved by the police, though they soon re-emerged on a slightly different basis. The matter had rested there as far as the BDF was concerned until 1900, when at the BDF's General Assembly, the Berlin primary school teacher Maria Lischnewska, a close associate of Minna Cauer, put forward an 'emergency motion' demanding co-operation with the women supporters of the SPD. This found no more favour with the conservatives than had the proposals of 1894. Helene Lange declared that 'the Federation is not a political body and therefore it cannot come to an arrangement with a political party'. The radicals were in a far stronger position in 1900 than they had been six years previously, and Lange's statement was greeted by 'laughter, applause and hissing'.[17] Nevertheless, Lischnewska's motion was defeated, and Helene Lange complained later that it had caused long debates and 'made necessary a great reduction of the time available for important commission work',[18] that is, for detailed debates on social problems such as prostitution and alcoholism which were covered by the BDF's specialist commissions. Like all the old guard of the BDF, the so-called 'moderates', Lange believed that social welfare, not political advancement, was the real task of the women's movement.

Clearly, too, the ideas of Lange and her supporters were so conservative that co-operation with the SPD was quite out of the question. With the emergence of the radical feminists as the driving force in the BDF from about 1900, however, things began to look very different. From the turn of the century there was a wide agreement of aims between the SPD women and the BDF. On the question of women's suffrage, in particular, where the bourgeois feminists, in contrast to the left-wing liberal parties, supported universal adult suffrage (from 1902 onwards, after a resolution to this effect by the BDF), their position was far to the left of any other political group save the SPD. Even if the BDF was not prepared to co-operate with the SPD, the separate individual organizations of the radical feminists could do so without requesting the BDF's permission. The German Union for Women's Suffrage was *de facto* a political organization that could only exist in areas such as Hamburg, Baden and Bremen, because the Law of Association forbade women to join it in Prussia. This meant that there was no legal objection or danger about such co-operation, at least for the female suffragists. Moreover, the very radicalism of the radical feminists placed them outside the bounds of respectable society and created a further bond between them and the Social Democrats. It was scarcely surprising, therefore, that despite their failure to persuade the BDF to co-operate with the SPD, the radical feminists attempted to institute this co-operation themselves in their own organizations. Thus the Union of Progressive Women's Associations, founded in 1899, incorporated in its Statutes the rejection of all attempts to divide the women of the middle class from their female comrades in the proletariat; and leading members of the Union sometimes participated in SPD meetings.[19] Later on, too, the radical feminists seemed to regret the break. It is interesting that Anita Augspurg and Lida Gustava Heymann were supporters of the Independent Social Democrats during the First World War, and that Heymann stood (unsuccessfully) for the National Assembly in 1919 on an Independent Social Democratic ticket.[20] Minna Cauer, too, wrote at the end of her life that she had always sympathized with the SPD and that the proclamation of the republic in 1918 realized 'the dream of a lifetime'.[21] Indeed, in 1911 she noted in her diary that she was actually considering joining the party.[22]

Feelings of solidarity with working-class women and despair with prospects of reform actually did lead on occasion to bourgeois feminists joining the SPD. The editor of the bourgeois women's suffrage magazine *Die Staatsbürgerin*, Adele Schreiber, took the plunge at the end of the First World War and represented the SPD in the Reichstag during the Weimar Republic.[23] Minna Cauer's successor as President of the Union of Progressive Women's Associations, Meta Hammerschlag, who already in 1906 referred to herself as 'not a socialist, but socialist-minded',[24] married the SPD politician Max Quarck and joined the party during the First World War.[25] The Berlin bourgeois suffragist Toni Breitscheid also followed her husband into the socialist camp by 1913.[26] Others made the move independently. Oda Olberg left the General German Women's Association in 1896 for the SPD. She later married Giovanni Lerda, an Italian journalist, and left Germany for Italy.[27] Clara Zetkin, the editor of the SPD women's magazine, had herself begun in the bourgeois women's movement. Regine Ruben, the Hamburg radical feminist, referred to herself in 1904 as 'half a Social Democrat'. The 'moderate' Alice Salomon attacked this statement as inconsistent. Either one was a Social Democrat, she remarked, or one was not; either one wanted to improve the social system through reform or one wanted to destroy it altogether through revolution. Between socialism and reformism there was, she thought, no compromise.[28] According to the SPD women's leader Clara Zetkin, however, Ruben was 'one of those female intellectuals who swing back and forth between feminism and Social Democracy. She may stand inwardly nearer to the latter but she is held back by material considerations, so that she feels unable to accept the consequences of her own train of though'.[29] By 1912, however, Regine Ruben had apparently cut her ties with bourgeois feminism, moved from Hamburg to Berlin, and joined the SPD, for we hear of her playing an active part in the party's campaign against inflation and speaking from the platform in a number of party meetings.[30]

Regine Ruben's dilemma, in which social and material considerations clashed with ideological ones, occurred in an even more acute form in the case of Lily Braun, the co-founder with Minna Cauer of the bourgeois feminist magazine *Die Frauenbewegung*. Like many other members of the radical feminist movement in the 1890s, Lily Braun sympathized with Social Democracy. But her sympathies went deeper than most. By 1895, she was clearly on the brink of abandoning bourgeois feminism and joining the SPD as an active member. It was social considerations that held her back, however, as she explained to the leading Social Democratic theoretician Karl Kautsky, in a characteristically revealing letter:

Social Democracy [she wrote] demands from its representatives that they 'stand on the ground of the class struggle'. I freely admit to you that neither my husband[31] nor I has understood this sentence . . . My view is this: there is certainly a class struggle between the working class and the bourgeoisie . . . Individual members of the bourgeoisie can be—and are—convinced that the aims of the working class can be achieved, they often say: 'What use is it if I now publicly go over to Social Democracy? My social equals will all turn their backs on me and I shall lose my income . . . If I stay where I am on the other hand, I can win my family, friends and social equals more and more for Social Democracy without their noticing it'.[32]

For someone like Lily Braun, of course, joining the SPD did involve real sacrifices. She had already estranged herself from her aristocratic Prussian family by entering radical intellectual circles in Berlin and marrying the leading member of the social-reformist and ultra-liberal Ethical Culture Society, George von Gizycki. Her hesitation over joining the SPD shows vividly how powerful were the social sanctions operating within German society against the members of the Social Democratic movement.[33] Socialism in her eyes was a movement to free the whole of mankind, 'and not simply one class at the cost of and to the detriment of the others', and she urged Kautsky and his colleagues to realize that 'these wicked "bourgeois" are human too'.[34] It was not long however before Lily Braun realized that it was impossible to work for the SPD without joining it and by 1896 she had left the bourgeois women's movement and joined the party. 'It will certainly amuse you', she wrote to her English friend Alys Russell, 'to learn that I am now publicly a "comrade", that is, I have joined the Social Democratic Party and severed my connections with the bourgeois associations. I intend in future to place my strength more and more in the service of the party'.[35] Subsequently she went on to embrace with real conviction a number of the party's Marxist beliefs.

Women such as Lily Braun and Regine Ruben were exceptions. What held feminists back from joining the only party that supported them was above all an inability to agree with the wider aims of Social Democracy. Although the radical feminists wanted to reform the political system of Imperial Germany, they certainly did not want a socialist revolution, with its expropriation of private property and its extension of the powers of the state; nor were they able to agree with the Marxist elements in the SPD's ideology. As individualists, the feminists were reluctant to submerge themselves in a movement which stressed the virtues of solidarity, collective action and mass support. The radical feminists went along with the Social Democrats in their criticisms of the German state and the political system; but their ways parted when it came to deciding what kind of social and political structures should replace them.

Increasingly, too, the suffragist leaders Augspurg and Heymann argued that the SPD, although theoretically in favour of women's suffrage, opposed it or neglected it in practice. Their view was shared by the suffragists in Berlin.[36] And it did indeed have a certain amount of justification. In the struggle over the revised franchise in Hamburg in 1905–6, for example, the SPD refused to demand female suffrage because it had no chance of being accepted.[37] Occasionally too, the suffragists were able to take advantage of the failure of the SPD to give its wholehearted support to campaigns for female suffrage. When the government of Oldenburg introduced a suffrage reform bill in 1907 the SPD neglected to use the opportunity to demand votes for women, and Lida Gustava Heymann and her aide Martha Zietz were able to mobilize the wives of SPD members in Wilhelmshaven in support of the Suffrage Union's own agitation.[38] Such incidents were rare, but they did give a certain credibility to the suffragists' attack on the SPD.

The radical feminists distrusted the politics of class struggle and argued strongly for a politics of disinterested 'idealism'.

Anita Augspurg, President of the German Union for Women's Suffrage, said that one reason why she supported the liberals was the fact that 'the Liberal People's Party simply seeks justice and progress and its political morality is not weakened by any politics tied to economic interests'.[39] This was doubtless an excessively rosy picture of the party; yet it expressed the fact that, for Augspurg and her followers, politics were about the freedom of the individual; to assert, as the SPD did, that individuals were not free, but were bound to classes by economic circumstances, was to deny the very foundation of the radical feminist ideology.

A further reason given by the radical suffragists for standing aloof from the SPD women from 1902 onwards was the trust the latter placed in solidarity with the men of their own party and class rather than with the women of other parties and other classes. Referring to the theories of the SPD women's leader, Clara Zetkin, Augspurg declared that

If Clara Zetkin expects that the men of a victorious, post-revolutionary Social Democracy will voluntarily extend to women the rights which [Social Democratic] women voluntarily deny themselves today, then she has not learned much from the lessons of history upon which she places so much weight. In the 110 years since the French Revolution . . . the men who fought for liberty, equality and fraternity have not changed in the least, as far as the rights of women are concerned, and they will not change in the next 110 years. But in a far shorter time, the women who fight shoulder-to-shoulder will undoubtedly win their own rights, and then use them for the cause of justice and social progress'.[40]

Augspurg was stating here the central tenet of feminism— that the division of society into men and women is more important than the division of society into social classes. It was a tenet that the SPD of course could not share.

According to Augspurg, in the SPD 'personal freedom is unknown; there, the system of absolute monarchy, of absolutism is the rule of the day'. This statement reflected the fact that the bourgeois feminists, even at the height of their attempts to win over the SPD women to some form of co-operation, were determined to retain their own distinctive political and social identity. For women like Cauer, Augspurg and Heymann, the defection to the SPD of individuals like

Regine Ruben and Lily Braun was a warning that too much emphasis on the similarity of aims between radical feminism and Social Democracy might eventually lead to the feminists' organizations being swallowed up by the SPD altogether. Many if not most of the radical feminists gained important emotional compensations for the tedium of the bourgeois women's conventional life through forming and running their own organizations; these would be lost if they subordinated themselves to the political discipline and male-dominated political movement of the Social Democratic Party.[41]

The radical feminists were thus forced to exist in a kind of political limbo, suspended uneasily between left liberalism and Social Democracy. They were rejected by both, yet they oscillated uncertainly between the two, as they expressed their sympathies now for one, now for the other, in the vain hope that they would be able to go into partnership without losing their identity or sacrificing their aims. It was a highly unstable situation, and one that could not last very long. While a steady trickle of individuals found their way into the Social Democratic Party, the greater proportion of radical feminists deserted their leaders and followed the left liberals in their rightward trek through their participation in government (1907–9) into the ideological tutelage of the neo-liberal imperalist Friedrich Naumann. In 1908 the radicals met their first real reverses at the BDF General Assembly; in 1910 the 'radical' feminist Marie Stritt was ousted as President of the BDF in a backstairs intrigue by the more conservative Gertrud Bäumer, a disciple of Friedrich Naumann; by 1913 the Suffrage Union had split into three separate organizations, the two largest of which had abandoned universal suffrage and opted for a property franchise, leaving the original leaders of the movement with only their principles and 2,000 followers. The sexual liberationist *Bund für Mutterschutz* had also split and lost much of its support in a series of scandalous lawsuits between the leading members. By the outbreak of the First World War, the bulk of the bourgeois feminist movement had come to adhere to a doctrine of national aggrandizement, constitutional liberalism strongly tainted with racist and eugenic ideology, and sexual conservatism, emphasizing the 'essential differences' between men and women, the primacy of women's duty to the state and *Volk* above individual desires, and the need to preserve marriage and family from those (like the *Bund für Mutterschutz*) who (it was argued) wanted to destroy them. It was a doctrine that bore little resemblance any more to the conventional bourgeois feminism that had dominated the BDF in the first decade of the twentieth century; and it further reduced the chances of co-operation with the women of the SPD.

III

If bourgeois feminists had reason to be reluctant to join with their socialist sisters, then so too did socialist women feel unable to co-operate with their feminist counterparts. The socialist women's movement in Germany was very small until about 1906, and was regarded with considerable suspicion by male party functionaries. The first task of its leading figure in this period, Clara Zetkin, was thus to prevent it from being absorbed by the more powerful BDF, and to allay the fears of SPD leaders by making clear the absolute commitment of the women's organization, which for legal reasons had only the loosest formal ties with the SPD itself, to the cause of Social Democracy. Zetkin fulfilled these objectives through strongly dissociating the SPD women's movement from its bourgeois counterpart in every respect. She argued that barriers of class were stronger than barriers of sex; collaboration with liberals would blur these vital distinctions and lead the SPD women's movement to forget its main aim, which was to work for a social revolution. 'Feminist ideas', as the radical SPD daily newspaper *Leipziger Volkszeitung* put it later on, 'are a great danger for the German [Social Democratic] Women's Movement . . . *There is no community of interests among women as a whole.*'[42] Bourgeois feminism, Zetkin argued, was the last stage in the process of emancipating private property from the legal controls that had shackled it in the feudal era, and of removing restraints on the ability of the individual to compete on equal legal terms with everyone else for employment and financial gain. Bourgeois women were now struggling for this freedom against the men of their own class.

Proletarian women, in contrast, were struggling with the men of their own class against the bourgeoisie as a whole. Bourgeois women were fighting against men; proletarian women were fighting against capital. Apart from these theoretical considerations, Zetkin was also able to argue in the 1890s that the practical demands of the bourgeois women were not radical enough for the SPD to support them even as reforms to lessen the evils of capitalism. The methods of the bourgeois feminists at this time too were not considered satisfactory; one could not expect class-conscious proletarian women to grovel before the Kaiser with humble petitions, said Zetkin in 1896.

Later on, however, as the feminists became more radical, this argument lost much of its force, at least until the feminists' move to the right after 1908 gave it back some validity. Zetkin therefore laid increasing emphasis on the revolutionary implications of female emancipation in order to distinguish Social Democracy from bourgeois feminism at a time when the distinction seemed to be getting blurred. Zetkin attended an international women's conference organized by the radical feminists in 1896. She used the occasion to denounce them, and to bring home to them the fact that their attempts to recruit working-class women to their organization (one of the main planks in their political platform) would be strongly resisted. It is, perhaps, hardly surprising that Zetkin went to these lengths, unusual though they were for her. For it was precisely at this time, when the radical feminists were first emerging as a political force, that the threat to the integrity of the SPD women's movement from the blandishments of Minna Cauer and her friends was most acute. The radicals, Zetkin asserted, were making a 'systematic' attempt to 'take the proletarian women in tow'; at the same time, the proletarian women's movement was threatening to 'form an alliance with the bourgeois feminist movement'. It was particularly for this reason that Zetkin stressed the differences between socialism and bourgeois feminism. By 1904, she could claim of the magazine she edited, that '*Gleichheit* has separated the proletarian women's movement . . . in principles as well as in tactics completely from any kind of bourgeois feminism.'[43] In the early 1890s, in contrast, the SPD women's movement had indeed been partially feminist in character, and the suppression or collapse of many of the early socialist women's societies in 1895–6 was probably seen by Zetkin as a blessing in disguise.

Zetkin argued that a policy of non co-operation would benefit the bourgeois women just as much as the proletarian. Association with Social Democracy, she claimed in a letter to Lily Braun in 1895, would gravely damage the bourgeois feminists' chances of getting their demands accepted by the government. Since Lily Braun was on the point of joining the SPD, but had not yet taken the plunge, the letter may have been framed so as not to offend her, for it was a refusal to help in a commission to be set up by the Berlin radical feminists to consider the working conditions of women factory workers. Yet there was some plausibility in the view that the women's movement would be taken less seriously by those it was trying to influence—in the first place, administrative authorities and legislative assemblies—if it was connected with Social Democracy, which was still considered to be a dangerously revolutionary political force.

In my opinion [wrote Zetkin] we ourselves should not be represented on the commission. Not that I'm afraid of the influence of the bourgeois members over the proletarian. There would be no chance of such an influence being exercised if we delegated Comrades Ihrer, Rohrlach and a few others to represent our side. But other considerations of principle and expediency speak against a mishmash commission . . . the more bourgeois the source from which the commission's conclusions emanate, the less they seem to be mixed up with agitatory/revolutionary forces, the more effect they will have on the authorities, and the more telling they will be in our agitation. I think that will make sense to you. If the commission conducts and reports its researches in a strictly neutral and objective way, this provides the guarantee that the commission is basically working for us even if we are not represented on it. Naturally I am prepared at all times to support the commission with my help and advice, because this would be in the interests of our movement. However I would criticize and oppose all co-operation between our comrades and the bourgeois elements on an official level.[44]

Zetkin's views were not accepted without opposition. In 1898–1902, joint meetings of SPD and bourgeois women did in fact take place, organized by Minna Cauer, in Hamburg and Berlin. The meetings caused the liberal daily, the *Berliner Tageblatt*, to comment that 'the bourgeois and proletarian women's movements, which are nowhere so deeply divided as here in Germany, now seem to be drawing closer together'.[45] And some SPD women enjoyed close contacts with bourgeois feminist organizations, above all with the *Mutterschutz* League. Henriette Fürth was very active in the League while remaining a party member and writing for the SPD 'revisionist' periodical *Sozialistische Monatshefte*.[46] Sometimes, too, the wives of leading members of the SPD were active in bourgeois feminism. Anna Lindemann, whose husband became SPD Interior Minister of Württemberg at the end of the First World War, was a leader of the Württemberg female suffragists.[47] And both the Bavarian SPD leader Georg von Vollmar and his wife were members of the bourgeois feminist movement in Munich.[48]

Before 1900, too, on some issues those SPD women who wanted to co-operate with the BDF enjoyed the support of the party newspaper *Vorwärts*. In 1896, for example, Zetkin published an article in *Vorwärts* arguing against Social Democratic participation in a petition for the reform of the Law of Association. The petition had been organized by two radical feminists and a member of the Social Democratic Party. Zetkin considered that it betrayed a 'thoroughly bourgeois character'. Its lack of socialist demands, despite the participation of a Social Democrat in its framing and despite the organizers' desire for it to be signed by socialist women as well as middle-class feminists, convinced Zetkin that bourgeois feminists were only prepared to use working-class women for their own ends and not to accept them as equal partners. Besides, asked Zetkin, if the Social Democrats as a whole refused to participate in political activities organized by bourgeois parties, why should women behave any differently? Were they to abandon their socialist principles just because they were women? Such an article was typical of Zetkin's denunciations of bourgeois feminism. The editor of *Vorwärts*, Wilhelm Liebknecht, felt obliged to append an editorial note, pointing out to his readers that:

Women are still in a completely different situation from that of men within the state. They are fully without rights, and, as far as the bourgeois women are concerned, politically speaking, completely uneducated. Every step towards self-reliance is a step forward . . . It really does make a difference whether such a petition as this is composed by men or by women.[49]

The newspaper again urged the socialist women to co-oper-ate with bourgeois feminists such as Minna Cauer in 1899.[50]

Zetkin was also criticized at the SPD women's conference in 1904 by the SPD sociologist Robert Michels, attending as a guest. He agreed that there were wide differences between the bourgeois and proletarian women's movements, but thought that they had much in common too. The SPD women should have taken part in the international bourgeois feminist conference of 1904, he argued, if only to put their views across and to remove misunderstandings and prejudices. After all, the SPD men had no objections to working with bourgeois politicians in the Reichstag. This speech—delivered by a speaker sent by the party rather than selected by the women's movement—gave rise to one of the very few real debates that took place at these conferences. Bourgeois women's congresses, said the SPD women's organizer and recruiting agent Luise Zietz, were not like parliaments, to which socialists were obliged to go to defend the interests of the working class in the legislative process; they were more like bourgeois party political congresses to which (naturally) socialists did not go. Besides, SPD women could not spare the time to discuss petty reforms with their enemies, who would in any case never listen to them. 'We have better things to do that to go to bourgeois conferences to stop bourgeois feminists from perpetrating stupid errors', she said. Experience showed, added Clara Zetkin, that the bourgeois feminists could not be detached from their class egoism by socialist speakers.[51]

Zetkin's views were accepted for two major reasons. First, her critics, who advocated co-operation with bourgeois feminists, were virtually all 'revisionists', associated with a minority in the party who wished to moderate the SPD's intransigence by repudiating some of the Marxist elements in its ideology.[52] Revisionism had been rejected by the party at a stormy congress in 1903, and this rejection enabled Zetkin to defeat her opponents fairly easily, especially since her control over the SPD women's magazine *Die Gleichheit* and the key Berlin branch of the SPD women's movement gave her a great deal of power in a situation where the movement's active members were to be counted in hundreds rather than thousands. Secondly, the doctrine of non-cooperation with bourgeois feminism grew in importance as the SPD women's movement grew in numerical strength, from about 1905 onwards (up to 1914, when it numbered about 175,000 women, compared to the BDF's 250,000 or so). For the movement's growth to mass proportions was based largely on the recruitment of the wives of male SPD activists, who felt it increasingly desirable that their families should share their own social and political ideas. This did not mean, of course, that the Social Democratic women's movement purely existed as a support for the ideology of male Social Democrats; it took a strong stand for the liberation of women on a number of issues, from the vote to the right to control contraception. This brought it into sharp conflict with the SPD men, who were constantly—and unsuccessfully—attempting to curb the autonomy and independence of the women's movement.[53] Yet it was only possible for the SPD women to create the necessary political elbow-room for themselves and to take a stand for genuine female emancipation if they constantly reiterated that the last thing they wanted to do was to abandon the labour movement of which they were a part and opt for bourgeois feminism instead. The social origins of the movement in the politicization of male Social Democrats' wives made it unlikely in any case that this would happen. The basis of the movement, after all, lay in solidarity with the men; a solidarity founded on a hard-fought position of relative autonomy, but solidarity none the less.

From a working-class perspective the bourgeois feminists also appeared to lack comprehension of the needs and aspirations of women engaged in manual labour. Certainly the German feminists, both moderate and radical, tended to have a more favourable attitude towards the idea that the state should intervene to improve the condition of working-class women than did their colleagues in England and America. The stock assumption of the SPD women, that the feminists were interested only in gaining a full share for themselves in the rewards of exploitation, and not in improving the condition of the working-class women, seemed less than fair. Many English feminists opposed the introduction of laws banning women from certain dangerous occupations, limiting their hours of work and so on because they thought that this would negate the principle that women should have the free choice of doing any job they wished, just as men did. But this was not the view of the German women's movement. The BDF petitioned the Reichstag in 1899 and 1905 for the extension of controls and safeguards to domestic labour and generally supported provisions for the protection of mothers working in industry. The radical feminists also established a Conference for the Protection of the Interests of Women Workers in 1907—another offshoot of the Union of Progressive Women's Associations. This was conceived as a kind of organizing body for liberal feminists interested in founding anti-clerical, liberal women's trade unions, though none was in fact formed. The radical feminist Maria Lischnewska also devoted much of her time to devising a scheme for training girls to skilled crafts. And the radicals produced a magazine for women workers from 1904. It was clearly then quite unjustified to accuse the bourgeois feminists of 'class egoism', of being interested only in improving their own social and political position at the expense of that of the women of the working class.[54]

Nevertheless, in the attitude of the radical feminists towards working-class women, a strong element of liberal individualism could be discerned. Käthe Schirmacher wrote as early as 1896, speaking for radical feminists in general, that the bourgeois women supported some of the SPD's demands for the protection of female labour 'because they want the free competition of all classes and both sexes, competition without restraints and barriers, the struggle for existence under just conditions'.[55] Augspurg and Heymann, indeed, went much further and opposed legal protection for women workers altogether, demonstrating once more that their liberal individualism was more consistent than that of their colleagues.[56] If, like Maria Lischnewska, feminists were interested in improving the lot of women workers, it was in the liberal tradition of helping individual working people to rise to the middle-class, or at least to the labour aristocracy, based on the liberal virtues of self-discipline and self-help. As Lischnewska put it, the aim was to 'help women to gain their independence'. The aim of the feminists, in sum, was to re-create working women in their own image.[57]

It was for this reason that the bourgeois feminists, both radical and moderate, concentrated so strongly on the need for after-school education *(Fortbildung)* for working-class girls. The motivation and attitudes behind the feminists' concern with the working classes were heavily influenced by maternalistic ways of thinking. Minna Cauer put the reason for her belief that the bourgeois feminists should pay more attention to the proletarian women than they did, in the following revealing way:

Because we are educated and better placed in life . . . we must understand the struggle of the lower orders and build bridges through sympathetic responses to their demands and silence when they attack us. We must never upset them, but despite the struggle which must now come, we must only use the most noble weapons.

Even for Cauer, therefore, sympathy with working-class women was quite consciously seen as a 'weapon' in the class struggle: and her concern never to 'upset' the women of the proletariat is symptomatic of the real fear which middle-class women felt of the power and radicalism of the Social Democratic women's movement. Cauer and her friends aimed above all to 'build bridges' to the revisionist wing of the Social Democrats and so encourage moderation in the party. Thus Cauer complained in 1903 that the SPD women's magazine *Die Gleichheit* preached class hatred to working women and criticized all social reforms suggested by others standing outside the SPD, 'instead of trying in the first place to improve, educate and elevate'. By 'improving' working women, it was thought, class hatred could be diminished and class barriers made easier for the individual to cross.[58] As in the case of the French controversy over domestic servants, however, socialist women saw only condescension and the representation of bourgeois class interests in such an attitude.

IV

The German Social Democratic women's movement not only imposed on itself a ban on official co-operation with the feminists, it also sought to internationalize this policy through the agency of the Socialist Women's International, founded and effectively run by Zetkin (its headquarters were in her home near Stuttgart). At its first congress in 1907, the International voted through a resolution proclaiming that 'socialist women must not ally themselves with the feminists of the bourgeoisie, but lead the battle [for the vote] side by side with the socialist parties'.[59] The French, represented by Madeleine Pelletier, attempted to object to the resolution, but the Austrian and German women eventually pushed it through with little real dissent. Ultimately, however, it scarcely needed enforcing. Under the leadership of Louise Saumoneau, as we have seen, the French socialist women too rejected any idea of compromise with bourgeois feminism. Socialist women in other countries were already taking a similar course. In Russia, for example, Alexandra Kollontai expended a good proportion of her very considerable energies on attacking bourgeois feminism and disrupting their meetings. At the great Russian feminist congress held in St Petersburg in 1908, similar scenes occurred to those which had already taken place at the German congress in 1896 and its French counterpart in 1900. Kollontai and the labour delegates tried to get the Congress to support their socialist demands, but without success. This was perhaps not surprising, since Kollontai's report to the congress declared that bourgeois feminists and working women had nothing in common and should not form a united all-women's movement such as the feminists envisaged.[60] As the report was read out, the feminists responded to its diatribes by foot-stamping and shouts of 'go away!'. One of the leading feminists, Anna Kalmanovich, delivered a bitter attack on the failure of the Second International to give practical support to women's suffrage, and this in its turn was met with interruptions and shouts from the labour delegates. For her part, Kollontai declared that 'between the emancipated woman of the intelligentsia and the toiling woman with calloused hands, there was such an unbridgeable gulf that there could be no question of any sort of point of agreement between them.'[61] In her book, *The Social Bases of the Woman Question* (1909), she relentlessly attacked the feminist movement, refusing to give it credit for anything, and portraying it as acting from ulterior motives, in the desire to shore up the class position of the bourgeoisie. Working women, she concluded, should not join in the feminist struggle for women's equality but had to fight alongside the men of the proletariat for the liberation of all humanity.[62]

Views such as these were by no means an inevitable extrapolation of the fundamentals of Marxism. Marx and Engels, for instance, were always quite clear about the legitimacy of socialists co-operating with non-socialists for tactical reasons, and Wilhelm Liebknecht was acting quite in accordance with their views in criticizing Zetkin's isolationist stance in 1899.[63] The other leading figure in German Social Democracy, August Bebel, had devoted substantial sections of his book *Woman and Socialism* to a very positive assessment of the nature and history of bourgeois feminism (and was criticized by Zetkin precisely on this ground).[64] The failure of feminism and socialism to join forces was not the outcome of Marxist philosophy. As we have seen, it reflected far more the deep social gulf between bourgeois and proletarian women in pre-1914 Europe, and owed much as well to the anxiety of male socialist leaders that working-class women would drift away from the socialist movement. Feminists were not simply serving bourgeois class interests, as the socialists maintained, but their feminism could easily be seen as running counter to working-class interests, especially where it involved the primacy of aims—such as equal but limited suffrage, married women's property rights, or the admission of women to universities and the professions—that were of little or no immediate concern to the women of the working class. For their part, it is hard to deny that socialist women like Zetkin and Saumoneau made too many concessions to the male leadership of their respective parties, even if there were cogent reasons for making some, and even though—at least in the case of Zetkin—they could be sharply critical of the leadership when it went directly against the principle of equal rights or tried to curb the autonomy of the women's movement.

How much difference did the failure to unite make to the cause of women's equality and emancipation? There were mutually hostile liberal feminist and socialist women's movements not only in Germany, France and Russia but in

Austria, Finland, Sweden and the United States as well. Yet in
Finland and the USA women had already achieved substantial
rights, including the vote (in some American states at least) by
1914. While the socialist women's movement in the USA was
perhaps too weak in comparison to the powerful bourgeois
feminist organizations for their mutual hostility to be of any
great significance, the same certainly cannot be said of
Finland. Yet Finnish women achieved the vote in 1906, the first
European women to do so. It was significant that the bourgeois
and socialist wings of the movement began to act in concert
when it became clear in 1905 that women's suffrage was a real
political possibility; so too did the bourgeois and socialist
women's movements in Sweden in 1909–12, in Russia in
March 1917, and indeed in Germany itself in 1917–18.[65] These
examples suggest that as far as getting the vote for women was
concerned, the division of the women's movement into two
mutually hostile wings was not a cause, but a product, of its
impotence. There is no doubt, for example, that when the
Kaiser promised political democratization in his 'Easter
message' of 1917, German women's organizations began to
feel that female suffrage had become a political possibility.

Yet in the case of Germany, these conclusions must be
thrown into question by the changes that had taken place in the
SPD women's movement since shortly before the war. After
1908, Clara Zetkin, who was becoming increasingly radical,
lost her former hold over the movement, and in 1917 she was
ousted from the editorship of *Die Gleichheit* and joined the
secessionist Independent Social Democratic Party along with a
number of other leading women activists, including Luise
Zietz.[66] Those who took over the majority SPD women's
organization included the very revisionists—notably Wally
Zepler—who had been arguing for co-operation with
bourgeois feminists for years. The Independent Social
Democrats were conspicuously absent from the joint
bourgeois feminist/Social Democratic meetings organized to
demand the vote.[67] Moreover, these developments led to a
permanent split within the BDF, as the right wing of the
bourgeois feminist movement left in protest against the
campaign. What had in fact happened was a process of
convergence which paralleled similar developments in national

politics: the liberals moved to the left, and the Social Democrats to the right, under the pressure of prolonged war; those who opposed this shifting of position moved out towards the opposite extremes of the political spectrum. Co-operation thus had as much to do with the general shake-up of the German left which took place in 1917 as with any sudden conviction on the part of women's organizations that female suffrage was just around the corner. Leaving the suffrage question aside, it seems quite probable that the struggle for legislative reform was hampered by the mutual hostility of feminists and socialists: far more important, however, in the end, were the general social and political conditions under which the struggle took place.

This means that some caution must be exercised in judging the relevance of the feminist/socialist debates of the pre-First World War period for political practice today. In the first place, attitudes and theories were conditioned by the nature of the social and political systems within which they operated. While the socialist women's refusal to co-operate with bourgeois feminists reflected both their need to identify strongly with a socialist movement whose leaders regarded them with suspicion and mistrust, and that movement's overall insistence on the complete separation of all its constituent parts from bourgeois organizations of any kind, the bourgeois feminists on their side held aloof from their socialist sisters not only because they wanted to retain overall control of their own affairs, without letting the male leadership of any political party dictate to them what they should or should not do, but also because they feared the social stigma and police repression that would be their lot if they joined forces with the SPD. Ideological influences—individualism versus socialism, reformism versus revolution—played a distinctive role of their own in helping to keep the two groups of women apart; but they also reflected differences in the social composition of the two movements, the radical bourgeois feminists being dominated by unmarried middle-class professional women, while the socialist women were mainly the wives of working-class socialist men. In the present day, though it is difficult to generalize across all the countries where women's movements now exist, many of these factors seem to be different. The experience of the last fifty years has made socialist women less sanguine about the prospects of revolution and less confident in the progressiveness of the working class in areas such as the role of women. Feminists are often less hostile to the general ideological orientation of socialist movements than were the liberal individualists of the pre-1914 era. Formal organizations and organized campaigns for legislative reform, though still important, play a smaller role in the present-day women's movement than they did in the past. The women's liberation movement in advanced capitalist economies is overwhelmingly middle-class in social composition; an equivalent of the mass working-class organization of the Social Democratic women's movement in Imperial Germany no longer exists; the changing class structure of advanced industrial society, with its large service sector, has provided a new, more unified social base for feminism. All these influences would seem to imply that the forces working against common action and unity within the women's movement are considerably weaker now than they were in the society which has been the subject of this chapter. Whether this is in fact the case, or whether the new conditions are, in their different way, as hostile to united feminist action as were the old, is perhaps a matter for further debate.

NOTES

This chapter is based on my article 'Bourgeois feminists and women socialists in Germany 1894–1914: lost opportunity or inevitable conflict?', *Women's Studies International Quarterly,* vol. 3 (1980), pp. 335–76, and draws on material first presented in my book *Sozialdemokratie und Frauenemanzipation im deutschen Kaiserreich* (Verlag J.H.W. Dietz Nachf., Bonn–Berlin, 1979).

1. See chapter 3 for a detailed exploration of socialist attitudes to women's suffrage.
2. Quoted in Charles Sowerwine, *Sisters or Citizens? Women and Socialism in France since 1876* (Cambridge, p.113.)
3. Sowerwine, *op. cit.*, pp. 110–28.
4. *ibid.*, p.127
5. *ibid.*, p.186. See also Marilyn J. Boxer, 'When radical and socialist feminism were joined: the extraordinary failure of Madeleine Pelletier',

in J. Slaughter, R. Kern (eds), *European Women on the Left* (Westport, Conn., 1981), pp. 51–74.

6. Steven C. Hause, with Anne R. Kenney, *Women's Suffrage and Social Politics in the French Third Republic* (Princeton, 1984), pp. 134–5.

7. *ibid.*, p.43. See also James F. McMillan, *Housewife or Harlot: The Place of Women in French Society 1870–1940* (Brighton, 1981), pp. 76–100.

8. Sowerwine, *op. cit.*, p. 79.

9. Hause and Kenny, *op. cit.*, p. 70.

10. Sowerwine, *op. cit.*, pp. 134–41.

11. *ibid.*, p. 135.

12. *ibid.*, p. 88.

13. *ibid.*, p. 89.

14. See below, pp. 69–75.

15. Sowerwine, *op. cit.*, pp. 129–30. See, more generally, Patrick K. Bidelman, *Pariahs Stand Up! The Founding of the Liberal Feminist Movement in France 1858–1889* (Westport, Conn., 1982); Marilyn J. Boxer, 'Socialism faces feminism: the failure of synthesis in France, 1879–1914', in M. Boxer and J. Quataert (eds). *Socialist Women: European Socialist Feminism in the Nineteenth and Early Twentieth Centuries* (New York, 1978), pp. 75–111; Steven C. Hause and Anne R. Kenney, 'The limits of suffragist behaviour: legalism and militancy in Franc, 1876–1922', *American Historical Review* 86 (1981), pp. 781–806.

16. ABDF 4(4); Cauer to Stritt (29 January 1904).

17. StA Hbg, PP, S9000/II: *Berliner Volkszeitung* (2 October, 1900).

18. *Die Frau*, 8(2), pp. 65–7 (November 1900).

19. *FB*, 5(20) (15 October 1899). In the same year, indeed the BDF asked the SPD leader August Bebel for his support in the Reichstag (IISG Amsterdam, NL Bebel 164: Stritt to Bebel, (18 November 1899)). See also StA Hbg, PP, S8897/III: *VW* (28 October 1907).

20. Lida Gustava Heymann, in collaboration with Dr. jur. Anita Augspurg, *Erlebtes-Erschautes. Deutsche Frauen kämpfen für Freiheit, Recht und Frieden 1850–1940,* (Meisenheim-am-Glan, 1972), pp. 167–8.

21. IISG Amsterdam, NL Kautsky, D VII 45: Cauer to Luise Kautsky (9 November 1921); IISG Amsterdam, Kleine Korrespondenz: Cauer to Redaktion 'Freiheit' (9 November 1921).

22. Else Lüders, *Minna Cauer, Ihr Leben und Werk. Dargestellt an Hand ihrer Tagebücher und nachgelassenen Schriften* (Gotha, 1925), entry for 20 March 1911 p.156. But cf. also *ibid.*, pp. 227–8.

23. Max Schwarz, *MdR. Biographisches Handbuch der Reichstage,* (Hanover, 1965) entry for Schreiber-Krieger, Adele.

24. UB Rostock, NL Schirmacher: Schirmacher to Schleker (3 October 1909). I am grateful to Amy Hackett for lending me her notes on the Schirmacher Nachlass, which I was not able to see for myself.

25. StA Hbg, PP, S8897/V: *VW* (2 July 1917).

26. StA Hbg, PP, S8898/IV: 'Frauen heraus!' 2 March 1913.

27. ABDF 5/II/4: Protokollbuch des Allgemeinen Deutschen Frauenvereins, II (7 January, 1896); Oda Olberg, 'Polemisches über

Frauenfrage und Sozialismus', *SMH* (1905) p.302.

28. Alice Salomon, 'Sozialdemokratie und Frauenbewegung', *Die Frau* (November, 1904), pp. 75–6.
29. IML/ZPA NL 5/45: Zetkin to Wilhelm Blos (27 December 1905).
30. StA Hbg, PP, S8897/IV: *HE* (27 October 1912), *VW* (25 September 1912).
31. Georg von Gizycki. She married the Social Democrat Heinrich Braun in 1896. See also Lily Braun, *Memoiren einer Sozialistin,* vol. II (Munich, 1909); and Alfred G. Meyer, *The Feminism and Socialism of Lily Braun* (Bloomington, Indiana, 1985).
32. IISG Amsterdam, NL Kautsky, D VI 584: Lily Braun to Karl Kautsky (16 May 1895).
33. Lily Braun, *Memoiren einer Sozialistin,* vol. I, *Lehrjahre* (Munich 1908), p.575.
34. IISG Amsterdam, NL Kautsky, D VI 584: Lily Braun to Karl Kautsky (16 May 1895).
35. Fawcett Library, London, Autograph Collection, col. VIII, part C: Lily Braun to Alys Russell (16 January 1896). For a fictionalized account of Braun's conversation, see Marianne Bruns, *Uns hebt die Flut* (Halle, 1952).
36. StA Hbg, S9001/I: *HN* (4 October 1903).
37. *Stenographische Berichte über die Sitzung der Bürgerschaft zu Hamburg im Jahre 1906:* 4. Sitzung, p. 113 (24 January 1906). For a more extended discussion of this point, see chapter 3, below.
38. StA Hbg, PP, S9001/II: *VW* (22 December 1907).
39. StA Hbg, PP, S9001/I: *Generalanzeiger* (10 May 1903).
40. (Anita Augspurg), 'Die Sozialdemokratische Frauenkonferenz', *FB* 8(20), 15 October 1902, p. 155.
41. StA Hbg, PP, S9001/I: *Hamburger Fremdenblatt* (3 October 1903). See Heymann/Augspurg, *Erlebtes-Erschautes,* for a graphic description of the feminists' personal rejection of the conventional life of middle-class womanhood; similarly, Lily Braun, *Memoiren einer Sozialistin,* vol. I, (aristocratic background).
42. StA Hbg, PP, S9001/III: quoted in *Berliner Neueste Nachrichten* (10 December 1913) (italics in original).
43. PTP 1896, p. 173; IISG Amsterdam, NL Kautsky, D-XXIII Nr 348: Zetkin to Kautsky (29 October 1901); *GL* 14(13), p. 102 (15 June 1904); quoted in Karen Honeycutt, 'Clara Zetkin; A Left-Wing Socialist and Feminist in Wilhelmian Germany' (Ph.D. Thesis, Columbia, 1975), pp. 168–78.
44. IML/ZPA, NL 5/44: Clara Zetkin to Lily Braun (8 August 1895).
45. StA Hbg, PP, S5466/I: *HE* (22 March 1900, 17 March 1900), *VW* (31 March, 1900), *Berliner Tageblatt* (31 March 1900). Subsequent meetings of this sort were rare. One was held in Hamburg in 1907. This gave rise to strong criticism by Zetkin and her associates of the revisionist Wally Zepler, the socialist participant. Cf. *ibid., VW* (28 February, 1907).
46. Cf. IISG Amsterdam, Coll. Henriette Fürth: Eduard Bernstein to Fürth (5 April 1907).

47. 'As wife of a "sozi"', wrote the 'radical' Käthe Schirmacher, 'Lindemann can achieve nothing in the provinces' (UB Rostock, NL Schirmacher: Schirmacher to Schleker, 13 March 1914).
48. IISG Amsterdam, NL Vollmacher, 135: Augspurg to Vollmar (14 May 1899, 18 September 1901, 8 January 1902); *ibid.*, 3157–3158: Verein für Fraueninteressen, München: Mitgliederkarten.
49. IML/ZPA NL 5/14: *VW* (24 January 1895).
50. StA Hbg, PP, S8897/III: *VW* (6 October 1899).
51. PTP 1907, pp. 342–9.
52. This was above all true of Lily Braun (see *Memoiren einer Sozialistin*); But the *Sozialistische Monatshefte* was also a 'revisionist' periodical. Wilhelm Liebknecht of course cannot be classed with the revisionists. Revisionist theory, rejected by the party, should not be confused with reformist practice, which became increasingly common in the years up to 1914.
53. See chapters 3 and 4, below.
54. *Jahrbuch der Frauenbewegung 1921* (Berlin/Leipzig 1922), pp. 43–5; *FB* 9(20), 157 (15 October 1903); Haupstaatsarchiv Stuttgart E151 cII Nr 238; StA Hbg; Senat, C1. II. Lit. Rf. Nr. 344, vol.1; StA Hbg, PP, SA 1417.
55. SMH 1896, p. 224.
56. Irmgard Remme, 'Die Internationalen Beziehungen der deutschen Frauenbewegung vom Ausgang des 19. Jahrhunderts bis 1933' (Phil. Diss., West Berlin 1955) pp. 114–5.
57. *FB*, 9(18), 138–40 (15 September 1903).
58. *FB* 9(11), 81 (1 June 1903); Else Lüders, *Minna Cauer, Ihr Leben und Werk. Dargestellt an Hand ihrer Tagebücher und nachgelassenen Schriften* (Gotha, 1925), p. 95.
59. Sowerwine, *op. cit.*, p. 118.
60. Richard Stites, *The Women's Liberation Movement in Russia. Feminism, Nihilism and Bolshevism 1860–1930* (Princeton, 1978), p. 218.
61. *ibid.*, p. 228.
62. *ibid.*, pp. 423–6.
63. Cf. Hans-Josef Steinberg, *Sozialismus und deutsche Sozialdemokratie* (Bonn–Bad Godesberg, 1968).
64. For a full discussion of Bebel's book, see my *Sozialdemokratie und Frauenemanzipation im deutschen Kaiserreich* (Bonn-Berlin, 1979).
65. For international comparisons, see my book *The Feminists: Women's Emancipation Movements in Europe, America and Australasia 1840–1920* (London, 1977), esp. pp. 211–28.
66. See Luise Dornemann, *Clara Zetkin. Leben und Wirken* (5th edn, East Berlin, 1973).
67. *Die Staatsbürgerin,* April 1918, pp. 9–10; May/June 1918, p. 24; July/August 1918, pp. 33–4.

3 Women's Suffrage and the Left

I

Many accounts of the women's suffrage movements of the late nineteenth and early twentieth centuries give the impression that 'votes for women' was a demand raised almost exclusively by women from the liberal middle classes. Here and there, perhaps, individuals or groups from the working class might attach themselves to bourgeois female suffrage movements, but the leadership and the political direction of these movements remained firmly in the hands of the better-off sections of the female population. For some countries, notably England and the United States, this picture is not wholly inaccurate, though even here work by historians such as Liddington and Norris is beginning to uncover substantial and active working-class participation. But when we turn to the European continent, a very different picture presents itself; for in a number of countries, the fight for women's suffrage was led not by middle-class, but by working-class women, and the largest and most determined women's suffrage organizations were not the liberal feminist societies of the bourgeoisie, but the mass socialist movements of the proletariat.

By far the most impressive—though by no means the only—example of a working-class female suffrage movement is to be found in the case of Imperial Germany, in the form of the women's section of the Social Democratic Party of Germany. In sheer size and strength of organization, the SPD was easily the greatest socialist movement of its day. Originating in the 1860s, it had acquired by 1891 a programme which contained a strong element of Marxism. Its leaders, notably August Bebel and the party theoretician Karl Kautsky, were in close contact with Engels until the latter's death in 1895. By 1905 the party had 384,000 members, and on the eve of the First World War it had no fewer than 1,086,000. In the German elections of 1912, the SPD secured some 4,250,000 votes and became the largest party in the German parliament (the Reichstag), although it was unable to form a government until the removal of the Kaiser and the establishment of a parliamentary constitution in the Revolution of 1918. It was during the course of that Revolution that German women got the vote; but remarkably, already by 1914 nearly 175,000 women were enrolled in the SPD as full-time members. This appears even more striking when it is realized that until 1908 women were forbidden by law to join political parties in most parts of Germany, so that the Social Democratic women numbered only a few tens of thousands until that date. Particularly after 1908, the Social Democratic women's organization easily stood comparison with the organizations of the middle-class feminists. The liberal female suffrage movement in Germany, for example, only numbered some 14,000 women in 1914, and although the main feminist movement, the Federation of German Women's Associations, contained about a quarter of a million women in its ranks by that date, most of them did not campaign for women's suffrage at all, and scores of thousands of them even opposed it.

The Social Democratic women were forced by the legal restrictions on their full membership of the party until 1908 to constitute their own organization, independent in many respects from that of the SPD itself. Even after 1908, though they were formally incorporated into the structure of the party, they still retained a good deal of independence, and continued to refer to themselves as the 'proletarian women's movement of Germany', as they had done before. In contrast to the bourgeois feminists, who only formally committed themselves to female suffrage in 1902, the Social Democratic women supported votes for women from the very beginning. However, it would be true to say that in the early years of the proletarian women's movement, in the 1880s and 1890s, their major concern was with the pay and conditions of female factory and domestic workers, a concern reinforced by the fact that many, if not most, of the leading SPD women were also active in the trades union movement. Gradually, after the turn of the century, this emphasis began to change. The SPD women's movement put more and more of its energy into campaigning for the right to vote. Of course, this reflected a general trend in the Social Democratic Party as well, since the party too was becoming increasingly preoccupied with the extension of voting rights, above all in Prussia, where the important provincial parliament (*Landtag*), representing over half the population of Germany, was elected on a property franchise which effectively excluded the working class and the SPD from any real measure of power.[1] This general trend was bound to be reflected in constituent parts of the SPD such as the women's movement. But female suffrage had its own special meaning for women as well.

Women's suffrage played an important role for the members of the women's movement—and indeed for all working-class women brought into contact with SPD propaganda on the subject—as the most potent and most public of all symbols of female independence and emancipation. For working-class women themselves, the increasing concentration of the party and the Social Democratic women's movement on demanding the vote brought with it an increasingly public insistence on women's equality; on the equal ability of women of all classes to understand politics, on the equal right of women to take part in them, and in the most practical sense on the equal assertiveness of women in politics even when they were still without the vote. It was above all the demand for women's suffrage that gave working-class women the chance to acquire political roles outside the home even more public than participation in meetings: roles that they could share by proxy even if they could not play them out in person. The SPD women staged their own silent demonstrations outside polling booths at election time (especially in 1911 and 1912) with banners and placards calling for women's suffrage; but above all their urge for political equality found its classic expression in the institution of the 'International Proletarian Women's Day'.[2]

The idea of the International Proletar
originated with Clara Zetkin, who
International Socialist Women's Confer
conjunction with a Congress of the Seco
women's demonstrations be held annually on
over the world, as an expression of the international soɪ
of socialist women in their struggle for the emancipation of the
female proletariat. Among the reasons for this proposal was
very probably a desire on Zetkin's part to regain some of the
power she had lost within the SPD women's organization since
1908, when she had been replaced as its effective leader by the
less radical Luise Zietz.[3] However, if Zetkin thought she was
going to turn the Women's Day to her own advantage she was
mistaken, for once it had been decided upon it was in effect
taken over by Zietz, who set about organizing it. Whatever
Zetkin's intention had been, Zietz—whose main talent lay in
her organizing ability—turned it into a day of mass demonstrations for women's suffrage. On the first Women's Day, held on
19 March 1911, forty-one mass meetings were held in Berlin
alone, and hundreds more meetings were held in the rest of
Germany. Many of them were filled to overflowing and men
were asked to leave so that more women could be admitted.
Five thousand women attended a meeting in the Berlin
working-class district of Wedding, and another five thousand
an assembly in Moabit, another proletarian quarter in the
capital city. At every meeting, after the speeches, resolutions
demanding the vote for women were passed unanimously amid
thunderous applause. All this was impressive evidence of the
strength of organization of the Social Democratic women's
movement, and underlined in the most effective possible way
the seriousness of its commitment to female suffrage.[4]

The next Women's Day, in 1912, was perhaps a little less
successful. The *Hamburger Echo*, the SPD's main newspaper
in Hamburg, Germany's second largest city, reported that
some of the meetings were badly attended, in contrast to the
previous year. At the central assembly point (the Trade Union
Hall), for example, only 300 people appeared, in contrast to
800 in 1911; and in the Eppendorf district, the numbers fell
from 230 to 140. Nevertheless, despite occasional reports to the
contrary ('unfortunately the meeting was not attended by the

mbers we would like to have seen'), the impression conveyed by reports is that most of the meetings were, as before, packed to overflowing. 1,200 people, mostly women, took part in an assembly in Essen, 2,000 in Breslau, 3,000 in two meetings in Bremerhaven, and 1,000 in a meeting in each of the towns of Leipzig, Erfurt and Brunswick.[5] However, this did not stop many of the leading men in the party from taking the opportunity to argue that there would be no point in holding a further Women's Day in 1913.

On 7 November 1912, at a sitting of the party council (*Partei-Ausschuss*), a body created by the party congress of the same year, and consisting of representatives of the local party organizations with the function of making recommendations on contentious issues which came up before the party's executive committee (*Parteivorstand*), Luise Zietz admitted that 'the last Women's Day did not turn out as we would have wished it to'. Conscious of a strong feeling in the executive committee (to which she belonged) that the Women's Day should be abandoned, Zietz attempted to suggest a compromise which would preserve the Women's Day while making at least some concession to its critics: 'We recommend', she said, 'that it be held not annually, but when it is needed', adding: 'It will take place next year, if only because of the forthcoming elections to the Prussian Parliament.' But the institution's critics were not to be put off so easily. One delegate, from Jena in Thuringia, remarked (beginning with a customary disclaimer), 'We Thuringians are friends of the women's movement. The Women's Days have only cost us money. Women's meetings prepared for a special purpose are more valuable. No Women's Day should be held next year.' Richard Lipinski, the delegate from Leipzig, added: 'We have had bad experiences with the Women's Days, with the exception of Leipzig itself. The women's meetings should not all be held on the same day.' Some, like the delegates from Brunswick and Magdeburg, remarked that it had been a mistake to hold the Women's Day on a Sunday in 1912. The Magdeburg delegate insisted none the less that 'the recruitment of women deserves more attention than it has got so far'; and Paul Löbe (Breslau) pointed out that 'the first Women's Day was very imposing and brought the party good results'. But most (including Löbe) agreed that the 1912 Women's Day had been, as the Stuttgart delegate said, a 'fiasco'. 'Interest in the Women's Day', concluded Georg Thöne (Cassel), 'has died down, so it must not be held every year.' In the end, therefore, 'the holding of the Women's Day next year was rejected by a great majority'.[6]

The leading women in the party refused to accept this decision. Clara Zetkin and Luise Zietz buried their differences and joined forces to reverse the vote. They managed to secure an emergency meeting of the party council, which usually met once a quarter, at the beginning of 1913. Zetkin declared:

Comrade Zietz and I have above all with regard to women comrades in other countries emphatically and exhaustively stated our reasons for holding the Women's Day this year as well, and for it to be given the strongest support. We have further given our grounds for holding it, if possible, on the same day as the one which women comrades in other countries have already chosen.[7]

This was an important point, and Zetkin used it at the special meeting of the party council on 31 January 1913, which she attended as International Secretary of the Socialist Women's Movement. A number of delegates were successfully convinced that the SPD would look foolish in the eyes of the international socialist movement if it pulled out of the International Women's Day at this stage, and a compromise was eventually agreed on. The council voted by 25 votes to 10 to uphold its earlier decision, but it also voted by a large majority that nationwide women's meetings should take place on 2-3 March 1913. Thus in effect, even if not in name, the Women's Day was saved.[8]

The women's demonstrations of 1913 played down their wider aspects and put an even greater emphasis than before on the demand for women's suffrage. Some of the meetings were better attended than in 1913. According to police reports, the number of people attending the meeting in the Hamburg Trade Union Hall rose from 300 to 550; and in other parts of Hamburg it rose too—in Harvestehude from 100 to 250, in Veddel from 38 to 100, in Fuhlsbüttel from 80 to 250, in Barmbek from 300 to 650, in Hamm and Horn from 120 to 330 and in Eppendorf from 140 to 350. In Berlin, the picture was more mixed: 2,000 came to the meeting in the Pharus Rooms as against 1,500 in 1913, in Britz the numbers were 170, compared with 150 in 1911, and in Niederschönhausen the numbers rose from 200 to 500. On the other hand, numbers sank in other parts of Berlin from 1912 to 1913: in Badstrasse from 2,000 to 1,000: in Neukölln from 5,000 to only 900, in Schöneberg from 1,000 to 600, in Oberschöneweide from 500 to 100, in Tegel from 500 to 200, and in Weissensee from 750 to 600. These figures were enough for the SPD's executive to decide once more that no Women's Day would be held in 1914. But once more the women opposed the decision; and once more they got their way, even if their victory was disguised as a compromise, as in 1913. This time the Women's Day was to be held as the opening day of a 'Red Week' devoted to a massive recruitment drive designed to shore up the SPD's membership figures, which were beginning to sag by this time. It appears from reports that participation was better than in 1913, but it is also clear that none of the Women's Days held from 1912 to 1914 was quite so successful as the first one held in 1911.[9] Yet none of them was so disastrous as to justify the institution's abolition. On the contrary, since a major feature of the meetings was the carefully orchestrated signing-on of new female members of the SPD and new subscribers to the SPD's women's magazine *Die Gleichheit*, all the Women's Days obviously played an important part in boosting the party's overall membership, for none of the meetings failed to recruit scores, if not hundreds, of new members to the party ranks.[10]

The real reason for the strong and persistent hostility shown to the Women's Day by the leading men in the party seems in fact to have been quite different, for perhaps the most important feature of the Women's Day lay not in the mass meetings, speeches and recruitment drives, but in the street demonstrations which occurred before and after the actual assemblies. Street marches, the common tactic of militant and constitutional female suffrage movements in England and America at this time, were considered almost revolutionary in Germany, and usually called forth a strong reaction from the police. The liberal feminist German Union for Women's Suffrage only ever held one street demonstration, and that was in carriages, not on foot. Yet spontaneous street marches took place at many of the major centres of the Women's Day in

1911. On 19 March 1911, for instance, when the meetings closed in Dresden, 500 women marched from their assembly hall in the suburbs of Preischen into the middle of the city, carrying a white banner emblazoned with the words 'Votes for Women!' (*'Heraus mit dem Frauenwahlrecht!'*). On the same day, 150 women also marched on the Town Hall in Hamburg to demand the vote, while similar processions were held in various parts of Berlin. In 1912 these street demonstrations were even more widespread. The women's march from the Trade Union Hall in Berlin to the Arnim Halls was described by the SPD's newspaper *Vorwärts* as being 'like a black snake'. Such demonstrations also took place in 1913 and 1914. In all of them, banners and placards were carried demanding the vote. Another report from *Vorwärts* gives an impression of the atmosphere of the Women's Day in 1914, in terms which place the participants very firmly within the social order:

2 o'clock. The meeting-hall has long since been filled to overflowing. But still new multitudes flock to the assembly place. Processions of up to 300 people have come together. Several ladies, clad in expensive furs, look curiously at the entrance to the meeting-place as they drive by. Ordinary women of the middle classes, on their way to gossip over a cup of coffee, open their mouths and pin back their ears in sheer curiosity and amazement. Three women from the *Lumpenproletariat* totter in front of one of the columns, their clothing torn, their appearance mute and hopeless, broken in body and spirit, victims of our so-glorious social order. Apathetically they pass by the entrance of the assembly hall. But behind them march the battalions of women workers, proud and confident of victory.

These women's suffrage marches did not take place without the interference of the police, who often appeared in force and attempted to break them up. Usually the women dispersed peacefully, but on occasion there were arrests, as in Düsseldorf in 1912, and there were also some instances of force being used, with the police employing truncheons to disperse the women.[11] Such incidents were all grist to the SPD's propagandistic mill: but in fact many of the men in the party were taken aback by the women's initiative in mounting these unplanned but undeniably impressive and courageous street processions. In Düsseldorf, for instance, the local party functionaries expressed their surprise that women were even capable of such spontaneous action.[12] The Women's Day, in fact, smacked to these men of female independence and 'feminism', which is why they proposed instead 'women's meetings prepared for a specific purpose',[13] for such meetings would be prepared for purposes decided by the local (male-dominated) party organizations and would remain firmly under the men's control. Clara Zetkin pointed to the special value which the Women's Day held for the women, and the contrasting hostility of male 'party circles', when she remarked 'that there is quite an aversion to the Women's Day in some party circles, while the women comrades in all areas are firmly convinced of its great agitational value'.[14] An additional cause for friction was the fact that the Women's Day was held in spring, and therefore constantly threatened to clash with the greatest Social Democratic festival of the year, May Day, which of course provided its inspiration. On this ground alone, many Social Democratic men argued, it was inadvisable to hold the Women's Day on a fixed annual basis. As one delegate from Offenbach remarked in the party council meeting of 31 January 1913, 'Whatever else happens, care should be taken to ensure that the Women's Day does not become a second May Day.'[15]

Opposition on the part of the men may well have been a reason for the fact that the Women's Days in 1912–14 were less successful than that of 1911. The overwhelming majority of Social Democratic women were married to Social Democratic men[16] and their husbands may well have tried to stop them going. The Social Democratic men were constantly attempting to suppress the independent institutions of the SPD women's organization, such as the Women's Bureau,[17] and they were acting consistently when they attempted to suppress the Women's Day as well. Moreover, there seems to have been something of an attempt by the men to take over the Women's Day themselves, for while in 1911 men were being ejected from the meeting-halls, by 1913 they were forming a sizeable proportion of the audience in many of the assemblies. According to the Hamburg police, for instance, some 420 of the 550 attending the Women's Day meeting in the Trade Union Hall in 1913 were men, in Eppendorf there were 130 men in an audience of 350, in Barmbek 150 out of 650 participants were men, in Hamm and Horn 100 out of 300, in Eimsbüttel 150 out of 350.[18]

Despite all this, however, the German Social Democratic women succeeded in holding their Women's Day demonstration for female suffrage every year from 1911 to 1914. Its importance transcended that of a mere recruitment drive, though of course it was this aspect which Zetkin and Zietz stressed when arguing its retention before the party council. The Social Democratic women fought so hard to retain the Women's Day because it was a symbol of their independence, a vehicle of their active involvement in politics, a means by which they asserted their right to stage dramatic and imposing political demonstrations, organized by themselves. International Proletarian Women's Day was also important because it was international. In Sweden successful women's demonstrations were mounted for the occasion in 1912 and 1913, while 2,000 people attended the first celebration of the event in Paris on 9 March 1914, and even the Russian women socialists managed to stage one in 1913, with meetings in Moscow, St Petersburg, Kiev, Samara and Tiflis, though the meeting in St Petersburg, by far the largest of them, had to be disguised as a 'Scientific Morning Devoted to the Women Question' and even then was quickly followed by reprisals from the police.[19] Though none of these could rival the German celebrations, all of them were as Zetkin intended held under the slogan 'universal suffrage', and gave socialist women the feeling that they belonged to a broad international movement all of whose branches were working towards the same goal (even if they seldom managed to co-ordinate their efforts and stage the demonstrations on the day intended, March 8). To assess the Women's Day purely in terms of its impact on political decision-making is to ignore what was perhaps its most significant feature, namely its importance for the thousands of working-class women who took part in it, watched it from the sidelines or read about it in the newspapers; a public demonstration of the fact that despite all the obstacles, women of the working classes were capable of organizing their own political movement and of adding their own distinctive voice to the chorus of cries for the democratization of European political systems. In the face of this urge to self-expression on the part of the proletarian women's movement, jealous and suspicious male party functionaries were in the last resort powerless to do anything.

II

Despite the lukewarm or even hostile reaction of male party functionaries to the International Proletarian Women's Day, the record of European socialism on the question of female suffrage was, on paper at least, a good one. Socialist parties in Europe before the First World War were virtually alone in the political world in including an explicit demand for female suffrage in their programmes. The Austrians demanded it in their Hainfeld Programme of 1888–9, the French socialists passed resolutions in favour of it in 1879, and again in 1906 and 1907, Lenin and the Bolsheviks endorsed it in 1907, having already written it into their programme at the second party congress in 1903, the Swedish Social Democrats included it on their formal list of aims, and the Second International proclaimed 'the necessity of universal suffrage for both sexes' at its Paris Congress in 1900. While occasional male voices could be heard within the socialist movement speaking out against votes for women, notably in France, they were never more than a small minority, and after the 1890s there was never any serious opposition to the principle of female suffrage in any European socialist party. The record of the German Social Democrats was good, but far from exceptional. According to its programme, approved at Erfurt in 1891, the party was firmly committed to demanding universal suffrage for both men and women, the latter being included specifically in the formula. This demand was strengthened by the passage of a motion at the party congress held in Dresden in 1903, committing the party to the explicit inclusion of female suffrage every time it campaigned for the reform of the franchise, which was restricted to adult males in national elections and further restricted by property qualifications in elections for the important provincial parliaments such as the Prussian one. The campaign for the reform of the Prussian franchise, in fact, occupied an increasing amount of the SPD's attention, above all from 1910 onwards, and it is seldom pointed out by historians that this campaign—with hundreds of street demonstrations, thousands of mass meetings and millions of propaganda sheets and placards—was also, in theory at least, a campaign for female suffrage. Finally, when the Social Democrats eventually came to power in the Revolution of November 1918, one of their first actions was to pass a decree enfranchising women, who were able to exercise their new right for the first time in the elections for the constituent National Assembly which met at Weimar at the beginning of 1919.[20]

Many leading socialists regarded female suffrage as a simple demand of natural justice, which had little if anything to do with Marxism or socialism as such. In France, indeed, it was feminists such as Hubertine Auclert and Madeleine Pelletier who joined the socialists mainly in order to persuade them to take up women's rights in their programmes, who were responsible for securing the socialists' commitment to female suffrage on principles that were as much feminist as socialist.[21] In Germany, when the SPD leader August Bebel introduced a motion for female suffrage into the Reichstag for the first time ever (in 1895) he justified it simply 'in the name of the legal equality of the sexes'. Women, he said, had the same interest in making the laws as did men, because they were equally affected by them, especially now that they were entering the labour market in such large numbers. Though this might sound Marxist in tone, it was by no means an exclusively Marxist argument—the bourgeois feminist movement also used precisely the same reasoning once it began to demand the vote—and it was a commonplace in nearly all sections of German society that political parties and political rights existed (among other things) to represent economic interests.

Women, said Bebel, were more morally upright than men. They had a better sense of justice. Giving them the vote would raise the tone of public life. It might be objected, he went on, that the vote was reserved for men alone because they alone performed military service. This was an important and widely held objection in a society as permeated by militaristic modes of thought as Imperal Germany. But, he said, women underwent similar dangers and all too often made similar sacrifices to those of the soldier in bearing the children upon whom the nation's future rested. This analogy was also a favourite after the turn of the century with the bourgeois feminists. Like many of the arguments Bebel employed, it was drawn from the great Anglo-Saxon pioneers of feminist thought in the nineteenth century, most notable of whom was perhaps John Stuart Mill. But Bebel was of course not alone in the SPD in employing such arguments. The party freely borrowed from bourgeois feminist ideology, even going so far on occasion as to adopt the reasoning of the most conservative wing of the bourgeois feminist movement, led by Gertrud Bäumer, who accepted that the sexes were fundamentally different in nature, but went on to claim that enfranchisement would allow the female sex to bring its own special qualities fully to bear on political and social life.

As one SPD newspaper declared in 1912:

Women have a fully valid right to political equality with men through the duties they carry out as mothers, housewives and taxpayers. . . . And they have not only recognized that the possession of the vote would give them more influence over legislation, and thus the ability to represent their own interests, they have also recognized that in exercising their rights as citizens they would themselves gain as personalities and at the same time add enrichment and variety to the culture of the society in which they would be active as full citizens through everything that the female nature has to contribute to it.

Social Democratic propaganda used the experience of countries such as Australia and the western states of the USA to imply that Germany was not keeping pace with the rest of the Western world, and to show the beneficial social, moral and political effects of female suffrage. Women, as men and women in the SPD said, were classed in the same category as criminals, infants and lunatics, which was absurd; they needed the vote as a natural right; and they deserved it by the services they performed for the nation. These were all stock arguments employed by bourgeois feminists the world over.[22]

Some German Social Democrats, the so-called 'revisionists', went even further towards the adoption of liberal arguments. The revisionists were followers of Eduard Bernstein, who at the end of the nineteenth century had tried to persuade the SPD that Marx's theories needed to be revised, in the light of what had happened since they were developed, by the abandonment of their revolutionary content. They believed in gradualist reformism along the lines of the English Fabians. It has sometimes been argued that the revisionists were anti-feminist; but in fact they were mostly strong supporters of liberal feminism, and many of them, such as Lily Braun, Eduard David and Georg von Vollmar, actually belonged to liberal feminist organizations.[23] The revisionist Edmund Fischer, who argued that woman's place was in the home, was an odd man out in this respect; and even he never suggested that women should not have the vote.[24] A more typical approach was that of Wally Zepler, who wrote a column on the women's movement in the revisionist periodical *Sozialistische Monatshefte*. The problem as Zepler saw it was that the enfranchisement of the entire female sex all at once, necessitating as it did the democratization of the male franchise as well, was a demand far beyond the bounds of practical politics. She sought to solve this problem by accommodating the demand for female suffrage to the form in which it was put by the most right-wing elements in the bourgeois suffragist movement, that is, merely to extend the existing, unequal franchise to women, in the hope that this would prove acceptable to the ruling classes. The political model to which the revisionists in this instance thought the German Empire might conform was that of Great Britain, where suffrage reform took place step by step over a long period, leading slowly but surely, it seemed, towards universal adult suffrage. In 1910 Wally Zepler criticized the demand for the immediate implementation of universal suffrage as unrealistic. She advocated instead a 'policy of the attainable', and urged the party to ask first for the extension of the existing franchise to women.[25]

But she was mistaken in calling this a 'policy of the attainable'. Not only was there no chance of the franchise being extended to Conservative and National Liberal women, whose parties vehemently rejected any such idea, but also, even if these women did get the vote, the chances were that this would strengthen rather than weaken the determination of the ruling classes not to extend full political rights to the rest of the female sex. For propertied women were just as determined as propertied men to resist the democratization of the Prussian franchise; and their enfranchisement would greatly increase the parliamentary strength of the parties they voted for. So Zepler's gradualist formula, which postulated the full enfranchisement only of propertied women and the extension of existing inequalities in voting rights to the female sex, as the 'first step' in a process which, once begun, would 'inevitably' lead to the advent of universal suffrage, in reality did nothing more than provide a recipe for the reinforcement of existing political and social antagonisms. In any case, these arguments were purely hypothetical. The party was not likely to give credence to Zepler's views. They were condemned everywhere outside the revisionist camp. As the SPD's main daily newspaper, *Vorwärts*, remarked, such thoughts were the means by which Social Democracy could be encouraged to follow German liberalism down the path of total ineffectiveness. The SPD never adopted Zepler's view; and the controversy merely indicated the weakness and isolation of the revisionist group even as late as 1910.[26]

At the opposite extreme from the revisionists were those on the left of the SPD who could not accept the liberal or ethical arguments for female suffrage put forward in the bulk of Social Democratic propaganda. Until 1902, these arguments were seldom challenged within the German party: the SPD enjoyed a virtual monopoly of the demand for votes for women, and could employ all kinds of arguments to justify it. But in 1902 the bourgeois feminists formed a German Union for Women's Suffrage, so that the SPD could no longer argue that it was merely taking up the demands which bourgeois liberals were too feeble to raise themselves. From this time onwards, therefore, the leading theorists of women's emancipation in the SPD were forced to think out their own particular and unique reasons for demanding votes for women, if only to make a clear differentiation between themselves and the bourgeois feminists of the German Union for Women's Suffrage. This trend was strongly reinforced from about 1905 by the crystallization of a radical revolutionary left wing of the party around figures such as Karl Liebknecht, Anton Pannekoek, Rosa Luxemburg, and Clara Zetkin.[27] In these circles, it was argued that female suffrage would help the political education and mobilization of women, and bring the socialist revolution nearer by adding further to the strength of Social Democracy. The liberal feminists too stressed that the best kind of political education was to be found in the exercise of political rights. Female suffrage would, they believed, of itself bring about major changes in the social and political system: for the left wing of the bourgeois feminist movement were supporters of a full institutional and parliamentary democracy with equal rights for all. In the circumstances of Imperial Germany this was a very radical idea, and the bourgeois feminists indeed argued that female suffrage would have revolutionary consequences. The SPD left, of course, never supposed that female suffrage would of itself bring about a revolution—it would only be one factor among many. As time went on, Clara Zetkin in particular laid growing stress on the utility of female suffrage as a means of political education. Its enactment, she believed, would enormously strengthen the solidarity of the working class by binding its women to socialist ideology through their participation in elections and their exercise of political rights.[28] This argument, of course, also served the function of presenting female suffrage to the men of the SPD as a policy which would benefit them, even if, in the form presented by Zetkin, it had most appeal to the revolutionary wing of the party. Although female suffrage was also a demand of liberal feminism, then, it appeared in this light as directly hostile to the interests of the bourgeoisie.

German socialists on right and left therefore found their own reasons for supporting votes for women before the First World War. So too did other socialist parties in Europe. In Britain, for example, the Independent Labour Party, under the leadership of Keir Hardie, officially committed itself to opposing any extension of the franchise that left women out of account; the maverick Social Democratic Federation, led by H. M. Hyndman, which opposed votes for women and even contained a prominent anti-feminist in the person of Belfort Bax, a leading member of the Men's Anti-Suffrage League, only had a limited influence and no mass support. All over Europe, socialist parties were formally committed to women's suffrage; in the Second International it was not a controversial issue. Differences began, as with so many other points on the socialist programme, when discussion descended to the level of practical politics; and here, as we shall now see, the record of European socialism was very different.

III

The main issue around which the debate on votes for women within the socialist movement revolved was in fact not its justice or utility as far as women were concerned, but rather its likely impact on the political system as a whole. This in fact was the aspect of women's suffrage which most concerned the men in the Second International. Given the ultimate aim of the socialist movement—the replacement of capitalism by socialism—what would happen to the existing social order if women got the vote? Would it bring the revolution any nearer? Was the demand for women's suffrage an obstacle to the achievement of the more limited aim of the removal of property qualifications for elections where they existed? These were the questions that most concerned socialist men.

A rare and interesting insight into the views of the rank-and-file German socialist man on these questions can be gained from the report of a Hamburg political police agent who, sitting incognito in a well-known haunt of the local Social Democrats, noted on 2 May 1902 the following:

In the period from 9.40 to 10.25, I visited the bar owned by Kelling, at No. 5 Süderstrasse. There were eleven workers there, sitting at various tables. One of them said the following: 'People are always working towards a state in which women will be given equality with men in public and political life. In my opinion this is wrong, because a woman never has a correct understanding of these kinds of matters. On the contrary, she must always be guided by the man on them, so she can never be made equal to men. Of course there are also women who possess energy and insight, but these are so few that they do not come into consideration. It would be better if people worked towards removing women from public life altogether and occupying them with domestic tasks'. Another worker said: 'There are lots of women who are very well-suited for public life. This can be best observed in the fact that they have forced their way into nearly every trade. Of course, these are only those trades in which excessively hard physical labour is not demanded of them; they will never be able to enter these trades since they lack the necessary physical strength by nature. Still, their number in other jobs is so great that they can be given equality with men, which is indeed merely a measure of justice towards women which they should have enjoyed long ago.' Another said: 'All of us here must support women's equality. The advantage which accrues to us from it is considerably greater than the disadvantage which it brings. If women are given equality with men in political life, our party will double in size at least. This ground alone would be enough to let all other reservations vanish. Whether or not the women understand politics is all the same to us; the main thing is, the majority of votes which are used at elections and so on is there. It's obvious that the workforce will come out of it better than the rich, and indeed this is the main reason why the rich resist recognizing the right of both sexes to equality.[29]

This shows the range of opinion within the party on this issue, though the men would probably have hesitated before giving vent to such views in public; but it also shows that along with the issues of principle involved ('a measure of justice') there were also powerful practical considerations ('our party will double in size at least').

As time went on, some voices on the emergent revolutionary left of the socialist movement began to cast doubt on the utility of female suffrage, and in Germany in the last years of peace they began to criticize the growing preoccupation of the Social Democratic Women's organization with the vote. What good, they asked, would it really do working women if they got the vote even in a bourgeois parliamentary democracy, let alone in the political system of Imperial Germany, where parliaments were virtually powerless? 'It would only be just if women were given the vote. But it is another question altogether when we ask if they could then entertain any great hopes for their emancipation. Our position with regard to parliamentarism is that our miseries will only be prolonged in this system.'[30] Without the deep-seated social, economic and institutional changes that only a full-scale social revolution could bring about, the vote would be of little use to women. And in any case, even female suffrage, as some Social Democrats pointed out, was not likely to be enacted before such a revolution occurred. 'What', asked the SPD daily the *Hamburger Echo* in 1911, 'can be expected in respect of female suffrage of a government that has never even supported universal suffrage for men on principle, that regards the existing Reichstag franchise as a "necessary evil", and that is certainly not inclined to reject the idea of putting an end to this suffrage?!'[31] There was another point, too, which did not escape even such a fervent enthusiast for women's suffrage as August Bebel, and that was, that the enfranchisement of women under any circumstances might well damage the interests of the SPD, given the fact that women were more influenced by religion than were men. In his Reichstag speech of 1895, Bebel conceded that it was probable that when they were eventually enfranchised, a higher proportion of women would vote for the Conservatives and the National Liberals than for the Social Democrats. In the end his prophecy came true, for the most popular political parties among women in the Weimar Republic were indeed the Conservatives (DNVP) and the National Liberals (DVP), both parties associated with the Protestant Church, and the Centre Party, which was associated with the Catholic Church, and the most unpopular parties were the Communists (KPD) and the Social Democrats themselves, both generally considered anti-religious parties. Bebel also said, however, that in the long run the balance would redress itself and the SPD would prove at least as popular among women as the other parties. Here too time is at last proving him right, though it has taken ninety years to do so.[32] The temporary disadvantage that female suffrage would bring to the Social Democrats, declared Bebel, in no way deterred them from advocating it, for there were—he said— too many arguments in its favour.

This was a good example of the ethical and utopian side of German Social Democracy, which insisted on matters of principle even to its own disadvantage. This aspect of Social Democracy owed a good deal to the belief, widespread among Social Democrats in the 1890s, that reforms such as the democratization of the franchise were impossible under the existing social system, and that a social revolution would not be long in coming. As time went on, and the immediate prospect of revolution receded, the leaders of the SPD came to put an ever-greater stress on the attainment of reforms within the Imperial German system. As a result of this, as a consequence of the secondary importance which female suffrage had as far as most Social Democratic men were concerned, and as a reflection of the largely instrumental terms, divorced from principle, in which Social Democratic men came to see the demand, the SPD men became increasingly prepared to drop female suffrage when what they conceived of as more vital issues were at stake.

In Hamburg in 1906, for example, the Hamburg Senate

introduced into the Citizens' Assembly (*Bürgerschaft*) a Bill to restrict the local franchise so as to remove the possibility of an SPD victory; and the Social Democratic spokesmen opposing the Bill did not go so far as to include votes for women among their demands. The SPD deputy Emil Fischer admitted in the debate

that the Social Democrats . . . demand according to their programme universal suffrage not only for the male, but also for the female population. . . . This . . . is a demand that is not at all Social Democratic, this demand is raised by good bourgeois women, who are much too respectable to call themselves Social Democrats. So, in this case . . . we are dealing not with a Social Democratic demand, but with a demand that has already become reality in many States, for example in Australia, in America, in England, where female suffrage has been introduced in municipalities. . . . [But] the Social Democrats are being extraordinarily modest, because they are not raising this demand in opposition to this proposed worsening of the franchise, but are contenting themselves with the demand for the extension of the franchise to all male citizens.

The reason for the Social Democrats' 'modesty' on this occasion, according to Fischer, was that 'if we were . . . so consequential as to demand what stands written in our programme . . . we would stand no chance of having our proposal accepted'. Moderate though it was, however, the Hamburg Social Democrats' proposal was doomed from the start. Their 'modesty' in refraining from adding votes for women to their demands did nothing at all to make their basic policies more acceptable to the Hamburg City Fathers, and their effort to prevent the amendment of the franchise to their disadvantage was a complete failure. Similar reactionary proposals in other parts of Germany called forth from the Social Democratic men a similar willingness to jettison the rights of women when their own rights were at stake.[33]
    More striking still in this context was the behaviour of the Social Democrats in the Revolution of November 1918. At the beginning of the month, when the SPD was still discussing with the Liberal and Catholic Centre Parties the democratization of the German constitution in preparation for peace negotiations once it had become clear that the war was lost, they did indeed suggest the enfranchisement of women. But the liberals Gustav Stresemann and Conrad Haussmann were strongly

opposed; and in order to reach agreement on the abolition of property franchises in Prussia and elsewhere, the SPD leaders agreed to remove female suffrage from the proposed Franchise Bill. Instead, they declared their intention of introducing it as an amendment when the Bill was put before the Reichstag. Here, in fact, because the Social Democrats were in a minority, and all other parties opposed the enfranchisement of women, it would have been doomed to failure. However, the Bill was never introduced, for within a short time the Revolution had broken out, and the Liberals and Catholic Centre had agreed to votes for women (and other measures to democratize Germany even further) in an attempt to pacify the vast crowds gathering in the streets and the workers' and soldiers' councils being set up all over Germany. This too was in vain, for within a short while the Reichstag had been swept away by the full flood of the revolutionary tide, and the workers' and soldiers' councils had established a revolutionary government (with the participation of the SPD), which immediately declared the enfranchisement of the adult female sex. Even at this stage, then, female suffrage retained its political instrumentality in the eyes of men: for the majority Social Democratic leaders, joining the revolutionary government largely in order to steer it towards political stability, saw the granting of the vote to women largely as a means of pacifying the masses and stealing the thunder of the far left. One of the majority SPD leaders told the revolutionary Kurt Eisner that his proposal to postpone the election of a national Constituent Assembly and continue the revolution by means of the workers' and soldiers' councils would mean the shelving of votes for women (for the councils were almost exclusively male in composition). In this way, therefore, female suffrage became a means of legitimating the limited and imperfect parliamentary democracy which the majority SPD grafted on to the capitalist system with such unseemly haste in the winter of 1918–19.[34]

This evident willingness of the German Social Democrats to jettison female suffrage in order to secure manhood suffrage was nothing unusual among the member parties of the Second International. In 1901 the Belgian socialists appeared to be on the brink of gaining universal manhood suffrage, since the measure was clearly supported by a large number of liberal deputies in parliament. But Belgium was a Catholic country and, as in France, liberals, who were generally anti-clerical, believed that the great mass of ordinary women were under the influence of priests and would vote for parties of the right if enfranchised. If German statistics of the 1920s are anything to go by, there was certainly a grain of truth in this, though such fears were equally certainly grossly exaggerated. During the Belgian debates of 1901, however, a conservative deputy sought to exploit these anxieties and wean the liberals away from suffrage reform by proposing an amendment extending the democratic suffrage to both sexes. This put the Belgian socialists in the position of either standing on their principles and losing the vote, or abandoning their theoretical support for female suffrage, now put to the test, in order to secure the enfranchisement of all adult males. They chose the latter course. More than this, they secured the agreement of the Belgian socialist women's movement to stop campaigning for female suffrage while the issue of manhood suffrage was in the balance.[35]

This decision was greeted by the main organ of the French women socialists, *la femme socialiste*, in the following terms:

We can only [it declared] congratulate the Belgian socialist women who have, by this decision, demonstrated a class consciousness which we would like to see imitated by the socialist women of France. By placing above one of their individual rights the interest of the Worker Party [which] is at the same time the interest of the proletariat of both sexes, they have given to all socialists an admirable example of solidarity.[36]

The same line was followed by the Austrians. Austria too had a limited, property-qualified franchise, but in the wake of the 1905 revolution in Russia the socialist party took advantage of the sudden apparent fragility of the Habsburg regime to launch a campaign for universal suffrage. The Habsburg government seemed more than likely to give in, since it was genuinely frightened of the spread of revolution, but once more, in order not to jeopardize this reform, the socialists decided to drop their demand (contained in the Hainfeld Programme of 1888–9) for votes for women and persuaded the Austrian socialist women's movement to do the same. These betrayals of principle were roundly condemned by the first congress of the Socialist Women's International, held at Stuttgart in 1907. Led by Clara Zetkin and the Germans, the congress voted by 47 to 11 to lay down the principle that socialist parties everywhere must always campaign for universal suffrage for both men and women, and not just for manhood suffrage; and at the full congress of the International Zetkin followed this up—against the opposition of the Austrians—by getting through a resolution laying down that 'whenever a struggle is to be waged for the right to vote, it must be conducted only according to socialist principles, i.e. with the demand for universal suffrage for both women and men'. It was indeed partly in order to secure the observance of this principle that the congress went on to establish an international women's secretariat run by Zetkin herself.[37]

These events were characteristic of the way in which the Germans tended to impose rigid policies on the International which neither the other member parties nor, ultimately, they themselves were prepared to observe when it really came down to it.[38] For Zetkin and the German women socialists, their loyalty to the labour movement needed to be reciprocated by the labour movement's loyalty to them; and it was precisely this kind of experience that fed the disillusion with the reformist tactics of the Second International that was to lead Zetkin towards the revolutionary left and eventually into the Communist Party. Gradualists might claim that once universal manhood suffrage had been achieved the socialists would gain more seats in legislatures and so there would be more likelihood of a vote in favour of women's suffrage getting through. But in practice this did not happen: the example of France showed that such a policy could be hampered by the limited interest of the party leadership and the limited size of the socialist vote, while the examples of Germany and Austria showed that it could—despite the intermittent support of the party for women's suffrage campaigns—be frustrated by the lack of power exercised by the legislature itself.

IV

Such, then, were the complexities and contradictions in the meaning of female suffrage for the socialist movement of the pre-1913 era. Votes for women, indeed, was not, either in

Germany or anywhere else, a simple demand, the supporters or opponents of which were motivated purely by a belief in or denial of equality for women. Nor were the consequences and meaning of the actual enactment of female suffrage simple matters either. The enfranchisement of women owed much of its general political significance to the historical context in which it occurred. In Germany in 1918, as we have seen, it formed part of an attempt to stabilize the political system, reduce social tensions and stop the revolution from going any further than the establishment of parliamentary democracy. It also made a real practical difference whether all adult women were enfranchised or just those who fulfilled the same property qualifications as existing male voters, for as the opponents of the advocacy of equal (as distinct from universal) suffrage for women realized, equal suffrage might have meant a step forward for the female sex, but it would have been a step backwards for the working class. What the Social Democrats had to decide, therefore, was whether the disfranchisement of women was such an outrage to natural justice and the democratic conscience that it had to be overcome even at the cost of harming the prospects for a socialist revolution (or, more modestly, the democratization of the male franchise); or whether, as others on the left came to believe both before 1914 and during the upheaval of 1918 itself, the revolution—or a democratic male franchise—came first, and had to be pushed through even at the sacrifice of the political equality of women.

The struggles waged over the Women's Day within German Social Democracy can be seen as symptomatic of the wider processes taking place in the development of the party as a whole. For in their way, the Women's Day and the enthusiastic demonstrations which attended it were part of a growing demand for equality and democracy among the Social Democratic rank and file, and indeed among wider sections of the working class. In its failure to fulfil this demand, in its growing indifference or even hostility to the democratic urge of large numbers of its supporters, the SPD party *apparat* was beginning well before 1914 to forfeit the loyalty of many working-class people. During the First World War and in the early years of the Weimar Republic these left the SPD for more radical parties, or abandoned the conventions of party politics in favour of direct mass action of a more spontaneous and informal kind. The attempts of the party bureaucracy to suppress the Women's Day, the collapse of the SPD's women's movement during the war, and the widespread women's riots which took place from 1915 to 1923, can all be seen as illustrations of this general process. Similarly, the reluctance of the French socialist movement to give active support to women's suffrage reflected the party's petty-bourgeois heritage and the dominance within it of parliamentary politics and electoral tactics; while the low priority which the Russians gave to rights such as the vote signified not only their belief that such issues were diversions from the central revolutionary task but also perhaps a more deep-rooted disdain for civil rights and parliamentarism in general.

So it is not enough for historians just to celebrate the labour movement's advocacy of female suffrage and applaud the rediscovery of the mass suffrage marches and demonstrations staged by the proletarian women's movement on International Women's Day. There was no necessary or automatic connection between Marxism or revolutionary socialism and women's suffrage. Indeed, it was precisely on the left that many of the most serious doubts about the value of the vote for women arose. On the other hand those who came to hold the real reins of power within socialist parties also came for opposite reasons to regard female suffrage as an expendable item on the party's list of demands, as so utopian and far-reaching that it held up the achievement of more practicable reforms. Uniting both views was the fact that they were held by men; and the controversies over the waging of serious campaigns for women's suffrage surely demonstrate that women had to fight for equality and independence within the labour movement just as much as they did in any other part of society.

NOTES

This chapter appeared in an earlier version as 'German Social Democracy and women's suffrage 1891–1918', *Journal of Contemporary History* 15

(1980), pp. 533–57, and draws on material first presented in my book *Sozialdemokratie und Frauenemanzipation im Deutschen Kaiserreich* (Verlag J. H. W. Dietz Nachf., Bonn–Berlin, 1979).

1. Dieter Groh, *Negative Integration und revolutionärer Attentismus. Die deutsche Sozialdemokratie am Vorabend des Ersten Weltkrieges* (Frankfurt-am-Main, 1973).
2. See Molly Nolan, 'Proletarischer Anti-Feminismus. Dargestellt am Beispiel der SPD–Ortsgruppe Düsseldorf 1890 bis 1914', in *Frauen und Wissenschaft. Beiträge zur Berliner Sommeruniversität für Frauen Juli 1976* (Berlin, 1977), for details of these demonstrations in Düsseldorf.
3. Luise Dornemann, *Clara Zetkin. Leben und Wirken* (5th ed., East Berlin, 1973), pp. 225–31.
4. StA Hbg, PP, S8897/IV: *VW* (15 March 1911, 21 March 1911); Versammlungsberichte in S8897/VI, VII. The reliability of these figures is discussed in my article 'Feminism and female emancipation in Germany 1871–1945: sources, methods and problems of research', *Central European History* 4 (December 1976), pp. 323–51.
5. StA Hbg, PP, S8897/IV: *HE*, 14 May 1912, *VW* (14 and 21 May 1912); Versammlungsberichte in S8897/VI, VII.
6. GLA Karlsruhe, NL Geck, 1907: Partei-Ausschuss (7 November 1912).
7. Zetkin to Ankersmit (7 January 1913), in W. Eildermann (ed.), 'Unveröffentlichte Briefe Clara Zetkins an Heleen Ankersmit', *Beiträge zur Geschichte der deutschen Arbeiterbewegung*, 9, 4 (1967), p. 664.
8. GLA Karlsruhe, NL Geck, 1907: Partei-Ausschuss (31 January 1913).
9. StA Hbg, PP, S8897/IV: *VW* (14 March 1913, 9 March 1914): Versammlungsberichte in S8897/VI, VII. For arguments over whether or not to hold the Women's Day in 1914, see *PTP 1913*, pp. 150, 377–84.
10. See the instruction on how to organize these meetings in Luise Zietz, *Gewinnung und Schulung der Frau für die politische Betätigung* (Berlin, 1914).
11. StA Hbg, PP, S8897/III: *VW* (21 March 1911), *Berliner Tageblatt* (20 March 1911), *HC* (20 March 1911); S8897/IV: *HC* (14 May 1912), *VW* (14 May 1912, 9 March 1914, 10 March 1914).
12. Nolan, *op. cit.*
13. See above, p. 70 and note 6.
14. Zetkin to Ankersmit (7 January 1913), in Eildermann, 'Unveröffentlichte Briefe', p. 664.
15. GLA Karlsruhe, NL Geck, 1907: Partei-Ausschuss (31 January 1913).
16. For evidence, see chapter 4.
17. Fricke, *op. cit.*, pp. 320–30.
18. StA Hbg, PP, S8897/VI, VII: Versammlungsberichte (March 1913).
19. Richard J. Evans, *The Feminists* (London, 1977), p. 169; Charles Sowerwine, *Sisters or Citizens? Women and Socialism in France since 1876* (Cambridge, 1982), p. 139; Richard Stites, *The Women's Liberation Movement in Russia. Feminism, Nihilism and Bolshevism, 1860–1930* (Princeton, 1978), pp. 283–4.
20. Charles Sowerwine, *Sisters or Citizens?* pp. 25, 114, 196; Wilhelm

Schröder, *Handbuch der Sozialdemokratischen Parteitage von 1863 bis 1909* (Munich 1910), p. 166; Stites, *op. cit.*, p. 242.

21. Sowerwine, *op. cit.*
22. *GL* 5, 6 (20 March 1895), pp. 43–5, and 5, 7 (3 April 1895), pp. 52–4, reprinting Bebel's speech; StA Hbg S8897/IV: *Fachzeitung für Schneider,* 5 May 1912, for the 1912 quotation.
23. See my book *The Feminist Movement in Germany 1894–1933* (London 1976), pp. 122, 124, 136–7, 140.
24. Edmund Fischer, 'Die Frauenfrage', *SMH* (1905), pp. 258–66.
25. *SMH* (1910), pp. 1130, 1454; *SMH* (1911), pp. 353–65.
26. Zepler had already advanced her proposal in less systematic form in 1908, and had met with an immediate rebuff. See StA Hbg, PP, S8897/III: *VW* (18 June 1908, 23 June 1908, 4 January 1910).
27. Carl E. Schorske, *German Social Democracy 1905–1917: The Development of the Great Schism* (New York 1955), for the general background.
28. Clara Zetkin, *Zur Frage des Frauenwahlrechts* (Berlin 1907). For the bourgeois feminists, who argued that female suffrage would bring an end to war and poverty, see Evans, *The Feminist Movement in Germany,* esp. chs 3 and 7.
29. StA Hbg, PP, S9001/I: Wirtschaftsvigilanzbericht (Schutzmann Hinz, 10 May 1902).
30. StA Hbg, PP, S8897/III: *Die Einigkeit* (24 December 1910).
31. StA Hbg, PP, S8897/III: *HE* (19 March 1911).
32. On voting patterns among German women after the introduction of female suffrage, see Brian Peterson, 'The politics of working-class women in the Weimar Republic', *Central European History,* (June 1977), 2, pp. 87–111, and Gabrielle Bremme, *Die politische Rolle der Frau in Deutschland* (Göttingen, 1956).
33. *Stenographische Berichte über die Sitzungen der Bürgerschaft zu Hamburg im Jahre 1906*, 4 (24 January 1906), pp. 113.
34. *Die Regierung des Prinzen Max van Baden*, bearbeitet von Erich Matthias und Rudolf Morsey (Quellen zur Geschichte des Parlamentarismus und der politischen Parteien, 1. Reihe, Bd. 2, Düsseldorf, 1961), pp. 598–9, 602; F. L. Carsten, *Revolution in Central Europe 1918–1919* (London 1972), p. 113, n. 17.
35. Sowerwine, *op. cit.*, p. 85.
36. Quoted in *ibid.*, p. 95.
37. Charles Sowerwine, 'The socialist women's movement 1865–1939', in Renate Bridenthal and Claudia Koonz (eds), *Becoming Visible: Women in European History* (2nd ed, New York, 1987).
38. See James Joll, *The Second International* (London, 1955).

4 Socialism and the Family

I

In the nineteenth century most people agreed on the central importance of the family for the social and political order. The family was still, though to a diminishing degree, a public institution; its formation was a matter for communal concern, its transactions were carried out under the public eye, and its activities played an important role in public life. As it has become removed from the public sphere, however, and transformed (at least in theory) into a place of refuge from the world outside,[1] so the family has also been removed from the historian's concept of past politics. Its incorporation into a 'private sphere' removed from society has been followed by its removal from history in a wider sense. This chapter takes up the neglected question of the connections between family and politics in the late nineteenth and early twentieth centuries, in particular by looking at the relationship between socialism and the family in theory and practice. Conservatives all over Europe castigated the socialist movement for allegedly wanting to destroy the family in order to make male workers more discontented by depriving them of the comforts of home and hearth.[2] And indeed there was some justification for the belief that socialists were hostile to the family as an institution. The classical texts of Marxism, so often cited by socialist theorists, presented the dissolution of the family under the impact of the spread of capitalist industry as a generally positive development. 'The emancipation of women', wrote Engels in *The Origin of the Family, Private Property and the*

State (1884), 'has as its first precondition the return of the
whole female sex to public industry, and . . . this again
demands the removal of the individual family in its character as
an economic unit of society'. Engels predicted that the
upbringing of children would be a public not a family matter in
the future socialist society.[3] Marx himself, in a much-cited
passage of *Das Kapital*, remarked that 'the dissolution of the
old family structure within the capitalist system' through the
employment of women and children outside the home
provided 'the economic basis for a higher form of the family',
and he added that the 'Christian-Germanic form of the
family', was as socially determined as any other, and just as
likely to be superseded.[4] August Bebel, the leader of the
German Social Democrats, in his book *Woman and Socialism,*
the most widely read of all Social Democratic tracts, repeated
these views at greater length and in more detail.[5] Lily Braun,
the author of the only other large-scale work on women and
society to come out of the German Socialist Women's
movement, argued, like Bebel and Marx, that the family would
give way in the future socialist society to communal forms of
social organization.[6] Likewise, in 1891, Clara Zetkin, who
subsequently became the leading theorist on women's
questions within the SPD, envisioned the rapid dissolution of
the family in the last phases of capitalism.[7] The key text of the
socialist women's movement in Russia, Nadezhda
Krupskaya's *The Woman Worker*, looked forward to a
socialist future when children would be cared for in communal
institutions, while Alexandra Kollontai, in a lecture on the
'Family Question' in 1908 and in numerous other writings, also
stressed the inadequacy of the family as an institution for
bringing up children and creating a truly collective
consciousness, and criticized the notion of monogamy.[8]
Socialists of all countries could look back to a tradition of
criticizing the family as a source of oppression that began with
Fourier, Owen, Saint-Simon and the utopian socialists in the
early nineteenth century.[9]

It was a corollary of these beliefs that the socialists too, like
their conservative enemies, believed that the spread of female
wage labour outside the home would lead increasing numbers
of women towards socialist commitments. Capitalism, they

held, was drawing more and more women into factory work and full-time employment. In doing so, it politicized them by exposing them to direct forms of exploitation in which the reasons for their oppression, both as women and as workers, became clear. By breaking down the sexual division of labour, capitalism forced women and men to undergo similar forms of exploitation, thus making clear to both their common interest in overthrowing the existing social order. As the employment of women in industry increased, so growing numbers of proletarian women joined their male working-class comrades in the fight for emancipation and social justice. Thus—in the eyes of the socialists—the political mobilization of working-class women was part of the same inexorable process of economically determined political and social change that would eventually bring them to power.

The place accorded to the family in the formal ideology of European socialism seems clear enough, then; but in view of the gulf between theory and practice noted by many historians of the movement, it should come as no surprise to discover that in day-to-day party life, attitudes to the family were very different. The following pages document this by examining in detail the sociopolitical processes and recruitment techniques that lay behind the rise of the German Social Democratic Women's Movement, by far the largest socialist women's movement of its day, before returning to a broader comparative perspective and asking whether its experience reflected more general aspects of socialist theory and practice.

II

The SPD in Germany recruited women to its ranks in growing numbers from the 1880s and above all the early 1900s onwards, until by 1914 there were no fewer than 175,000 women in the party. Did this reflect, as was so widely believed, the dissolution of the family under the impact of capitalism? Important evidence is provided by the information we possess on the social composition of socialist women's organizations. On 16 June 1886, for instance, a straw poll revealed that all fifty women at a meeting of a socialist women's educational society in Hamburg, at that time the main centre of the nascent socialist women's movement in Germany, were married.[10] After this, the Hamburg society carried out a more detailed survey. Completed in October the same year, it revealed that only sixteen of the society's members were factory workers. Thirty-three did some form of paid domestic work, while no fewer than seventy-four did not work at all.[11] At a much later date, a survey of eight of the SPD's 'Women's Reading Evenings', designed for the political education of Social Democratic women, showed that the overwhelming majority of participants were married and did no paid work.[12] To a large extent, then, it seems that the Social Democrats were recruiting housewives rather than factory workers.

We can see this much more clearly, in fact, when we turn from the rather scattered and unsatisfactory statistical evidence to an examination of the actual techniques which the SPD used in trying to attract women to its organization. The initial appeal of the SPD to the uncommitted was made through mass public meetings,[13] which were carefully designed to provide entertainment—rousing songs, fiery speeches, colourful banners and so on—as well as to arouse political enthusiasm. During the meetings, volunteers stood ready in the wings with membership forms, waiting to swoop on the audience the moment the speeches finished.[14] The subjects announced as the topics for the women's meetings were very revealing of the direction in which the party was launching its appeal. The major issue after the turn of the century was the inflation of food prices, which the SPD ascribed to high corn import tariffs and low meat quotas imposed in their view to protect large farmers against foreign competition.[15] In 1905–6, for example, the SPD in Hamburg, at that time the only big city in which it was legal for women to join the party, held the following meetings for women: six on 'The trade treaties and women', three on 'Our daily bread', three on 'Podbielski, the Hamburg beef cattle exhibition and the meat shortage', two with the title 'Hunger and whips', two on 'How the German Michel's' (the equivalent of John Bull) 'bread basket is being hung even higher', and two on 'Can women still keep house properly in view of the high food prices?' Apart from these, all of which referred in one way or another to the high cost of food, there were two meetings on primary education and three on a current scandal about brutality in the army, all of which could be seen as appealing to women as the mothers of schoolchildren or conscripts; and finally there was one meeting attacking the Christian religion's attitude towards the female sex.[16] Similar examples could also be taken from subsequent years, and from the experience of other towns and cities.[17] In Dortmund, for example, an industrial town dominated by iron and steel, mining and building, and with relatively few employment opportunities for women, the police reported in 1907–8 that the SPD had launched an intensive recruiting drive to bring women into the party, and that its success was due to the high price of food.[18]

Another important means of recruitment and mobilization was through the SPD women's magazine, *Die Gleichheit* ('Equality') which from the turn of the century onwards was increasingly directed towards a popular audience, more and more of whom were not members of the SPD.[19] In 1905, while remaining officially, a 'Magazine for the Interests of Women Workers', it began to include regular supplements for mothers and children. From about the same time, as its editor Clara Zetkin had hoped, its circulation begain to increase sharply and it moved from a situation in which it made regular deficits to one in which its profits were reasonably healthy.[20] Here too, then, the mass recruitment of women began when campaigns and propaganda were explicitly directed towards their interests as housewives and mothers, rather than towards their interests as workers. It seems, therefore, that the political mobilization of working-class women in Wilhelmine Germany did not take place as a direct and immediate result of politicization through the experience of exploitation in the factory labour force. Actual mobilization did not generally occur until women were married and out of full-time industrial employment. In 1907, for example, while 70 per cent of women employed in German industry were below the age of thirty, surveys of the age structure of female party members showed that only 30 to 35 per cent of them fell into this age group.[21] This becomes even more paradoxical if we take into consideration the fact that the unmarried woman worker was likely, despite long hours, to have more leisure time available for political activities than the married woman in her thirties or forties with small children and a household to look after. Yet many married women entered the SPD from 1905–6 onwards, paid regular membership dues, attended weekly meetings, went to mass demonstrations, helped the party organization at election time and involved themselves actively in party affairs, while few younger unmarried women did.

The most important clue to understanding this phenomenon lies in the fact that the SPD women were overwhelmingly the wives of men already active in the party. Local evidence is unambiguous on this point. Thus the Hamburg political police noticed in 1886 that the husbands of the members of the socialist women's organizations were 'all known to be zealous Social Democrats'.[22] The 1911 survey of women's reading evenings in Berlin showed that the great majority of the participants had husbands in the SPD; many of the husbands were also in the trade unions.[23] On the eve of the First World War, a survey of the 11,684 female members of the SPD in Hamburg revealed that only 1,601 were engaged in paid employment: as the historian of the Hamburg party in this period concludes, 'the majority of female members were the non-working wives of the organized comrades'.[24] And at an earlier date, a social investigator of working-class life noted that young women workers were largely unpolitical, and added: 'those who really possessed a knowledge of the teachings of Social Democracy were the married women, who were brought into the ferment of agitation by their husbands and finally in this way they took part in it themselves'.[25] Similarly, a recent study of the SPD in the South German state of Baden has concluded of the period before the First World War that 'the Social Democratic women's movement was formed to a decisive degree by married women . . . A strong part was taken by the wives of the local party leaders'.[26] On a more general level, too, there was increasing recognition by party workers that the women in the SPD were mostly the wives of men already active in the labour movement. Since this contradicted the ideology of the SPD by disproving the theory of direct mobilization through factory work, it was the source of a certain amount of embarrassment and disquiet. One of the leading SPD men in Leipzig, for example, asked with evident irritation in 1913: 'Whom do we have, then, in the organization? The wives and daughters of party comrades, but not women factory workers.'[27] The women themselves were equally concerned. In the same year, 1913, the SPD women's organization in Berlin held a conference in which a special session was devoted to the topic 'How do we recruit unmarried women workers?' The speaker began by saying:

For the most part it is only the wives of our comrades who belong to the party organization. The great mass of female industrial workers is still lacking. I think we've been somewhat remiss in directing our women's recruitment efforts too much at women in their role as housewives and mothers. Our propaganda addresses itself too much to the housewife and mother. We don't have material for agitation among unmarried women workers.[28]

The leading recruiter of women for the SPD, Luise Zietz, also admitted in the same year that she had only really succeeded in winning over women with husbands already active in the party.[29] How this situation was to be remedied, however, nobody could convincingly say; and the SPD women's organization continued to be a movement of party wives right up to the First World War.

Now of course there are a number of problems with the evidence which I have presented for this statement. It is, inevitably, drawn from scattered sources. In the final analysis it is perhaps suggestive rather than convincing. Certainly this is a subject on which a great deal more research is called for. But it is significant that all the concrete evidence which we possess does actually point in the direction I have indicated. No one contradicted those leading SPD activists who complained that women workers were not being recruited. There are no figures available which indicate that the SPD's women members in any part of the Empire were predominantly engaged in full-time wage labour. There is no evidence to suggest that any more than a handful of them joined the party independently of their husbands, let alone in opposition to them. This is not to say, of course, that SPD women were never confronted with the exploitative power of capitalism as workers as well as in their role of housewives at some stage of their lives. Most of them must have undergone full-time employment before marriage and this may well have been a source of later commitment. Moreover, it is clear that at some stage during their married life most of them would have taken part-time casual jobs to help out in times of economic difficulty for the family. It may well be the case that the evidence which I have cited underestimates the numbers of working women in the SPD because at least some wives of Social Democratic men may have concealed their involvement in the labour market for fear of compromising their husbands' respectability. And in addition to this, of course, it may well be that for some of them at least, political considerations, even if only of the vaguest sort, may have played a role in the choice of marriage partner. In many ways, women had a lot to gain by joining the SPD, and would have realized this when considering commitment. None the less, when all these various reservations and provisos have been made, the point remains that there was no simple one-way process of the politicization of women through their emancipation from the family unit and incorporation into the productive process outside the home. On the contrary, such evidence as we have suggests that the decisive act of political mobilization—joining the party—took place within the framework of the family. It reflected the realities of women's role within the working-class family as much as, or even more than, their earlier experience as full-time wage labourers, or their continuing engagement in part-time, casual employment. Not only did the party address itself to women in their roles as mothers, consumers and wives, to a greater extent than it concerned itself with them in their role as wage-earners, but as often as not, this was the kind of appeal which proved most effective in arousing their interest.[30]

III

Of course, this angling of the SPD's appeal to women reflected the extent to which the men who dominated it accepted the conventional bourgeois concept of the sexual division of labour and the nature of sex-role divisions—women in the home, men out at work. Yet the men of the SPD had good reasons of their own for desiring the recruitment of women into the party. Had they been as hostile to women's involvement in politics as were their counterparts in the French labour movement, for example, then it is hardly likely that women, however strong their own reasons for committing themselves to socialism, would have entered the party in such massive numbers. But there is no doubt that the women who joined the SPD were actively encouraged to do so by their husbands save in a very small minority of cases. Again, a few local examples may serve as illustrations. Thus the 1911 analysis of members of the eight Berlin women's reading evenings already referred to showed that only 3 per cent of them were attending against their husbands' wishes. The analysis was carried out by women for women, so it probably reflected the true situation.[31] The attitude of many male activitists in the party was well conveyed by Karl Böttger, a speaker at a meeting of the SPD women's group in Lindenhof, an industrial suburb of Mannheim, in 1912, when he remarked that 'you're a bad comrade if you stand at the top and can't even manage to bring your wife into the association'.[32] In earlier years, up to 1906, the SPD women constantly complained about the indifference shown by their male comrades towards the recruitment of women.[33] But this constant insistence that it was wrong for men to take this attitude was bound to have an effect. Indeed, there is evidence that in the case of Dortmund the local party was spurred into launching a drive to recruit women precisely by this kind of complaint, which implied that it was backward, old-fashioned and inactive.[34] As time went on, then, it seems that the prejudice against the recruitment of women was gradually eroded.

One reason for this was a growing impatience with the hostility which working-class women often displayed towards the involvement of their menfolk in socialist politics. Joining the SPD in Imperial Germany could have severe consequences—it could lead to arrest and imprisonment, for even after the lapsing of the Anti-Socialist Law in 1890, police harassment of socialists, using a whole battery of legal pretexts, was very widespread; or it could lead to dismissal and, if the worker rented company housing, eviction by the employer, for many industrialists refused to tolerate active Social Democrats in their workforce. The economic consequences of all this for the working-class family were clear above all to the housewife, whose role it was to keep the family fed and clothed. A local newspaper commented with some feeling after the defeat of a miners' strike in Zwickau in 1900:

> Women do not want to know about politics and organization, they do not 'understand' it all; they appreciate a Mayday festival, with singing and speeches and dancing, that makes sense to them, but they do not appreciate political and trade union meetings, working-class women seem to lack the capacity to think in abstract terms. The female members of a workers' family become directly hostile, however, when a strike threatens or breaks out. They see only the missing weekly pay-packet of their husband, brother or father, not the circumstances which lead him to strike, and what the strike hopes to achieve . . . They think he has been 'stirred up' by others and 'forced to strike', compelled to be idle, and because they cannot get any money from him during the strike, they drive him from his comrades' side into the ranks of the strike-breakers, blacklegs and Judas Iscariots![35]

Further evidence of this can be found in workers' auto-biographies.[36] A recent analysis of thirty-three auto-biographies of pre-1914 Social Democrats has found that not one of the writers had experienced any sympathy from his mother for his decision to join the party. One writer commented that his mother had made life hell for him after he joined the SPD. Another reported that his mother had said to him on hearing the news, 'Out, you godless boy! You're not going to eat with us in the kitchen any more . . . I'm not going to let the children be corrupted by someone who'll end up in gaol or on the gallows.' Several writers mentioned that their political convictions were opposed by their wives as well as by their mothers. Two of them actually divorced for this reason.[37]

These experiences indicated another way in which women were believed to damage the interests of the labour movement: by bringing up children in opposition or indifference to the tenets of socialism. According to the sexual role division common in the German working-class home in the late nineteenth century, the care of children was left almost exclusively to women: the men spent most of their leisure time in all-male pubs, singing clubs, sports associations or, of course, political meetings. While father was out helping to run the SPD, mother or grandmother was at home making sure the children did not follow in his footsteps. To a movement as concerned as the SPD was with the future, this was a serious problem. It was present above all in Catholic areas, where working-class women continued to support the church long after a large part of the male population had gone over to the SPD. Even in the Weimar Republic, when women had the vote, the Catholic Centre Party was supported by proportionately more women than men at the polls in these areas, while the reverse was true of the SPD.[38] In an area such as Düsseldorf, indeed, the loyalty of women to the Catholic Church in the 1890s was so strong that the men in the SPD regarded it as a complete waste of time even to try to recruit them to the party.[39] The same pattern could be observed, though to a much lesser extent, in Protestant areas.[40]

The turning-point in the SPD's attitude towards the recruitment of women is hard to pin down precisely, and varied from area to area, but as the national statistics suggest, it can most plausibly be dated to the years 1905–6. An important role here was played by the great miners' strike of 1905, when the active participation of women in support of the strikers made a strong impression on observers, who contrasted it with the women's hostility to the last great strike, that of 1889, as well as with their attitude in many small strikes such as the one in Zwickau in 1900, mentioned above. This support, of course, had its ideological limitations: one commentator described 'how they streamed in their thousands to the women's meeting and often a dozen of them marched on to the platform one after another and gave their opinion: "Fight to the end, God and the Kaiser will take care of us."' These assemblies made what the same writer called an 'eternally unforgettable impression' on the labour movement in the area.[41] They seem to have convinced the men that there were positive advantages to be gained by the recruitment of women. The will to support the labour movement was clearly present in large numbers of women; all it needed was to be given a more permanent and more politically educated form. It was after the strike of 1905 that the first successful women's recruiting drives were launched in places such as Bochum and Dortmund, in the Ruhr,[42] and significantly they were virtually the first to be aimed directly at housewives and mothers.

Not only the men, but also the women of the SPD were quite explicit that the major purpose of the political mobilization of

working-class women was to strengthen the ideological
solidarity of the Social Democratic family. Thus at a meeting
of a local branch of the SPD's women's association in
Mannheim, for example, the participants resolved in 1905 to
take note of the fact that 'we women are at last waking up and
not leaving it to the men alone to fight for the general well-
being of the family'.[43] The SPD women were constantly
insisting that their intention was to fight 'shoulder to shoulder'
alongside the men in the party to achieve a general
improvement in the life of the working class, and they were
always careful to reassure the party that they had nothing
whatever to do with the 'bourgeois women's rights enthusiasts'
of the liberal feminist movement, whose fight was directed not
against capitalism, but against men.[44]

Clara Zetkin argued that socialist women should support the
commitment of their husbands in political life.[45] Beyond this,
too, as a member of the Mannheim-Lindenhof SPD women's
society remarked in 1911—'women can contribute a great deal
towards making their children familiar with our efforts from
an early age'.[46] Zetkin too emphasized that a major purpose of
the political mobilization of women, as of young people,
therefore, was to provide backing for the Social Democratic
man in his struggle against government, police, capital and
reaction, by sealing off his family as far as possible from
outside influences.[47] His wife was to be removed from the
reactionary influence of the church, and she in her turn was to
immunize their children against the nationalistic and
conservative ideology purveyed in the schools.[48]

IV

When we turn from high socialist theory to the everyday
practice of the Social Democratic movement, therefore, we
find, not hostility towards the family, but an overriding
concern for its integrity and solidarity. Indeed, it is not
difficult to find SPD members—both male and
female—deploring the effects of industrialization on the
family as sharply as any romantic conservative. Early tracts
and manifestos of the socialist women's movement are full of

outrage that every woman who was neither an heiress nor married into a propertied family was compelled to work,[49] that woman's work spelled ruin for the family,[50] and that men often had to look after the home; and the aim of the movement was declared to be the creation of 'circumstances in which a woman can fulfil her duties as wife and mother'.[51] A local SPD women's branch in Hamburg looked forward in 1894 to a time 'when our men will earn more, so that we don't need to work any more and can devote ourselves more to bringing up our children'.[52] A male speaker in the Mannheim–Lindenhof women's branch in 1910 met with no contradiction when he envisaged a time when men would earn enough for their wives not to have to work.[53] It was a common complaint that capitalism had driven women out of the home; and many ordinary party members evidently thought that the socialist revolution would put them back there.

The accommodation of the Social Democrats to the institution of the family, and their conversion to the view that family solidarity should be strengthened, can be viewed as a response to the common accusation that their main aim in this area was to subvert the family rather than maintain it. It can also be regarded as part of a complex sociopolitical process, commented on by many historians, through which the Social Democratic movement, denied influence on the political system, ostracized by respectable middle-class society and cut off from full participation in national life, turned in on itself and built up a social subculture, a 'society within a society', in which all social activities could be carried out within the orbit of Social Democracy, thus keeping the movement's members uncorrupted by contact with 'bourgeois society' until the coming of the revolution. By the early twentieth century, it has been argued, it was possible for a male Social Democrat to live almost his entire life within this subculture; he could eat food bought in a Social Democratic co-operative, read nothing but Social Democratic newspapers and magazines, spend his leisure time in a Social Democratic bicycling or gymnastics club or a Social Democratic male voice choir, drink in a Social Democratic pub and be buried with the aid of a Social Democratic burial society. It was only a small step from this to make him a happy home life in a Social Democratic family, with a Social Democratic wife and Social Democratic children.[54] However, the precise political meaning and significance of this elaborate subculture are complex and difficult to unravel. Some historians—indeed so many that their views can now be described almost as an orthodoxy—have argued that the Social Democratic subculture closely resembled the dominant culture of Imperial Germany despite the superficial differences and apparently irreconcilable hostility between them, and instead of sealing off the party from bourgeois influences, the SPD subculture acted as an unconscious transmitter of the dominant values of Wilhelmine Germany to the new working class. The party's emphasis on the importance of the family as an institution would seem to be a classic instance of this contribution to the embourgeoisement of the proletariat. The party was inculcating reverence for the bourgeois family ideal in the working classes; it was even trying to insist on the need for the family to be as cohesive and unified as possible in its outlook on life.[55]

It could also be argued that the SPD was trying to import the bourgeois reverence for the family into its own organization as a whole, rather as the dominant culture of Wilhelmine Germany argued that the state was but a larger version of the family, and should be bound by the same values and modes of behaviour. The Austrian socialist leader Viktor Adler commented in 1915 for example that the SPD provided for its members 'the family home and the stuff of life'.[56] In this larger family of the SPD as a whole, the women's and youth sections occupied the same subordinate and supportive positions as women and children were supposed to occupy within the individual household.[57] The recruitment of women and young people, however much effort was devoted to it, always appeared as a secondary objective in the eyes of male party activists: 'One should try to organize the men', a women delegate to the party congress in 1906 reported the men of her local party organization as saying; 'then after that one could approach the women'.[58] Clearly it would not do to recruit women and children unless the adult male membership of the local party organization was already numerous and firmly established. Once in the party, women were expected to maintain a low profile; as even Clara Zetkin's statements tend to suggest, their role was intended to be a supportive one. Women who tried to take an active role in running general party affairs ran into a lot of opposition from the men. There were few more hated people in the party than Rosa Luxemburg; and at a lower level, the experience of Klara Haase, a more humble party activist, when she was elected to the committee of the First Berlin Reichstag constituency party organization, was probably far from untypical.[59] She wrote later:

I came to the first session and the men tried to show their courage by using the vilest expressions and the foulest words in order to annoy me. However, I sat down and made a list of all these words with the corresponding names beside them. At the end, I said: 'If you men think you can frighten me off, you'd better take note: I'm going to take this list in person to the Party Executive tomorrow so that it can see what sort of people it's dealing with!' . . . After that, they were very decent to me.

In addition, of course, many SPD men must have been worried that it would arouse sexual gossip and suspicion if they spent long hours closeted behind committee-room doors with young, umarried (or even married) women to whom they were in no way related. The result of all this, however, was that the women did not take a significant part in general party affairs. Instead, they had their own areas of competence within the party. They were made responsible for so-called 'women's questions', children's welfare, family affairs, legal protection for women workers, consumer interests, health and so on. As a consequence they lacked a voice in party affairs as a whole. Here too, therefore, they could be seen as extending their prescribed role within the family, itself denied by bourgeois values and norms, to their activities in the party in general.[60] In these ways, therefore, Social Democratic attitudes to the family would seem to bear out many of the claims advanced by historians of the party in recent years: the divorce of theory and practice, the creation of a sealed-off subculture, the failure of ordinary party members to grasp Marxist ideology, and the function of the party as a contributor to the embourgeoisement of the proletariat.

In fact, however, this is only part of the picture; and the

conclusions which have been drawn from the notion of a Social
Democratic subculture are open to question. In the first place,
it is incorrect to emphasize exclusively the subordinate nature
of women's role in the party. Women joined the Social
Democrats for their own reasons. They were not mere ciphers,
enrolled in a cause in which their role was purely passive and
supportive. Membership in the party, whatever its limitations,
did represent a significant gain in status for working-class
women. And although the SPD women were largely confined
to 'women's questions', they asserted themselves in this area
with a vigour, a determination and an independence which
clearly antagonized male party leaders. Despite formal
incorporation into the party on the passage of the Imperial
Law of Association in 1908,[61] the women continued in effect to
run an autonomous women's organisation within the party.
The SPD men did everything they could to stop this. In 1912
they closed the Women's Bureau, the only central institution
of the SPD women in Germany as a whole.[62] After 1908, the
male party leadership was so hostile to the holding of separate
national SPD Women's Conferences, previously held every
other year, that only one more was ever held before the First
World War, in 1911. The local women's conferences which
replaced them were supposed to have the advantage that they
were put on by local party organizations, and so more easily
controlled by the men, but even here the fact that they were led
by women brought calls for their abolition. As one local party
leader put it: 'The Women's Conferences are a dubious
institution. We now have a unified organization, into which
the women have been incorporated. But the women still believe
in many cases that they form a special organization on their
own.'[63]

In the same way, most party leaders viewed the existence of a
separate socialist youth movement with profound distrust. 'If
we had such a movement', remarked Hermann Molkenbuhr in
1904, 'we would have to fight against it, since all the efforts of
the Party are directed towards centralization and greater
unity.' The trade unions were particularly hostile to the SPD's
youth movement. When in 1908, worried by the anti-
militaristic tone of the movement, the government banned all
people under the age of eighteen from taking part in political

activities, the party and the unions moved to bring the youth organization under tighter control by placing its branches under the aegis of the local party organizations. None the less, youth groups within the SPD continued to show signs of radicalism and rebellion, and clashes with the parent organization were frequent, rising to a new pitch of intensity during the First World War, when the youth organizations in towns such as Hamburg were centres of opposition to the moderate policy of the party majority.[64] Similarly (though to a much greater extent), the complaints of party leaders about the women's separatism after 1908 indicate that the women were not entirely unsuccessful in defending their autonomy within the SPD.

The position in particular of women in German Social Democracy should be seen in terms of a process of conflict and bargaining with the men in the party, in which both sexes made their own demands, yielded some and saw the realization of others. If the political mobilization of women involved their acceptance of the male-dominated family, then it was a negotiated acceptance, in which the end result was a significant shift in the balance of power between the sexes within the labour movement as a whole.[65] The redefinition of women's roles which occurred, in other words, was a result not of the simple co-opting of a passive mass of women who supinely acquiesced in the perpetuation of their own subordination, but rather the outcome of a constant process of conflict, of resistance and accommodation, in which the terms of women's subordination were constantly being renegotiated.[66]

V

Similar ambivalences may be observed in the position of women in the Social Democratic Party—Bolsheviks and Mensheviks—in Russia. Before the Revolution the party was forced by Tsarist repression to function clandestinely, and it never had the chance to become a large, mass movement on German lines. Even so, its lack of any real interest in the systematic recruitment to the party's ranks was remarkable. Alexandra Kollontai's efforts to organize a club for women workers in the aftermath of the 1905 Revolution met with indifference or even hostility from the Petersburg Committee of the Social Democratic Party. Indeed, although the Committee agreed to make its premises available for one of Kollontai's meetings, she later recalled that when she arrived she found the room locked and a notice on the door with the words 'Meeting for Women Only—Cancelled/Tomorrow, Meeting for Men Only'. The Bolsheviks failed to address any of their propaganda specifically to women at this period, and it was not until September 1913 that the party decided to make a real effort in this direction. Lenin and the other leading Bolsheviks tended to regard such campaigns as diversions from the revolutionary effort, and they too were adamantly opposed to any separate women's movements. Kollontai, who was at that time still a Menshevik, managed to organize a women's socialist club, but it ran into the obstacle of state repression and ceased to exist in 1908. In 1913–14, Bolshevik and Menshevik women, encouraged by the exiled leadership in Zurich, formed a women's club in St Petersburg and organized celebrations of International Proletarian Women's Day, but these too were quickly repressed by the police.[67]

It was only in 1917 that the Bolshevik women's movement revived, and this time, as distinct from the pre-war attempt to appeal to women workers, party propaganda concentrated on the issues of price inflation and the damage being caused to family life by the continuation of the war, as well as the conditions under which women workers were suffering. By this time Kollontai had become a Bolshevik, and, like Zetkin, she persuaded the party to tolerate a Women's Bureau by reassuring it that it would not exhibit any 'feminist' tendencies. It is clear that the existence of an autonomous movement was, as in Germany, an important element in the party's success, for in the field of moblizing working-class women it was effectively unrivalled in 1917. After the October Revolution a whole package of emancipatory legislation was passed and the women's section became a large movement dedicated to backing this up by mass propaganda and organization at the local level. Particularly noteworthy were the efforts of the women's sections in raising consciousness among Muslim women in Central Asia, in the teeth of fierce and often brutal opposition from Muslim men. Opposition and obstruction came from Bolshevik men both locally and (as with Zinoviev, Rykov and Ryazanov) centrally too. Accusations of 'feminist tendencies' were made at the party congress in 1923 and by 1930, with the rise of Stalin, the women's sections were abolished. This paved the way for the 'sexual Thermidor', as the Stalinist regime proceeded to reverse the legislation of the post-revolutionary period by, in 1936, tightening divorce law and abolishing abortion on demand. *De facto* marriages lost the legal status they had so recently gained, and in an atmosphere of 'revolutionary sublimation' even equal co-education was abolished. These measures were partly intended to increase the birth rate, but above all they were undertaken in the name of the 'strengthening of the Soviet family', as *Pravda* put it. In 1935 *Isvestiya* declared it was time 'to declare frivolity in family affairs a crime', and the new policy—backed up by family welfare provisions which partly mitigated its effects— emphasized the need to shore up the stability of the family rather than—as previously—the need to create equality within it.[68]

Both in Germany and Russia, therefore, though in different ways, socialism came to view the family in a fundamentally positive light, and the same can be said too, most probably, for socialism in Austria and other countries. Was this a departure from the canons of classical socialist theory? In fact, Marxist writing on the family was not as hostile to the institution as first impressions often led conservatives to believe. Neither Marx nor Engels nor Lenin had a great deal to say on the subject, and much of what they did have to say was rather vague. As Clara Zetkin once remarked, the Marxist classics were more important as sources of general ideas and methods with which to approach the problem of women and the family, than as providers of specific analyses on the subject.[69] Nevertheless, three general points do emerge from their writings. First, as we have seen, they were all convinced that after the revolution, society would take over some of the functions of the family, notably childcare, but also to some extent housework and cooking. This did not mean, however, that all family ties would be dissolved. On the contrary, the second point of general agreement to emerge from classical Marxist theory was that monogamy would not disappear under socialism; as Engels declared in *The Origin of the Family*, men would actually become more monogamous, not less, after the revolution, because socialism would allow human consciousness, and with it mutual and permanent love between two individuals, to develop to the full. As Kautsky declared in the Erfurt Programme, 'Socialists . . . maintain that ideal love, just the reverse of a community of wives and of all sexual oppression and license, will be the foundation of matrimonial connections in a Socialist Commonwealth, and that pure love can prosper only in such a system'.[70] Although, as Richard Stites remarks, 'when we step onto Russian soil, we find the atmosphere considerably more foggy', largely because of the tradition of sexual freedom bequeathed by the nihilists, still, Lenin is on record as having said that adultery was beyond the pale even under socialism. Marxists, including Lenin, did of course approve of divorce, but only because they were very critical of the idea of a 'loveless marriage' and advocated instead a permanent union based on love.[71]

Thirdly, although Marx, Engels, Bebel and Zetkin all insisted that the decline of the existing form of the family under capitalism heralded the emergence of a new form of the family under socialism, this insistence only took up a small part of the space which they devoted to the subject. What they paid most attention to were the harmful effects which capitalism had on the existing family structure; and it was all too easy for ordinary Social Democrats to forget the dialectic of decay and renewal and concentrate their attention exclusively on the former, especially because Marxist accounts of the decay of the existing family were rich in moral indigation, heavily laden with shocking examples, concrete and passionate at the same time, while accounts of the future family structure, by contrast, were necessarily pitched at a rather vague and abstract level. Both Marx and Engels in the *Communist Manifesto,* and Bebel in *Woman and Socialism*, depicted in lurid detail the moral collapse of bourgeois and proletarian family ties under the influence of capitalism; and their detailed analysis of the evils of female factory labour could all too easily be interpreted as the obverse of a tacit plea for returning women to the home. Ordinary Social Democrats tended to select from the range of ideas available to them those which emphasized the damage done by capitalism to proletarian family life, and drew the conclusion that everything possible should be done to maintain or restore the family's integrity. Significantly, the more the leading theorist on women's questions in international Marxism after Bebel, Clara Zetkin, came into contact with the views of ordinary party members on this subject, the more she was forced to modify her original beliefs. In 1896 she confessed that her earlier statements on the family had claimed with 'one-sided sharpness' that the family had no future because it was being undermined by the development of capitalism. Instead, as we have seen, from 1896 onwards she fully accepted the validity of the family as an institution.[72]

In Russia in the 1930s the family was seen in instrumental terms, as a means of shoring up the stability of the Stalinist regime. In the pre-1914 German SPD, more complex social processes were at work. Contemporary social surveys suggested that as men's wages rose, their wives tended to work less outside the home. Wives provided 3.5 per cent of the income of skilled workers' families in the 1890s but 7.7 per cent of the income of unskilled workers' families. Even unskilled workers, however, if they earned over 1,000 marks a year, tended to have wives who did no paid work.[73] A survey carried out in 1899 among married women factory workers found that over half of them worked because their husband earned too little to support the family, and many more because he was chronically ill or unemployed.[74] It seems likely, therefore, that the husbands of SPD women came from the better-off sectors of the working class. Many of these men, as the insistence of SPD propaganda and comment on the paramount importance of the wives of leading officials and activists joining the party suggests, were undoubtedly paid officials in the party or the unions. Others were benefiting from the long period of rapid increases in real wages which set in at the end of the 'Great Depression' in 1896.[75] Among the groups represented by the SPD, patterns of leisure were beginning to change. The all-male clubs and activities which dominated social life both among old-established artisan communities, reflecting the tightly knit organization of craft work, and in the newer industrial districts, where the population was predominantly

young, male and unmarried, were declining in importance as
artisan culture disintegrated and the balance of age and sex in
the new industrial areas became more even as the new
communities gained a measure of permanence and stability.
These men began to spend an increasing amount of their leisure
time within the home, so that the political opinions and
attitudes of wife and family, which they might not previously
have had the inclination to notice, now began to acquire a new
importance.[76] Seen in a wider social perspective, then, the
emergence of a mass socialist women's movement in Germany
could appear as part of the growth of a 'respectable' upper
stratum of the working class.[77]

Jane Humphries has recently remarked that 'all too
frequently in the modern literature, the family is seen as
engendering false consciousness, promoting capitalist
ideology, undermining class cohesion and threatening the class
struggle. In short, it stands charged with being a bourgeois
institution acting in collaboration with capital against the real
interests of the working class.'[78] This is not how it appeared to
the socialist movement in Europe before the First World War.
The mere fact that the official idealization of the family in
Imperial Germany was turned against the ruling classes by the
Social Democrats indicated that the proletarian family was no
simple vehicle for the downward transmission of bourgeois
values. Yet Humphries' claim that the family was on the
contrary an essential element in the economic defence and
solidarity of the proletariat ignores the explicitly educational
and socializing functions of the family as envisaged by the
German Social Democrats; much more importantly, it glosses
over internal divisions within the working class—vital for the
understanding of political behaviour—and presents the family
in far too unproblematic a way. A more fruitful way of
approaching the working-class family is to see it as the object
of a struggle between rival political creeds for its allegiance, the
permanent scene of a conflict between rival political
ideologies. To some extent, this conflict was fought out
between forces imported into the family from outside:
socialism and unionism, brought in by the father, religion
brought in by the mother, nationalism and monarchism
brought in from school by the children. But real conflicts of

interest within the family (ignored in Humphries' model) were also involved: conflicts of authority between man and wife, parents and children, and economic conflicts between the primary breadwinner and the housekeeper. It was precisely to help resolve such conflicts that the Russian reforms of the 1920s and the egalitarian campaigns of the Bolshevik women's sections were launched.

Both the Bolsheviks and the German Social Democrats, however, were ultimately somewhat ambivalent towards the family as an institution. Socialist attitudes towards the family were not just developed in isolation by Marxist theorists and imposed on the labour movement from above; they were worked out by ordinary Social Democrats themselves in the course of trying to explain, and ultimately to change, the conditions of their own existence; they were fought out in a series of conflicts of interest within the labour movement, and between the labour movement and the dominant culture; they were developed in response to the perceived needs of propaganda and political stability or change. They were an amalgam of personal and political experience, theoretical understanding, and parts of the cultural apparatus of the society in which the socialists lived, so it is difficult to talk of a simple contradiction between theory and practice, or to argue that a creeping reformism was the main characteristic of the evolution of German Social Democratic ideas about the working-class family, or, as Richard Stites has pointed out, that the 'sexual Thermidor' was exclusively the creation of Stalinism. Rather, here as in other spheres, we should pay more attention to the changing conditions under which socialist attitudes developed, and the ways in which they related to the changing exigencies of politics and everyday life in nineteenth- and twentieth-century Europe.

NOTES

This chapter is a revised version of 'Politics and the family: Social Democracy and the working-class family in theory and practice before 1914', in Richard J. Evans and W. R. Lee (eds), *The German Family: Essays on the*

Social History of the Family in 19th and 20th-century Germany (London, 1981), pp. 256–88 and draws on material first presented in my book *Sozialdemokratie und Frauenemanzipation im deutschen Kaiserreich* (Verlag J.H.W. Dietz Nachf., Bonn–Berlin, 1979).

1. Jürgen Habermas, *Strukturwandel der Öffentlichkeit. Untersuchungen zu einer Kategorie der bürgerlichen Gesellschaft* (Neuwied–Berlin, 1969), pp. 55–63, 171–9.
2. Evans, 'Politics and the family', pp. 256–62, for examples of such views.
3. Marx–Engels, *Ausgewählte Schriften*, vol. 2, (East Berlin, 1963), p. 216.
4. *Das Kapital* (Berlin, 1955), vol. I, p. 515.
5. August Bebel, *Die Frau und der Sozialismus* (50th edn, Berlin, 1970).
6. Lily Braun, *Die Frauenfrage: ihre geschichtliche Entwicklung und wirtschaftliche Seite* (Leipzig, 1901).
7. Clara Zetkin, *Die Arbeiterinnen- und Frauenfrage der Gegenwart* (Berlin, 1891).
8. Richard Stites, *The Women's Liberation Movement in Russia. Feminism, Nihilism and Bolshevism, 1860–1930* (Princeton, 1978), pp. 242, 258–69.
9. Barbara Taylor, *Eve and the New Jerusalem: Socialism and Feminism in the Nineteenth Century* (London, 1983); Claire Goldberg Moses, *French Feminism in the Nineteenth Century* (Albany, N.Y., 1983).
10. StA Hbg, PP, V43: Versammlungsbericht (16 June 1886).
11. StA Hbg, PP, V43: Versammlungsbericht (13 October 1886); StA Hbg, PP, S1053: *Bürgerzeitung* (26 June 1886 and 17 October 1886). According to the latter, the figures were: 33 domestic workers, 16 artisans, 49 'women workers' (*Arbeiterinnen*) and 74 without employment.
12. *GL*, Vol. XX1 (14 August 1911).
13. Cf. Jochen Loreck, *Wie man früher Sozialdemokrat wurde* (Bonn, 1977).
14. See the elaborate instructions for the holding of such meetings in Luise Zietz, *Gewinnung und Schlulung der Frau für die politische Betätigung* (Berlin, 1914).
15. Cf. the advertisement and reports in StA Hbg, PP, S8897.
16. StA Hbg, PP, S8897: Versammlungsberichte (1905–6).
17. In 1912, there was a campaign of mass women's meetings in Berlin against rising food prices (Staatsarchiv Hamburg, PP, S8897: *VW* (25 September 1912).
18. Ralf Lützenkirchen, *Der sozialdemokratische Verein für den Reichstagswahlkreis Dortmund-Hörde* (Monographien zur Geschichte Dortmunds und der Grafschaft Mark, Vol. II, Dortmund; 1970), pp. 114–32.
19. This was because an increasing proportion of each edition of the magazine was taken up by bulk orders from the unions.
20. Evans, 'Politics and the family', table 9.1, p. 281.
21. *ibid.*, pp. 281–2.
22. StA Hbg, PP, S1053: Hamburg police to Berlin police (3 November 1886).

23. *GL,* Vol. XXI (14 August and 18 August 1911).

24. Volker Ullrich, *Die Hamburger Arbeiterbewegung vom Vorabend des Ersten Weltkrieges bis zur Revolution 1918/19* (Hamburg, 1976), p. 77.

25. M. Wettstein-Adelt, *Dreieinhalb Monate Fabrikarbeiterin* (Berlin, 1893), p. 71.

26. Jörg Schadt (ed.), *Im Dienst an der Republik: die Tätigkeit des Landesvorstands der Sozialdemokratischen Partei Badens 1914–1932* (Veröffentlichungen des Stadtarchivs Mannheim, 4, Stuttgart, 1977), p. 42 and note 86.

27. GLA Karlsruhe, NL Adolf Geck, 1907: Stizungen der Kontrolkommission: Partei-Ausschuss (7 November 1913). The speaker was Richard Lipinski.

28. StA Hbg, PP, S8897: *VW* (17 November 1913).

29. *Die Neue Zeit,* vol. XXXI (12 September 1913), p. 881.

30. These points are made in response to criticisms of an earlier version of this argument, made by Willy Albrecht *et al.,* 'Frauenfrage und deutsche Sozialdemokratie vom Ende des 19. Jahrhunderts bis zum Beginn der zwanziger Jahre', *Archiv für Sozialgeschichte,* Vol. XIX (1979) pp. 459–510, esp. pp. 472–3.

31. See the interesting discussion of these reading evenings on pp. 193–200 of Jean H. Quataert, *Reluctant Feminists in German Social Democracy 1885–1917* (Princeton, 1979). The original figures are in *GL* vol. XXI (14 August 1911, 28 August 1911).

32. Stadtarchiv Mannheim, Kleine Erwerbung No. 43: Protokollbuch des Sozialdemokratischen Frauenvereins Mannheim, Zahlstelle Lindenhof (13 December 1912).

33. Molly Nolan, 'Proletarischer Anti-Feminismus. Dargestellt am Beispiel der SPD–Ortsgruppe Düsseldorf 1890 bis 1914', in *Frauen und Wissenschaft. Beiträge zur Berliner Sommeruniversität für Frauen Juli 1976* (Berlin, 1977), p. 386; StA Hbg, PP, V43: Versammlungsbericht (15 December 1886): *Parteitagsprotokolle, 1894,* p. 179; 1896, p. 170; 1906, pp. 407–9.

34. Lützenkirchen, *Der sozialdemokratische Verein, loc. cit.*

35. StA Hbg, PP, S8897/III: *Sächsisches Volksblatt,* cited in *Fachzeitung für Schneider* (21 April 1900).

36. For an introduction to this rich literature, see Wolfgang Emmerich, *Proletarische Lebensläufe* (Reinbeck bei Hamburg, 1974).

37. Loreck, *Wie man früher Sozialdemokrat wurde,* pp. 238–9.

38. Gabrielle Bremme, *Die politische Rolle der Frau in Deutschland* (Göttingen, 1956); Brian Peterson, 'The politics of working-class women in the Weimar Republic', *Central European History,* X (June 1977), 2, pp. 87–111.

39. Nolan, 'Proletarischer Anti-Feminismus', p. 366.

40. Bremme, *Die politische Rolle der Frau in Deutschland.*

41. Erhard Lucas, *Arbeiterradikalismus. Zwei Formen von Radikalismus in der deutschen Arbeiterbewegung* (Frankfurt-am-Main, 1976), p. 66, citing Anton Erkelenz, *Kraftprobe im Ruhrgebiet* (Düsseldorf, 1905), p. 49.

42. Lützenkirchen, *Der sozialdemokratische Verein* (for Dortmund);

reports in Münster/Bochum Staatsarchiv Münster RA/I/96 and Stadtarchiv Bochum 480 (for Bochum: I owe these last references to the kindness of Stephen Hickey).

43. Stadtarchiv Mannheim, Kleine Erwerbung No. 43: Protokollbuch des Sozialdemokratischen Frauenvereins Mannheim, Zahlstelle Lindenhof, minute for June 1905 meeting.

44. The classic statement of this view can be found in Clara Zetkin's speech to the 1896 Party Congress, printed in Clara Zetkin, *Ausgewählte Reden und Schriften,* vol. I (East Berlin, 1953).

45. *GL*, vol. VIII, no. 2 (19 January 1898), pp. 9–10.

46. Stadtarchiv Mannheim, Kleine Erwerbung No. 43: Protokoll buch des Sozialdemokratischen Frauenvereins Mannheim, Zahlstelle Lindenhof, minute of meeting on 6 April 1911.

47. *GL*, vol. VIII, no. 2 (19 January 1898), pp. 9–10.

48. Brief (if simplistic) delineations of the officially-prescribed role of church and Volksschule in: Hans-Ulrich Wehler, *Das deutsche Kaiserreich 1870–1918* (Göttingen, 1973).

49. StA Hbg, PP, V43: *Bürgerzeitung* (27 February 1886).

50. StA Hbg, PP, V43: Versammlungsbericht (23 February 1887)

51. StA Hbg, PP, V46: *HE* (19 November 1889).

52. StA Hbg, V581: Versammlungsbericht (18 October 1894).

53. Stadtarchiv Mannheim, Kleine Erwerbung No. 43: Protokollbuch des Sozialdemokratischen Frauenvereins Mannheim, Zahlstelle Lindenhof, minute of meeting of 7 December 1910.

54. For a critical discussion of the idea of a Social Democratic 'subculture', see Vernon Lidtke, *The Alternative Culture* (New York, 1985).

55. *ibid.*; and particularly in Peter Lösche, 'Arbeiterbewegung und Wilhelm-inismus: Sozialdemokratie zwischen Anpassung und Spaltung', *Geschichte in Wissenschaft und Unterricht*, 20 (1969), pp. 519–33; also in Dieter Groh, *Negative Integration und revolutionärer Attentismus. Die deutsche Sozialdemokratie am Vorabend des Ersten Weltkrieges* (Frankfurt-am-Main, 1973) (using the phrase 'Verbürgerlichung des Proletariats'); more generally, in the various essays in Hans Mommsen (ed.), *Sozialdemokratie zwischen Klassenbewegung und Volkspartei* (Frankfurt-am-Main, 1974). For a more sustained critique of the concepts of 'subculture' and embourgeoisement in contemporary German labour history, see my essay on 'The sociological interpretation of German labour history' in Richard J. Evans (ed.), *The German Working Class 1888–1933: The Politics of Everyday Life* (London, 1982).

56. Quoted in Alex Hall, *Scandal, Sensation and Social Democracy. The SPD Press and Wilhelmine Germany 1890–1914* (Cambridge, 1977).

57. Cf. Alex Hall, 'Youth in rebellion: the beginnings of the socialist youth movement 1904–14', in Richard J. Evans (ed.), *Society and Politics in Wilhelmine Germany* (London, 1978), pp. 241–66.

58. *PTP* Mannheim (1906), pp. 407–9.

59. Friedrich-Ebert-Stiftung, Bonn-Bad Godesberg; Archiv der Sozialen Demokratie, NL Gerda Weyl; Lebenserinnerungen von Klara Weyl.

60. See also the conclusions of Nolan, 'Proletarischer Anti-Feminismus'.
61. Diefer Fricke, *Die deutsche Arbeiterbewegung 1896–1914* (Berlin, 1976), gives the relevant documents (p. 325). The Law of Association (1908) made it possible for women to join political parties in all parts of Germany.
62. Fricke, *op. cit.*, p. 329.
63. *GLA* Karlsruhe, NL Adolf Geck, No. 1907: Sitzungen der Kontrollkommission: Partei-Auschluss (7 November 1913).
64. Hall, 'Youth in rebellion', Fricke, *Die deutsche Arbeiterbewegung;* Johannes Schult, *Geschichte der Hamburger Arbeiter* (Hanover, 1967).
65. For the idea of the negotiated acceptance of bourgeois values and institutions by the working class, see Frank Parkin, *Class Inequality and Political Order* (London, 1972), pp. 79–102.
66. For the application of this approach in the context of women's history, see for example Linda Gordon, *Woman's Body, Woman's Right. A Social History of Birth Control in America* (Harmondsworth, 1977), esp. pp. xiii-xiv.
67. Stites, *op. cit.*, pp. 243–58.
68. *ibid.*, pp. 301–6, 317–421.
69. *ibid.*, pp. 258–89.
70. *ibid.*, p. 259.
71. *ibid.*, pp. 258–87. See also Alfred G. Meyer, 'Marxism and the women's question', in D. Atkinson, A. Dallin and G. Lapidus (eds), *Women in Russia* (Stanford, 1977); Meyer's account of Marx and Engels is more convincing than his account of the later development of Marxist ideology in this area.
72. *GL* vol. VI, no. 25 (9 December 1896) and no. 26 (23 December 1896), pp. 197–200 and 203–7; see Chapter 1, above, for more detail.
73. Peter N. Stearns, *Lives of Labour. Work in a Maturing Industrial Society* (London, 1975); see also the same author's 'Adaptation to industrialization: German workers as a test case', *Central European History,* vol. III (1970), pp. 303–31.
74. Rose Otto, *Über Fabrikarbeit verheirateter Frauen* (Stuttgart/Berlin, 1910), pp. 114–15.
75. Ashok V. Desai, *Real Wages in Germany 1871–1913* (Oxford, 1968); Thomas J. Orsagh, 'Löhne in Deutschland 1871–1913: Neuere Literatur und weitere Ergebnisse', *Zeitschrift für die gesamte Staatswissenschaft* 125 (1969), pp. 467–83. Otto, *Über Fabrikarbeit,* shows that the husbands of women factory workers were overwhelmingly employed in poorly-paid or casual jobs (they are described as 'factory workers', 'day-labourers', 'other workers' etc., rather than being assigned to specific trades requiring training).
76. See Wolfgang Nahrstedt, *Die Entstehung der Freiheit. Dargestellt am Beispiel Hamburgs* (Göttingen, 1972), esp. pp. 217–26 and 183–91; also Robert Q. Gray, 'Styles of life, the "labour aristocracy" and class relations in later nineteenth century Edinburgh', *International Review of Social History,* vol. XVIII (1973), pp. 428–52; and Gareth Stedman Jones, 'Working-class culture and working-class politics in London

1870–1900: notes on the remaking of a working class', *Journal of Social History,* vol. VII (1974), pp. 460–508. I owe this point to work in progress by David Crew.

77. E. J. Hobsbawm, 'The labour aristocracy in nineteenth-century Britain', in E. J. Hobsbawm, *Labouring Men* (London, 1964), pp. 272–315.

78. Jane Humphries, 'Class struggle and the persistence of the working-class family', *Cambridge Journal of Economics,* vol. 1, no. 3 (1977), pp. 241–55.

5 Women's Peace, Men's War?

Feminism today has close associations with pacifism. At Greenham Common in England the women's peace camp has provided not only a permanent reminder of the dangers of nuclear missiles but also a living example of specifically feminist forms of political protest and action. In the Federal Republic of Germany feminists have been prominent in the Green Party and have taken a lead in the party's opposition to nuclear weapons. Similar examples could be adduced from elsewhere. Uniting all these movements is a belief that women are imbued with a peaceful, humane, non-aggressive and life-giving outlook which makes them inherently opposed to violence and war. Such a belief is not new, as feminist historians such as Anne Wiltsher, in her recent study of feminist opposition to the First World War, have begun to discover.[1] Darryn Kruse and Charles Sowerwine have similarly noted, in a new study of the Women's International League for Peace and Freedom, founded in 1915, that feminists in the early twentieth century used the 'separate spheres' argument for this purpose. If, as the social convention of the time assumed, women's role was primarily to keep the home safe and pure, their mission also lay in extending this spirit of peace and harmony into the world at large. Thus feminists of many kinds took the view articulated by Jane Addams in 1915, that 'as women we are the custodians of the life of the ages and we will no longer consent to its reckless destruction'.[2]

This Chapter takes up these ideas and provides an account of the opposition offered by feminist and socialist women in Europe to the First World War. That opposition, courageous and determined though it was, failed; and it is not enough simply to record and celebrate it, it is also important to understand why it did not succeed. The attempt to reach this understanding involves more than a critical (though I hope, still sympathetic) approach to feminist pacifism; it also involves setting that phenomenon in a wider context of feminist and socialist attitudes to war and peace, and studying it against the background of society and politics in Europe during the First World War. Simply writing a selective history of those feminists and socialist women who opposed the war runs the risk of delivering a distorted picture of the relationship between feminism and pacifism, unless it is linked, at the very least, to a wider view of the historical context.

I

Connections between feminism and pacifism were already visible in Europe before 1914. In 1899 and 1907 feminists organized worldwide women's demonstrations for peace, and indeed in 1902 radical German feminists suggested, though without success, that this event be made annual.[3] In 1909 a feminist observed that 'the women's movement in all countries . . . is becoming more and more interested in the idea of international understanding'.[4] This growing interest had three main sources. The first lay in the female suffrage campaign which was gathering strength in many European countries in the years before the First World War. Feminists were shedding their reluctance to fight for the vote, and the numbers of women who supported the idea were increasing rapidly, helped after 1905 by the worldwide publicity gained by the English suffragettes and their campaign of militancy, led by the Pankhursts. Feminists basically demanded the vote as a fundamental human right, as a matter of justice, but they also argued that if it were granted, the creation of a female electorate would bring about a range of social and political reforms, stemming from women's interest in a more just and humane society. In the atmosphere of rising international tension prevalent in Europe before 1914, these reforms included the reversal of the arms race and the guarantee of peace. Thus in 1912 the Russian League for Women's Equality argued in a petition to the Duma (the Russian Parliament) that women should have the vote because it would bring a solution not only to social problems such as alcoholism and prostitution but would also cause the defeat of militarism and the end of international tension.[5] The French Union for Women's Suffrage declared in 1913 that 'the women's vote will assure the establishment of important social laws', and these included not only health and welfare, temperance and the protection of young women against prostitution, but also legislation 'to prevent wars and to submit conflicts among nations to courts of arbitration'.[6] Five years before, in 1908, the German Union for Women's Suffrage had drawn up a similar list of reforms, claiming among other things that 'Women's Suffrage encourages peace and harmony between different peoples'.[7]

A second source of pacifist commitment before 1914 came from the growing interest of many feminists in problems of motherhood. With a decline in the birth rate in many European countries and the virtual end of the age of epidemics (such as cholera, typhoid and smallpox) that had so often made life cheap in the nineteenth century, came a growing public interest in reducing the scourge of infant mortality and the beginnings of a successful movement to protect maternity and improve infant health standards, encouraged both by state legislation and by voluntary associations. The rise of eugenics and 'Neo-Malthusianism' reinforced the new focus on motherhood. Increasing numbers of feminists argued that childbirth and child-rearing were becoming a matter of choice, and began to explore the implications of the new situation. Thus the Russian feminist Sofiya Zarechnaya, writing in 1910, suggested that birth control would make human life rarer, and so society would be less willing to squander it in war. She added that having fewer children would enable women to take a fuller part in politics, and this too would bring what she thought of as feminine forces of justice and love to bear on state policy.[8] Similarly, in Germany the Neo-Malthusian Helene Stöcker, leader of the League for the Protection of Motherhood and Sexual Reform, was also a convinced pacifist. She had a general belief in the need to release Nietzschean forces of love and understanding in the world of nations as well as in the world of individuals. Often, of course, the advocates of these two views of feminist pacifism were indistinguishable: it was mainly a matter of where they placed their emphasis; certainly some of them, like Stöcker, appear to have been brought to pacifism mainly by their interest in motherhood.[9]

The third, less obviously ideological source of feminist pacifism lay in the international contacts that had grown up in the feminist world in the years after the founding of the International Council of Women on the initiative of American feminists in 1888. By the eve of the First World War this organization had member councils in sixteen European countries. In 1904 the more radical feminists broke away and founded an International Women Suffrage Alliance, which by 1914 had member societies in twenty different European countries. These organizations were only loose federations, and because of the widely differing views of their member societies on many issues, they were never able to agree on a firm programme of action, although more specialized international feminist associations dealing with subjects like the white slave trade or temperance reform usually were.[10] However, their existence gave many feminists the feeling that they were engaged in a common struggle that united them with their sisters abroad. The many international congresses held by these organizations strengthened this feeling by fostering personal contacts and friendships between feminists in different countries. All this encouraged them to take an interest in lessening international tension and provided them with a network of international contacts that would prove very useful when it came to improvising a feminist campaign against the war.

Pacifism was by no means a central issue on the feminist platform before 1914, but with the outbreak of war it immediately became a concern of overriding importance for many feminists. A congress of the International Woman Suffrage Alliance was due to be held in the autumn of 1914, and when it was, inevitably, cancelled, a group of female suffrage activists began to try to arrange one themselves. Their aim was to re-establish the international contacts that had been so abruptly broken off, and to launch a general feminist campaign for peace. In February 1915 some of these women managed to meet in Amsterdam, and they succeeded in organizing an unofficial International Women's Peace Congress, held at The Hague in April 1915. The congress was attended by participants from Britain, Austria–Hungary, Germany, Belgium, Italy, Norway, Sweden, Poland, Brazil and the Netherlands. It was thus one of the earliest meetings of pacifists from belligerent countries. The congress successfully avoided any mutual recriminations, and wisely excluded questions of war guilt and atrocities from its deliberations, and agreed to establish national working groups which formed the basis of the Women's International League for Peace and Freedom. It passed resolutions against secret treaties and annexations, and in favour of a League of Nations, universal disarmament, international arbitration and the democratic control of foreign policy. Such ideas were being widely discussed in pacifist circles at the time, and were influential during the eventual peace settlement.[11]

The most interesting aspect of the Hague Congress, and of feminist pacifism during the war in general, lay in the close links it drew between women's subjection and the triumph of militarism. As Darryn Kruse and Charles Sowerwine have pointed out,[12] this idea was not new; but in tracing back its origins, they exaggerate the extent to which nineteenth-century feminism was based on a notion of the special qualities of women and forget that its fundamental thrust was towards the achievement of rights on the grounds of individual human equality. The war marked an important change in this respect, especially for the more radical, suffragist wing of European feminism. To be sure, the argument that women's suffrage would have a civilizing influence had already been widely employed; but now the feminist pacifists radicalized it and moved it to the very centre of their ideology. Women's suffrage, the Hague Congress argued, was the quickest way to bring the war to an end; more than that, the war itself, many of the participants argued, was men's work. In France, the radical feminist Madeleine Pelletier denounced the war in August 1914 as an instrument of men's power over women.[13] In Germany the suffragist leader Anita Augspurg branded it a product of 'men's politics' and declared in October 1914: 'Under men, murder is being committed on a scale more vast and more gruesome than the world has ever known.' The war, said another German feminist, Lida Gustava Heymann, was a 'men's war' between 'men's states'.[14] The Russian suffragist Mariya Porkrovskaia concurred in regarding the war as men's work. Women were not to blame. On the contrary, she wrote, 'only they can annihilate the power of brute force, the mania for world domination which creates slavery and war'.[15] The Hungarian women's suffrage leader Rosika Schwimmer took the lead in spreading such ideas to audiences in Sweden and the United States. All over Europe, therefore, a feminist pacifist campaign, with the twin objectives of votes for women and an end to war, was under way by early 1915.[16]

Yet despite the courage, vigour and persistence of the women who led it, the campaign met with very little success. The war went on for another three and a half years, and most European countries seemed no nearer to granting women the vote in April 1918 than they had been in April 1915. The first and most obvious reason for the campaign's failure lay in the hostile reaction it aroused in belligerent governments. Already in April 1915 they had attempted to prevent feminists from their respective countries reaching the Hague Congress. In Britain they cancelled North Sea ferry sailings, or switched them unannounced to other ports.[17] In Germany, they adopted the more bureaucratic tactic of stopping the women at the border and questioning the validity of their papers. Sterner measuers were taken too. The German authorities censored the feminists' magazines and pamphlets, and when the women tried to counter this by a letter-writing campaign, their correspondence was placed under surveillance. Activists like Lida Gustava Heymann were placed under restriction, banned from speaking in public and in some cases subjected to house searches and police harassment. The feminists' efforts to lobby European governments after the Hague Congress met with a generally frosty reception. As the war went on, governments made it increasingly difficult for them to maintain their international contacts. Attempts to hold a second women's peace congress foundered as the authorities made it clear that their tolerance of 1915, limited though it had been, would not be repeated on a subsequent occasion.[18] In almost all European countries in any case, political activity of any kind was actively discouraged, and feminism was no exception. The feminists were therefore crippled by government limitations on their freedom of action.

A second reason for the campaign's failure lay in the fact that the feminists found it difficult to join forces with other wings of the pacifist movement. Pacifist organizations in general were aware of the need to recruit women to their cause, especially since the departure of so many men to the front. And although opposition to conscription was an issue that applied only to men, it was a serious cause in Britain alone, because all other European countries had a tradition of conscription and allowed little or no room for the idea of conscientious objection. So most pacifist organizations concentrated in fact on very general issues, in which women's interest was hardly less than men's. Correspondingly, the Union of Democratic Control in Britain encouraged women to take on positions of responsibility in the movement. Some, like Helena Swanwick, succeeded in taking advantage of this, while in Germany the feminist Helene Stöcker was also prominent in the leadership of the pacifist 'New Fatherland League'.[19] Such organizations generally supported female suffrage and co-operated with the feminist pacifists in joint petitions and appeals. But most pacifist organizations remained resolutely male-dominated and were unable to accept the feminists' linking of war and masculinity. Nor were the feminists or the pacifists able to agree with the socialist movement against the war, which saw it as the product of capitalist imperialism. The issue of feminism was thus one factor contributing to the internal division that characterized the pacifist movement during the war.

By far the most important reason for the failure of the feminist-pacifist campaign lay in the fact that it had very little support among women, even among feminists themselves. Feminist organizations that espoused pacifist views at the beginning of the war quickly lost members. It was only through engaging in social welfare work, remarked the German feminist-pacifist Lida Gustava Heymann, that many of the branches of the anti-war German Women's Suffrage League were able to keep even 10 per cent of their members.[20] The League was itself the smallest of three suffragist organizations in Germany; the other two, numbering 12,000 women combined (as against 2,000 for the League) in 1914, both supported the war and indeed joined forces in 1916.[21] As for the umbrella organization of German feminism, the Federation of German Women's Associations (*Bund Deutscher Frauenvereine,* or BDF), numbering 250,000 women in 1914, it roundly condemned the peace movement and branded participation in the 1915 Hague Congress as 'incompatible with the patriotic character and the national duty of the German women's movement . . . [and] with any responsible position and work within the Federation of German Women's Associations'. Its leading figure, Gertrud Bäumer, had condemned pacifism, 'cosmopolitan aims and internationalist policies' in 1910 as 'outmoded', and the Federation went on in 1917–18 to issue formal rejections of Wilson's Peace Note, the Armistice Terms, the Treaty of Versailles and the League of Nations. Yet it was simultaneously campaigning for votes for women, so it certainly could not be accused of having abandoned its feminism altogether. In 1899 and 1907 it had even refused to support international women's demonstrations for peace, declaring that they threatened Germany's interests (most notably Tirpitz's naval armaments programme). It was not surprising that it was criticized in international feminist circles for its nationalism.[22]

The German feminists probably were more nationalist than their counterparts elsewhere, but it should not be imagined that feminist movements in other countries were much more sympathetic to pacifism. It was noticeable, for instance, that not a single French feminist found her way to the Hague Congress in 1915.[23] Despite their previous belief that women's suffrage would ease international tension, French feminists of all persuasions rallied round the flag in August 1914, stopped their feminist campaigns, devoted themselves to war work, and closed down their peace sections. Those who disagreed and joined the pacifist movement, like Jeanne Halbwachs and Gabrielle Duchêne, remained isolated individuals. Even Madeleine Pelletier soon gave up her opposition to the war in the face of feminist chauvinism, and went back to university to study chemistry. Not one prominent female suffrage leader in France opposed the war.[24] The main feminist organizations issued a joint declaration rejecting all contacts with feminists from enemy countries until they had criticized their countries' war crimes.[25] 'Our feminine and feminist societies have unanimously decided that they cannot participate in an international congress', they told the organizers of the Hague Congress in 1915, 'French women', wrote one feminist, '. . . united with those who battle and die, . . . do not know how to talk of peace.'[26]

Nor did any feminists come to the Hague Congress from Russia. Here too all the feminist organizations supported the war. Here too they condemned the Hague Congress as a piece of folly which merely served the interests of the Germans.[27] Feminists threw themselves into welfare work and organizing the home front. Many feminists saw important opportunities here. Mariya Porkrovskaia, whose pacifism made her unusual among Russian feminists, nevertheless saw the war, despite its cruelty, as giving women access to all kinds of jobs from which they had formerly been excluded.[28] The League for Women's Equality declared in August 1915 that it was women's duty to unite in the service of the fatherland, but added that 'this will give us the right to participate as the equals of men in the new life of a victorious Russia'.[29] They claimed their reward in the February Revolution of 1917, when 40,000 women marched in Petrograd to press the revolutionary government to give women the vote, which indeed it did. It was noticeable that the demonstrators were carrying banners demanding not only 'votes for women' but also 'war to victory'. Such an instrumental view of war work was certainly present among the feminists of other countries too. Yet on the whole it was submerged beneath a wave of genuine patriotic feeling. 'Duties', as one French feminist observed, 'called louder than rights',[30] and indeed the British constitutional suffragist leader Millicent Garrett Fawcett declared roundly: 'let us prove ourselves worthy of citizenship, whether our claim is recognised or not'.[31]

In Britain too, as this suggests, the vast majority of feminists supported the war. The lead, as before 1914, was given by the militants. On the outbreak of war, the Pankhursts suspended their militant campaign and began instead to campaign for conscription. Christabel Pankhurst said: 'All—everything— that we women have been fighting for and treasure would disappear in the event of a German victory'. English women, she declared, had more rights than women in any other country—a claim which she would have rejected as absurd only a few weeks before. The Pankhursts went on to wage a campaign against strikers, 'shirkers' and 'Bolsheviks' in the factories. In short, they and many of their supporters turned from militants into super-patriots.[32] The militants had about 7,000 supporters on the eve of the war; the main non-militant National Union of Women's Suffrage Societies had about 50,000, and it too supported the war effort under the leadership of Millicent Garrett Fawcett.[33] Like other feminist societies, it busied itself with welfare work. A few prominent members, like Helena Swanwick, split off to join the peace campaign and attend the Hague Congress, but the overwhelming majority remained committed to the war effort.[34] The major opposition to the war from among the British feminists came from the non-violent radical suffragists organized in the Women's Freedom League, a group roughly comparable to the German Women's Suffrage League led by Augspurg and Heymann. Of a similar stamp was the Hungarian women's suffrage movement, led by Rosika Schwimmer. It was another small, beleaguered but determined group battling for a democratic and pacifist vision in the face of a massive nationalist feminist majority in the rest of the country's women's movement.[35] Feminist pacifism was thus the creed of a minority, of a tiny band of courageous and principled women on the far-left fringes of bourgeois-liberal feminism.

II

In many ways the situation of the Socialist Women's International was very different to that of international feminism on the eve of World War I. Like its parent body, the Second International, the socialist women's movement was formally committed to the maintenance of peace, but for reasons that differed quite strongly from those of the feminists. The Second International believed, or professed to believe, that a war would be an imperialist venture in which the

European working class would be sacrificed as cannon-fodder to the interests of international capitalism. The socialist women's movement shared this belief, perhaps with more sincerity than its parent body. Certainly when the war broke out the two organizations embarked on sharply divergent courses. While the leaders of the Second International everywhere forgot their commitment to peace and fell into line behind their respective countries' war effort, the leading figures in the Socialist Women's International all remained true to their faith. Louise Saumoneau in France, Alexandra Kollontai, Nadezhda Krupskaya and Inessa Armand in Russia (or in the exiled leadership of the Russian socialists, in Zurich), Clara Zetkin and Luise Zietz in Germany, all opposed the war from the start.[36] While the International Woman Suffrage Alliance abandoned its plans for a congress, the leadership of the Socialist Women's International went ahead. Central to this decision was the attitude of Clara Zetkin, the Secretary, founder and effective leader of the organization.[37]

Zetkin's radicalism was increased, rather than diminished, by the advent of war. Shortly after the Austrian ultimatum to Serbia on 23 July 1914, she travelled to Brussels to address the Bureau of the Second International. But it refused her demand for immediate action to prevent the war and decided instead, on 29–30 July, to call a full Congress of the International, in the mistaken belief that the matter was not urgent.[38] Zetkin then returned to Berlin, where she conferred with other members of the far left of the SPD, to which she had belonged for the previous nine years or so. On 1 August she went back to her home near Stuttgart. When war broke out she was deeply shocked: 'I thought I would go mad, or that I would have to commit suicide', she wrote later.[39] On 19 September, she attacked in unmeasured terms the failure of the SPD to oppose the war. In a private letter of that date, she wrote that she had still not got over the 'political and moral bankruptcy of Social Democracy'. She complained that the 'inner hollowness of very many editors and leading comrades' was creating an 'unbelievably low level' of comment in the party press.[40] On 3 December she registered, in another letter, her determination at least to maintain the standard of the German SPD women's magazine, *Die Gleichheit*, of which she had been editor for over two decades. The party leadership, she said, was 'ever more quickly and completely throwing overboard everything that remains from the proud past and tradition of Social Democracy'; the least *Die Gleichheit* could do was to counter this by gathering together the 'decidedly left-wing' elements in the party, and by keeping up the flow of socialist comment on developments as they occurred.[41]

Even this, however, proved difficult, since like every other paper, *Die Gleichheit* was strictly controlled by the military censors. Moreover, shortly after the outbreak of war, Zetkin's house was searched by the police because she was suspect both as a 'known revolutionary' and as a woman with Russian contacts (with Kautsky, she looked after the money of the Russian revolutionaries in Germany).[42] The military authorities, who were given wide-ranging powers over the whole of civilian life in Germany under the state of siege declared by the government on 31 July,[43] imposed strict censorship on *Die Gleichheit*. Zetkin was tireless in her attempts to use the magazine for criticism of war. '*Gleichheit*', wrote the censors, for their part, later in the war, 'has always created a lot of difficulties'. They insisted on removing from the magazine references to International Women's Day, and to increases in food prices; Zetkin issued the magazine with blank spaces where material had been removed by the censors. The first issue after the outbreak of war was confiscated. Zetkin was as angry with the censors as they were with her.[44] Nevertheless, she managed to use the magazine quite effectively for conveying her opposition to the war, as long as she stayed away from the topic of food shortages and rising prices. In a letter of 12 March 1916 to the military authorities in Stuttgart, the chief censor in Berlin pointed out that 'it would attract considerable attention both at home and abroad' if the next number of the magazine were suppressed altogether. It would be best to let it appear, with two articles cut entirely and others amended considerably. The point was that

In the first place . . . inflammatory statements about rising food prices, and everything that endangers public security, should be cut. On the other hand, it is not necessary to suppress all references to female suffrage, though of course in this respect too, consideration for the preservation of the

Burgfrieden demands moderation. But the demand for the achievement of female suffrage by legal means cannot in itself be completely eliminated.

Clearly, the major fear of the authorities was the danger of food riots; demands for political reform, on the other hand, were taken less seriously.

Zetkin was determined to do something more decisive than merely continue the struggle through the mutilated pages of *Die Gleichheit*. Since the national organization of socialist women was no longer open to her influence, she decided to call an international conference of socialist women, to replace the one originally scheduled for August 1914, but postponed because of the outbreak of the war. Zetkin sent out the invitations personally because she was unable to print them in *Die Gleichheit*. The conference was held on neutral ground, in Bern, on 26–28 March 1915. It was attended by some seventy women from France, Russia, Belgium, Germany, Austria, Hungary, Poland and Switzerland. It was the first meeting of an international socialist body since the outbreak of the war, and it presaged the emergence of the larger international revolutionary meetings known under the name of the 'Zimmerwald movement', in which a leading part was taken by the Bolshevik exiles led by Lenin. At this early stage, in March 1915, however, the Bolsheviks—represented at the women's conference by a delegation headed by Nadezhda Krupskaya—were unable to make their influence felt. They urged on the German delegates a clean break with the SPD leadership and a policy of 'revolutionary defeatism' in which the SPD opposition would be pledged to work illegally for a revolution to stop the war and destroy the capitalist system. Zetkin rejected these proposals; she wanted to postpone the break with the SPD majority, and to avoid as far as possible going beyond the bounds of legality. A compromise resolution was agreed which in most points reflected Zetkin's views. It declared that the war was being fought not to defend the German people but to enrich arms manufacturers and other capitalists. The real enemy of Germany was not England or Russia but 'all those who create their riches from the misery of the masses and build up their power in oppression'. Men had been forced into silence by being called to the front; it was therefore up to women to try to bring the war to an end. Thus although the resolution was not a feminist one (unlike those passed at the Hague the next month), it did address itself to women.[46]

Clara Zetkin and her fellow German delegates, for the most part young activists in the Berlin women's movement (Käthe Duncker, Margarethe Wengels, Lore Agnes, Toni Sender, Martha Arendsee and Bertha Thalheimer) returned to Germany and began to distribute the resolution, contained in a peace manifesto drawn up by the Bern Congress.

Up to now [wrote Zetkin on 22 April 1915] we have distributed some 100,000 copies of the manifesto in more than 40 different places; 30,000 of them in Berlin and its environs alone . . . In the first place, we limited ourselves in most places to the distribution of the manifesto among the organized women comrades, but now the mass distribution can quietly and calmly proceed on its way.[47]

Zetkin hoped that mass meetings would take place to discuss the manifesto, and that these would lead on to demonstrations which would eventually bring the war to an end. By late July, she reported that 300,000 copies of the manifesto had been distributed in more than 100 different places. A number of meetings had already been held, under harmless-sounding titles, designed to deceive the authorities, and many resolutions had been forwarded to the SPD party executive. Zetkin reported with enthusiasm that 'women everywhere are wholeheartedly supporting our resolutions', and that it was women who dominated the submission and discussion of the Bern peace resolutions at most local party meetings.[48]

However, all this activity was abruptly brought to an end by the authorities. Already on 9 April 1915 Zetkin was complaining that her letters were being opened; on 23 July she reported that her house had been searched by the police once again; and on 29 July she was arrested and taken to Karlsruhe gaol, where she was charged with treason. Others responsible for distributing the resolution were also apprehended, including some eighteen women who, according to the Social Democratic diarist Eduard David, were arrested in Berlin on 8 May.[49] Zetkin herself was interrogated a number of times by the authorities. Her statements give an interesting indication of her intentions. At the first interrogation, which took place on 29 July,[50] Zetkin disclaimed all responsibility for the resolution or for its distribution, though she agreed with its contents and accepted responsibility for the conference as a whole. She denied any intention of distributing it to the troops, and pointed out that she had rejected the proposal of the Russian delegates at the Bern conference that revolutionary methods should be used in bringing about a peace. The resolution would not harm Germany, since it was to be distributed in all belligerent countries. Nor, she added, would the distribution of the resolution have any effect on the troops' morale, since in her view war and militarism created a psychological milieu among the troops which no other outside infuence could affect. A lawyer had assured her that it contained nothing illegal. The resolution was intended for women only. It had been distributed only to members of the SPD; but Zetkin hoped that bourgeois women would join with the women of the working class in a nationwide movement for peace which the government would be unable to ignore—a remarkable reversal of her previous policy of non-co-uperation with bourgeois feminists.[51] The movement, said Zetkin, would be called into life by person-to-person propaganda, the press, and mass meetings.[52]

In the second interrogation, on 30 July 1915,[53] Zetkin went somewhat further in accepting responsibility for the resolution and its distribution. In additional interrogations on 6, 7 and 9 August, she supplied more details, without substantially changing her story. She again denied having composed the resolution, but took full responsibility for its distribution. The intention was that this distribution would be followed by meetings of SPD women to discuss the resolution—a tactic which Zetkin, in a letter to Alfred Henke in Bremen asking him to call such meetings in his district, had optimistically described as 'extraordinarily effective' on 22 April.[54] These in turn would lead on to mass demonstrations. 'I personally', declared Zetkin, 'thought of peaceful demonstrations of women parading through the streets with banners carrying slogans for peace.' Her aim, she said, was to convince women that the war was an imperialist war of aggression, which would benefit capitalism and harm the workers—though she added that she believed the Kaiser and Bethmann Hollweg had been forced to declare war by circumstances, even though they as individuals had genuinely desired the maintenance of peace.[55] It was the women themselves who were to force the government to seek peace; Zetkin denied the intention or the possibility of persuading them to exert pressure on their male relatives at the front in this direction. Peaceful demonstrations by women were the means to achieve peace; no government would dare use force against them. Revolution, she declared, was out of the question. Revolution required force and violence, and these could not be exerted by women. The men who had command of the means necessary to bring about a violent revolution were all at the front.

The decisive action of the authorities was undoubtedly the major factor in the failure of Zetkin's plans. But the authorities were helped by the fact that the SPD party executive strongly opposed the Bern conference, rejected its resolutions, and refused to do anything that would jeopardize its good relations with the authorities. Moreover, apart from Zetkin herself, none of those arrested was in any way a prominent figure in the party.[56] The authorities found it all the more easy to prevent Zetkin continuing her campaign since Zetkin herself soon fell ill in prison. Shortly after her arrest, the SPD executive had provided Zetkin with a lawyer—Hugo Haase, the leading figure in the moderate wing of the party opposition. Zetkin was reluctant to accept Haase's appointment, since Haase was—in her view—much too moderate a political figure. Nevertheless, after some hesitation, she had agreed.[57] Haase visited her on 23 September to arrange details of her defence and found her 'in comparatively good health'.[58] On 12 October however, she was unexpectedly released, on bail paid by the SPD publisher Dietz, on grounds of ill-health.[59] Zetkin suspected that this had been arranged by the SPD executive acting in collusion with the authorities in order to prevent further outbursts by her supporters in the Berlin women's movement.[60] The circumstances were all the more suspicious since the others detained with Zetkin had not been released. Haase and the executive, however, were actually making every effort to secure the release of Zetkin's companions in gaol;[61] the SPD executive was careful, at least in the early years of the war, not to use its new position in the political system to ask for special favours. Moreover, Zetkin really was ill. Several months after her release in prison on medical grounds, she was still reporting that her doctor had forbidden her to travel from Stuttgart to Berlin, warning her that this would bring with it the risk of a serious heart attack.[62] When, in January 1917, she eventually undertook a short journey from her home, she suffered what seems to have been a stroke, and her left side was temporarily paralysed. Even in August 1918 she was forced to declare that she was still far from fully recovered.[63]

There were several reasons, therefore, why Clara Zetkin proved unable to mobilize the women's movement against the war. First, the authorities moved quickly to scotch the plans which she had helped to formulate in Bern. Secondly, the SPD party executive joined the authorities in actively opposing these plans. Thirdly, there were too few prominent women in the movement who were prepared to fall in with Zetkin's scheme, and her arrest and imprisonment left the women's peace movement without a leader. Finally, Zetkin herself fell ill at the crucial juncture and was unable to take an active part in politics from the autumn of 1915 until the end of the war. Had she been fully fit, however, she would most probably have received similar treatment to that meted out to Rosa Luxemburg, and she would have spent the rest of the war not on her sick-bed but in prison.

The only other prominent woman in the party who could conceivably have taken Zetkin's place was Luise Zietz, who had been women's organizer of the SPD since 1908. Zietz was a member of the party's executive committee, and belonged to the left-centre group within the party. She had already clashed with the majority of the executive and complained about the control it exercised over her activities. Nevertheless, Zietz considered that the doctrine of collective responsibility obliged her to abide by its decisions, even when she disagreed with them. This sense of party loyalty was very strong in Zietz, and it took a long time before she eventually overcame it. Zietz was against the war from the start, so she opposed the voting of war credits in the SPD's executive committee on 31 July 1914, and continued to support within the committee the tiny minority who opposed the war. 'Only Frau Zietz still goes along with Haase through thick and thin', noted Eduard David in his diary on 7/8 August 1914.[64] But she did not oppose the committee's stand in public. Such a step she regarded as the worst kind of breach of discipline. On the contrary she followed the committee's instructions and threw herself into organizing the SPD women in the establishment of welfare services for working-class women.

While the authorities regarded Zetkin's action in organizing the International Women's Conference and attempting to popularize its decisions as treason, the SPD party executive treated it as a breach of party discipline. On 7/8 April 1915, the SPD's chairman, Friedrich Ebert, complained in the party executive committee that Zetkin had been carrying on preparations for the conference without the committee's knowledge or approval. It was monstrous, he said, that the party members should simply ignore the known wishes of the party leadership in this way. The member of the party committee responsible for women's affairs was Luise Zietz. Characteristically, she took up a position halfway between Ebert and Zetkin. According to Eduard David, Zietz supported the Bern conference in the executive committee,[65] but at the executive's meeting on 7–8 April 1915, she criticized the way in which Zetkin had ignored the party executive in arranging the conference. However, she made clear her sympathy with the conference's line, and reiterated these views at the executive on 27 July. Like Zetkin, although rather more gradually, Zietz too saw her freedom of manoeuvre increasingly limited by the actions of the authorities and the party executive. As late as October 1915, Zietz went on one of her whirlwind recruiting tours, in the Lower Rhine, 'bringing new life into the women's movement' in such places as Düsseldorf, Solingen and Wuppertal;[66] at the same time, however, she became increasingly critical of the food situation, and spoke in alarming terms in September and October on the growing shortages and rising prices. The authorities, always worried by such talk, began to impose bans on her speeches. By 1916 she was banned from making public speeches altogether.[67] The ban made Zietz's position as leader of the SPD women's movement impossible. She could no longer carry out the recruitment drives that were essential for keeping the movement going.

At the same time, the party leadership and the trade unions were moving to reduce the influence of *Die Gleichheit*. In July 1915, the trade unions decided to withdraw their bulk orders from *Die Gleichheit* and to set up their own magazine, the Trade Union Women's Paper *(Gewerkschaftliche Frauenzeitung)*. Early in 1916 the first issue appeared, edited by Gertrud Hanna. It avoided socialist theory and political controversy. Local assemblies of women were organized by the party executive and the unions to arrange the transfer of subscriptions from *Die Gleichheit*. Even in Zetkin's own area, where the party had been one of the earliest to split, the local SPD women of Württemberg met and resolved that *Die Gleichheit* could no longer be regarded as representing the interests of the working women of Germany. While the new magazine, thanks to bulk orders from the unions, reached a circulation of 100,000 by the end of 1917, *Die Gleichheit*, deprived of these orders and further hampered by the decline of recruitment drives, suffered a rapid decline in its readership. From a circulation of 124,000 in July 1914, the magazine lost over half its readers by December of the same year—the result of the economic and social dislocation of the first wave of mobilization. Many women, it was clear, could no longer afford to buy *Die Gleichheit*. Circulation fell further in 1915, then more sharply still in 1916 and 1917. As many as 70,000 subscriptions were said to have been lost in 1914–17 because of the withdrawal of the unions' bulk orders.[68] By 1917 it was reaching a mere 19,000 subscribers.[69]

At the end of 1916, the party executive officially expelled Luise Zietz, and a women's protest meeting held in January 1917 against this step simply increased Zietz's alienation from the party leadership. Many oppositional party members of both sexes had already been expelled from the party following the holding of a separate conference by the oppositional members early in January.[70] The opposition reacted with the foundation of a new political party, the Independent Social Democratic Party of Germany *(Unabhängige Sozialdemokratische Partei Deutschlands,* or USPD), which took place in Gotha on 6–8 April. Zietz opposed the use of this

name for the party but nevertheless joined it. She became one
of the USPD's two secretaries (with Wilhem Dittmann), and
was elected to the party's central committee.[71] Clara Zetkin
also joined the new party as a founder-member, although she
was too ill to attend the Congress.[72] On 18 May, little more than
a month after the foundation of the USPD, the Majority SPD
executive moved to take over those magazines and newspapers
which had fallen into the hands of the opposition. Clara Zetkin
and her staff were dismissed from *Die Gleichheit* without
notice.[73] In the first issue of the women's supplement to the
USPD newspaper *Leipziger Volkszeitung*, which now served
Zetkin as a substitute for *Die Gleichheit*, Zetkin argued that
the major reason for her dismissal had been the fact that *Die
Gleichheit* was an international as well as a national organ of
the women's movement—

this, and the fact that *Die Gleichheit* was edited by me, the international
secretary. I edited the paper in accordance with the principles and decisions
of our international women's conference and the great general international
socialist congresses. Through long study and co-operation with leading
women comrades of all countries I had gained a general view of the entire
socialist women's movement. Into my hands ran the connecting threads, the
informative reports, the stimulating encouragements.

Now this was over. Zetkin tried to use the new periodical for
the same purpose.[74] But she could not but be aware of the fact
that in the USPD as in the old party, it was not she, but Luise
Zietz, who led the women's organization; and Zetkin's
freedom of manoeuvre was further restricted by her continued
ill-health, which prevented her from doing any more than
engaging in journalism.

These developments proved disastrous for the socialist
women's movement. If the women's organization of the SPD
had been increasingly tightly bound to the parent party after
1908,[75] it had at least been able to preserve a modicum of
autonomy, which it had used to struggle for women's rights,
often against strong opposition from the male-dominated
party hierarchy. The split of 1917 robbed the socialist women's
movement of the last vestiges of autonomy. The Majority SPD
and Independent (USPD) parties were each naturally
desperately anxious to tie their women's sections as closely as

possible into the fabric of the parent organization. They were deeply suspicious of any hint at autonomy, let alone of co-operation with the rival movement in the cause of women's rights. Thus it was only after strong pressure from Zietz and her female supporters that the USPD founded an Imperial Women's Committee *(Reichs-Frauenausschuss)* to co-ordinate the activities of its female membership; the main argument used was that without such a body, the women would have no influence on the party at all.[76] There was no question of this body constituting the leadership of an autonomous women's movement. Its *raison d'être* was the party split over war aims, not any quarrel over women's emancipation. On the side of the Majority Social Democrats, the reformist social worker Marie Juchacz[77] took over both Luise Zietz's leadership of the women's organization with its seat on the party executive, and Clara Zetkin's editorship of *Die Gleichheit*. Juchacz declared that the magazine had lost most of its readers because it had been too highbrow. She attempted to make it more popular and to avoid 'radical phraseology'. A Majority SPD women's conference, which Luise Zietz had repeatedly called for in the party executive committee but which had been refused until Zietz had left the party and with the emergence of the USPD made one necessary,[78] was held on 7–8 July 1917 in Berlin, attended by thirty-eight women delegates from local party organizations. The conference was controlled by reformists such as Juchacz and by revisionists such as Wally Zepler, and strongly supported the war effort. Thus the split in the women's movement, the rightward shift of the reformist SPD women under Juchacz, the mutual hostility of the Majority and Independent Social Democratic women, and the subordination of women's rights to other political issues, added to the continued state repression of organized campaigns, recruitment drives and oppositional journalism, to render the socialist women's organization ineffective in political terms after the end of 1915.

Though the SPD women activists had enjoyed the support of almost 175,000 women before the outbreak of war, they soon realized that the mass membership of their movement was melting away before their very eyes. In the first two years after the outbreak of the war, when the SPD freed its members from the compulsion to pay dues, the female membership of the party fell rapidly. As the party executive remarked, the payment of the subscription was often the only connection that women members had with the party organization. This connection lapsed in many areas in 1914 and 1915, bringing the overall membership of the SPD women's movement down from 174,754 in 1914 to 134,663 in 1915 and 107,336 in 1916. At the same time, the circulation of *Die Gleichheit* fell even more rapidly—from 124,000 to 58,000 immediately on the outbreak of war, and to 35,000 by 1916. The real collapse, however, came with the split of the movement in 1917, since those women who had continued to belong out of habit now had to make a positive decision. It has often been maintained that women went over to the USPD in unusually large numbers, and this may have been true of those involved in the national leadership. Certainly Zetkin and Zietz joined the USPD as did Margarethe Wengels and Mathilde Wurm. But others, such as Ottilie Baader, stayed. In some areas, notably the Upper Rhine, where male membership increased by 5.44 per cent in 1916–17 and female membership decreased by 78.2 per cent, it looks as though the women acted independently and left the SPD en bloc for the opposition. In 1916 the average female membership of the areas which suffered heavy losses to the USPD in 1917 was 27.34 per cent of the total, slighly higher than the average of 24.81 per cent for female membership in the party as a whole. In absolute terms, these areas lost 38,138 women in 1916–17; 12,937 of these women were in the Berlin women's movement.[79]

But in general the differences between behaviour of the women members and the men members of the SPD in 1916–17 were slight. The view that the socialist women mostly joined the USPD turns out to be something of a myth, as indeed is the assumption, often found in the literature, that the socialist women's movement was on the left wing of the party before 1914.[80] Looked at in numerical terms the socialist women's movement was split right down the middle in 1917. By the end of that year, there were some 66,608 women in the majority SPD. Figures are not available for the USPD, but a guess is possible. In the early years of the Weimar Republic, the female membership of the USPD stood at 15 per cent, that of the SPD at around 20 per cent, so by analogy, if the female membership of the SPD in 1917 was 25 per cent then that of the USPD should have been around 20 per cent. If we take the customary figure of 120,000 for USPD membership in 1917–18, this gives us a figure of about 24,000 women in the USPD, substantial enough to pose a serious threat to the SPD women's organization, which was between two and three times as large; but the bulk of socialist women remained in the majority party and so supported the war.[81]

III

The leader of the French socialist women's movement, Louise Saumoneau, also opposed the war from the very beginning. On 29 July 1914 she called an emergency meeting of the Group of Socialist Women, which urged women to 'rise up in a mass to form a living barrier against menacing and murderous barbarism'.[82] But one of Saumoneau's associates was arrested for trying to distribute the document containing the Group's resolution, and the Group had to abandon its plans for a meeting on 3 August. It was unable to publish its regular magazine, and Saumoneau had to hold committee meetings in her flat. However, Saumoneau did manage to attend the Bern conference in March 1915, and returned with a French version of the manifesto, which she now tried to distribute. Saumoneau and her associates left copies of the manifesto in public places in Paris overnight, and led the police quite a dance as they tried to locate and gather them up each morning before any members of the public had a chance to read them. In August 1915 Saumoneau was arrested and, admitting responsibility for the leaflets, was released. The authorities evidently wanted to avoid giving her publicity and making her into a martyr. However, on 27 September, more than a hundred more copies of the manifesto were discovered scattered around the tenth *arrondissement*, and she was arrested again. This time Saumoneau was imprisoned in Saint-Lazare, an institution usually reserved for prostitutes, and it was nearly two months before protests from within the French socialist movement obtained her release. Like Zetkin, she too was exhausted by the experience and needed several months to recover.[83]

Police repression, in France as in Germany, veered between the fear of creating martyrs and the desire not to let them get away with it. On occasion it could be harsh indeed, as with the passing of a three-year prison sentence on the socialist Hélène Brion in 1917 for 'defeatism'. Saumoneau and her supporters claimed already in November 1915 to have distributed 30,000 copies of the Bern manifesto, and they continued to distribute tracts, to write letters of solidarity to Zetkin and other anti-war socialist women, and to try—often unsuccessfully—to hold meetings. But they were in a very weak position. The Group of Socialist Women was very small. It had fewer than 1,000 members, compared to the 175,000 who belonged to its German equivalent. As in Germany, the socialist party leadership supported the war and gave no encouragement to those who opposed it. As in Germany, too, tensions over the war increased internal divisions within the party as time went on. The Seine federation of the French socialist party voted on 9 December 1915, by ten to one for 'war to the bitter end', against a peace resolution brought in by Saumoneau. But already Saumoneau and her allies had been voted off, or withdrawn from, the executive committee of the Group of Socialist Women, which dissociated itself formally from the Bern conference and declared that although Saumoneau was attending it, she represented nobody but herself. By withdrawing from the Group in January 1916, Saumoneau and her allies, its original driving force, ensured that it subsided into inactivity. Although they founded a new women's organization of their own, and celebrated International Proletarian Women's Day in 1917, the leaders, including Saumoneau, became increasingly absorbed in the complex factional struggles, made far worse by the polarizing effects of the Bolshevik Revolution in October–November 1917, which were tearing the French socialist movement apart. That a break as clean as that of the Majority and Independent Social Democrats in Germany was not achieved in France acted as a further deflection of the energies that might otherwise have gone into mobilizing women against the war.[84]

Although the socialist women who opposed the war were to a large extent generals without an army, out in the country there were plenty of potential recruits. In Germany the allied blockade brought food shortages even as early as February 1915, and rationing and inflation were the result. By 1918, it was estimated that the official rations only covered a half to two-thirds of daily calorie requirements. In this situation, women soon began to buy food on the black market, where prices were often twice as high as the official rates. The black market soon rivalled the official one as farmers sought to avoid selling their produce cheaply to officials. By 1915 whole columns of women and children were reported to be descending upon farmers and demanding potatoes and other foodstuffs at the lowest possible prices, or even simply stealing them under threat of force.[85] From here to actual riots in the towns was only a small step. There were women's demonstrations in Berlin in March and May 1915, and in November 1915 a series of food riots took place in Berlin, Aachen, Cologne, Leipzig and Münster. On 9 February 1916, a crowd of women gathered before the town hall in Hanover shouting 'smash everything to pieces, demolish the lot!' The police chief, knowing that to use force would be to play into the hands of enemy propagandists, persuaded them to disperse. Women rioted in Leipzig, Offenbach and Worms in May-June 1916, and on 17 and 18 June 1916, women rioted on the Marienplatz in Munich and smashed a number of windows. On 6 July 1916, some 2,000 women, accompanied by 50 to 60 sympathetic soldiers, rioted in Nuremberg after the shops had run out of eggs and butter. They pelted the police with horse dung and cobblestones, but eventually dispersed. In August the demonstrations spread to the North German port of Hamburg, where on 18–19 August women and children looted fifty-seven food stores in the city; thirteen women and young people were wounded by police sabres, some severely; there were thirty-seven arrests and the cavalry was called in; on 25 August a threatened repetition of these events was prevented by the police in what observers described as a brutal manner; at the same time, in the Ruhr industrial town of Hamborn women were observed pelting the police with stones during another riot. In the late autumn and early winter things quietened down, but on 13 January 1917 1,000 women, accompanied by children, smashed in the windows of the town hall at Harburg, an industrial suburb of Hamburg, and pelted the police with empty bottles. The crowd, 'especially women', as the police noted, shouted 'hunger!'. On 16 January 1917, a further twenty-two windows in Harburg Town Hall were smashed by another crowd of rioting women. On 30 and 31 January, food stores in Hanover were smashed and plundered by women. The authorities called in troops to restore order. Fifteen women and two men were arrested. In Munich, the police narrowly prevented similar rioting, but in Hamburg another 105 food stores were smashed and looted in riots which spread quickly to the city's suburbs in late February.

In the same month, an incident occurred which revealed in graphic detail the difference between the behaviour of working-class men and working-class women in a food crisis. In Wilhelmsburg, as the food situation became quite desperate, the men decided to take action. They marched in a disciplined column to the town hall, elected a deputation, presented their wishes to the Council, and then dispersed. The exclusion of women was a foretaste of the 1918 Revolution, when not a single woman had any part in the Workers' and Soldiers' Councils, the Revolution's central institutions. While this was going on, women, accompanied by children, were looting and plundering a total of eleven food and bread stores. The following month, in Nuremberg, similar scenes occurred. The mayor, Otto Gessler, requested the local (male) trade union leaders to calm the situation, but they declared themselves unable to help, even though they agreed fully with the authorities that such riots should if at all possible be prevented. The reason, as the leader of the local Christian Metal Workers' Union remarked, was that 'we are not just dealing with men and with reasonable people, but in many cases with women and young boys, who do not think about what they are doing, but act instinctively . . .'. Here was another reason compelling women to take action on their own. On 24 May 1918 some 2,000 to 3,000 women and children accompanied 150 soldiers in a march on the town hall in Erlangen, in Bavaria, and broke the town hall windows. The demonstration had begun when the soldiers had discovered that they were not going on leave, as they had been told, but were being sent to the front instead. The presence of the much larger number of women and children, however, was in all likelihood a consequence of food shortages. On 22 May demonstrators in Ingolstadt in Bavaria set fire to the town hall; the army was called in, and used tear gas to disperse the crowd. Ninety-seven demonstrators were arrested; thirty-five of them were women, thirty-nine of them were under seventeen. The origin of the demonstration lay in an incident in which the police had arrested and beaten up a war invalid, but here too food shortages probably underlay the riot. A further, similar demonstration, though of a less violent sort, took place in Munich in August, and other women's demonstrations, with riots and looting, took place in Aachen, Brunswick, Mannheim and towns in Upper Silesia.[86]

Here were working-class women engaging in direct political action to secure their immediate needs; their desperation with the course the war was taking must surely have communicated itself to others, including the troops with whom they came into contact. Moreover, strikes of women munitions workers were also far from uncommon; numerous instances were recorded in 1917, and women also called attention to themselves in the January strikes of 1918. This crescendo of discontent was eventually to reach a climax in the massive wave of popular protest which found its expression, after the military defeat, in the Revolution of 1918–19 and events such as the Ruhr civil war of 1920. Yet it was essentially unrelated to the organized Social Democratic women's movement, despite the fact that the same issues—food prices and anxiety about the fate of sons in the army—lay behind the mobilization of women in both cases. When Luise Zietz led a women's invasion of an SPD executive meeting in October 1915 to demand that the party leadership try to stop the war, one of her supporters declared: 'It is necessary to gain control of the spontaneous mass movement against dearth, to organize and lead it. Then it may develop into a powerful popular movement against dearth and for ending the war.'[87] Yet as soon as Luise Zietz began to do this by speaking in public on food shortages and rising prices, the authorities, as we have seen, banned her meetings. In similar fashion they had deleted all references to these subjects in *Die Gleichheit*. The authorities were very careful to stop any attempts to encourage further riots and demonstrations and they seem to have been quite successful in this.

Leading socialist women such as Zetkin and Zietz were further cut off from reaching a mass base by the decentralization of the Social Democratic women's movement after the full integration of women into the party in 1908. With some difficulty they had managed to preserve autonomous institutions such as International Proletarian Women's Day and special SPD women's conferences,[88] but they had been unable to prevent the absorption of local women's organizations into local party branches. The national network of women's organizations was destroyed, and the results were seen well before 1914 at party congresses, as women delegates ceased voting as a block and voted along the same lines as their local (male) party instead. This meant not only that—as we have seen—women on the whole went with their local party on the split of 1917, but also that Zetkin and Zietz and their fellow opponents of the war lacked an independent grass-roots organization capable of channelling mass female discontent along the lines they desired. Finally the SPD women's movement itself, though very large, had never reached more than a fraction of the women of the working class. The situation was ultimately not so very different from that described by the head of police intelligence in France in September 1915: 'There does exist a pacifist movement . . . But this movement has not been able to get beyond the bounds of the economic and political organizations [i.e. the unions and the party] whose membership is moreover greatly reduced, and it remains unknown to the masses of the labouring population.'[89]

Only in Russia did a successful union of socialist militancy and working-class discontent occur. Food riots were common in Russia as well as Germany in 1915 and 1916; a typical incident was that which followed the suspension of meat sales in Petrograd on 6 April 1916, when women looted and smashed a meat market, folllowed by bread riots in Moscow two days later. Although the organized socialist women's movement had virtually ceased to exist and most of its leaders were in exile or in gaol, on 23 February 1917 (International Women's Day in the Russian calendar) women workers at the Vyborg textile factory in Petrograd went on strike, and marched to the city centre, where they were joined by housewives from food queues. Looting took place and the women played an important role in winning over or disarming the tsarist troops. The regime was far weaker and more vulnerable than its German counterpart, and proved unable to cope. 23 February was the first day of the February Revolution. It set off the chain of events that led within a short space of time to the overthrow of the Tsar. It was the Bolshevik women's organizations, revived in March, and now joined by Alexandra Kollontai, which managed to channel this discontent into further political action as the Provisional Government (backed by the feminists) continued to fight the increasingly hopeless war against Germany. As a result, women took a notable part in supporting and supplying the Bolshevik forces in the October Revolution, in staffing the Proletarian Red Cross, and indeed in fighting alongside the men themselves. Even here, however, it was noticeable that a politically organized struggle against the war only began after the collapse of the tsarist state, not before.[90]

IV

On the whole, therefore, neither the feminist pacifists nor the leading socialist women of the day were able to mount an effective protest against the war. They were hampered by state repression, internal divisions, lack of support from their own party, the difficulties of establishing contact with the mass of working-class women, and, in the case of the socialists, the growing primacy of other issues. Most of all they were hampered by lack of support from within their own ranks. The great majority of socialist women and the overwhelming majority of feminist women supported the war effort and rejected the idea that women were naturally inclined to favour peace. Indeed, some went even further and argued that women's innate characteristics were actually anti-pacifist, suggesting, for example, that mothers had a natural desire to

defend their children, and that this was expressed on a larger
scale in their support for the war. Some German feminists
argued by 1914 that the essence of being female lay in
motherhood; and the losses of manpower caused by the war
gave women the opportunity to fulfil themselves.[91] Others
considered self-sacrifice to be a primary female characteristic,
and here again the war was providing undreamed-of
opportunities for the full realization of the female essence. The
mainstream feminist movement in Germany acted on these
beliefs by organizing a special campaign to persuade women to
have children, and by propagating the idea of a 'Women's Year
of Service' to the community, the female equivalent of
conscription. In 1919 the programme of the German feminists'
umbrella organization, the BDF, said women had a 'special
task' in showing a 'spirit of self-sacrifice' that would
encourage German men to bury their party differences in the
interests of national regeneration.[92] Similarly, French
feminists insisted that women's special mission lay in securing
the nation's future by having more children. Here too,
motherhood and a spirit of self-sacrifice were portrayed by
feminists as the essence of the female character.[93]

It is difficult to understand these ideas unless we realise that
'first-wave' European feminism was closely connected with the
ideology of bourgeois nationalism. In France the organized
feminist movement emerged in the 1870s as part of a broader
resurgence of republican patriotism in the wake of the Franco-
Prussian War; in Germany it originated in the liberal
nationalism of the 1848 Revolution and revived at the height of
the liberal nationalistic upsurge of the mid-1860s; in Russia it
began in the wake of a debate on the role that women had to
play in the regeneration of the nation after the defeat of the
Crimean War (1854–6). In other countries the connections
were even more obvious, as feminists organized on the basis of
women's role in transmitting the national cultural heritage to
the younger generation, as in Finland, or identified with the
movement for national self-determination to such an extent
that nationalist aims almost took precedence over feminist
ones, as in Bohemia.[94] By the early 1900s, however, the
connection between nationalism and feminism was being
challenged by a minority of pacifists within the feminist

movement, while an even larger group of socialist women rejected notions of the female character and mission and argued for the primacy of class consciousness and proletarian solidarity instead. Still, the ideology of the socialist women made it easier for them than for the feminists to oppose the First World War when it came, and there seems little doubt that for all its failures and inadequacies it was the proletarian women's movement that stood a better chance of mounting effective resistance to the militarism and chauvinism that swept Europe between 1914 and 1918.

We should be sceptical, therefore, of claims that women are necessarily opposed to war, that women's natural functions (especially childbearing) and general disposition predestine them to support the pacifist cause. These are claims that the great majority of feminists in Europe between 1914 and 1918 would certainly have rejected, and which the vast majority of female opponents of the war, those in the socialist movement and the working class, believed to be largely irrelevant to their cause. Arguments that take their starting-point in allegedly innate female qualities are always vulnerable to different views of what these qualities are. They carry with them the seeds of dangerous concessions to anti-feminism, for if women's innate qualities are different from men's, why should they have equal rights? Feminist pacifists in Europe in the 1930s often had to experience their own arguments turned against them in this way. Whatever connection there is, or has been, between pacifism and feminism, is political and ideological, not 'natural' or inevitable. Pacifists tended to come from a limited but distinct strand of feminist ideology on the democratic left of the movement, just as anti-war women in the socialist movement tended to come from socialism's left wing. The views of the feminist pacifists were limited in their appeal because the historical links between nationalism and feminism were still strong in the late nineteenth and early twentieth centuries. Since then, however, the context has changed. The origins of contemporary feminism in (among other things) the student and anti-Vietnam war movements and non-violent civil rights protests of the 1960s have strengthened the pacifist–feminist connection, while in advanced industrial countries at least the connection between nationalism and feminism has largely disappeared. Much of the anti-war heritage of socialism, with its emphasis on the role of capitalism and profit in the generation of the arms race, has also found its way into the contemporary peace movement. It is a mistake for historians to project this changed situation back into the feminist past; but by the same token, the changing context also gives us, perhaps, some hope for the future.

NOTES

This article draws on material first presented in my book *Sozialdemokratie und Frauenemanzipation im deutschen Kaiserreich* (Verlag J.H.W. Dietz Nachf., Bonn-Berlin, 1979).

1. Anne Wiltsher, *Most Dangerous Women* (London, 1985).
2. Darryn Kruse and Charles Sowerwine, 'Feminism and pacifism: "woman's sphere" in peace and war', in Ailsa Burns and Norma Grieve (eds), *Australian Women: New Feminist Perspectives* (Melbourne, 1986).
3. See my book *The Feminist Movement in Germany 1894–1933* (London, 1976), pp. 269–70.
4. *ibid.*, p. 210.
5. Richard Stites, *The Women's Liberation Movement in Russia. Feminism, Nihilism and Bolshevism, 1860–1930* (Princeton, 1978), p.221.
6. John C. Fout and Eleanor Riemer (eds), *European Women: A Documentary History* (New York, 1984), pp. 79–81.
7. *Evans, The Feminist Movement in Germany*, p. 77.
8. Stites, *op. cit.*, pp. 180–1.
9. Evans, *op. cit.*, pp. 215–16.
10. See my book *The Feminists* (London, 1977), pp. 246–53.
11. For accounts of the congress, see Wiltsher, *op. cit.*; Evans, *The Feminist Movement in Germany*, pp. 219–20; Kruse and Sowerwine, *op. cit.*; and Lela B. Costin, 'Feminism, pacifism, internationalism and the 1915 International Congress of Women', *Women's Studies International Quarterly*, 5 (2/4), 1982, pp. 301–15.
12. Kruse and Sowerwine, *op. cit.*
13. Steven C. Hause, with Anne R. Kenney, *Women's Suffrage and Social Politics in the French Third Republic* (Princeton, 1984), p. 193.
14. Evans, *The Feminist Movement in Germany*, pp. 218–9.
15. Linda Edmondson, *Feminism in Russia 1900–1917* (London, 1984), p. 160.
16. Wiltsher, *op. cit.*
17. *ibid.*, pp. 88–91.
18. Evans, *The Feminist Movement in Germany*, pp. 221, 218.

19. *ibid.*, p. 216; Marvin Swartz, *The Union of Democratic Control in British Politics during the First World War* (Oxford, 1971), p. 57.
20. Evans, *The Feminist Movement in Germany,* pp. 216–17.
21. *ibid.*, p. 107.
22. *ibid.*, pp. 220, 210.
23. Hause and Kenny, *op. cit.*, pp. 192–4.
24. *ibid.*
25. James F. McMillan, *Housewife or Harlot? The Place of Women in French Society 1870–1940* (Brighton, 1981), p. 112.
26. Hause and Kenney, *op. cit.*, p. 194.
27. Edmondson, *op. cit.*, p. 158.
28. Stites, *op. cit.*, p. 283 n.8.
29. *ibid.*, p. 282.
30. McMillan, *op. cit.*, p. 112. See also Charles Sowerwine, 'Women against the war: a feminine basis for internationalism and pacifism?', *Proceedings of the Annual Meeting of the Western Society for French History*, 6 (1978), pp. 361–71.
31. Evans, *The Feminists*, p. 197.
32. Brian Harrison, *Separate Spheres: The Opposition to Women's Suffrage in Britain* (London, 1978), p. 199.
33. Jill Liddington and Jill Norris, *One Hand Tied Behind Us. The Rise of the Women's Suffrage Movement* (London, 1978), p. 253.
34. *ibid.*
35. Cf. Wiltsher, *op. cit.*
36. Stites, *op. cit.*, pp. 284–8; Charles Sowerwine, *Sisters or Citizens? Women and Socialism in France since 1876* (Cambridge, 1982), pp. 143–59; see also my book *Sozialdemokratie und Frauenemanzipation im deutschen Kaiserreich,* Ch.6.
37. For another account of socialist women and the war in Germany, see Heinz Niggemann, *Emanzipation zwischen Sozialismus und Feminismus. Die sozialdemokratische Frauenbewegung im Kaiserreich* (Wuppertal, 1981), pp. 169–81.
38. Georges Haupt, *Der Kongress fand nicht statt. Die Sozialistische Internationale 1914* (Vienna, Frankfurt, Zurich, 1967) for Zetkin's movements during this period.
39. Clara Zetkin, *Ausgewählte Reden und Schriften*, vol.I (East Berlin, 1953), p .656: Zetkin to Heleen Ankersmit (3 December 1914).
40. GLA Karlsruhe, NL Geck: Zetkin to Adolf and Marie Geck (19 September 1914).
41. Zetkin, *Ausgewählte Reden*, I, 639–56: Zetkin to Ankersmit (3 December 1914).
42. Dieter Groh, *Negative Integration und revolutionärer Attentismus. Die deutsche Sozialdemokratie am Vorabend des Ersten Weltkrieges* (Frankfurt, 1973), p.673, n.71, citing Zetkin to Unknown (2 August 1914), IML/ZPA, NL 5 III—A/12, B1.72.
43. See W. Deist, (ed) *Militär und Innenpolitik im Weltkrieg 1914–1918* (2 vols, Düsseldorf, 1970–1).
44. Militärarchiv Stuttgart, Stellv. Gkdo. XIII. (Württ). AK, Bund 60,

passim; IML/ZPA, NL 5/66, p. 12; *GL* 25/4 (1914); Luise Dornemann, *Clara Zetkin. Leben und Wirken* (5th edn, East Berlin, 1973), pp. 270–7; Zetkin to Ankersmit (2 September, 1914) in W. Eildermann (ed.), 'Unveröffentlichte Briefe Clara Zetkins an Heleen Ankersmit', *Beiträge zur Geschichte der deutschen Arbeiterbewegung*, 9 (1967), 4, p. 668.

45. HStA Stuttgart, Stellv, Gkdo. XIII. (Württ.) AK, Bund 60: Kriegspresseamt/Oberzensurstelle Nr. 6644 O.Z. The *Burgfrieden* ('peace in the siege') was the nationally-agreed suspension of party-political strife.

46. Dornemann, *op. cit.*, pp. 271–9, giving the edition of the pamphlet as 200,000; IML/ZPA, NL5/66, pp. 1–10; Horst Lademacher (ed.), *Die Zimmerwalder Bewegung. Protokolle und Korrespondenz* (Paris/The Hague, 1967), vol.I, pp. 36 n.14, 493–4; vol.II, pp. 8–10, 11, 43 n.2, 71–2 n.1, 90–2; F. Adler, *Viktor Adler: Briefwechsel mit August Bebel und Karl Kautsky* (Vienna, 1954), pp. 617–19.

47. FES/ASD Bonn, NL Henke 1/43: Zetkin to Henke (22 April 1915).

48. Zetkin to Ankersmit (23 July 1915), in Eildermann (ed.), *op. cit.*, pp. 767–80.

49. Zetkin to Robert Grimm (9 April 1915), in Lademacher (ed.), *op. cit.*, p. 43; Zetkin to Heleen Ankersmit (23 July 1915), in Dornemann, *op. cit.*, p. 279; S. Miller (ed.), *Das Kriegstagebuch des Reichstags-abgeordneten Eduard David* (Düsseldorf, 1966) p. 126.

50. Not, as Lademacher *op. cit.*, states, on 30 July.

51. See Chapter 2, above.

52. IML/ZPA, NL 5/66, pp. 1–10.

53. Printed in *Dokumente und Materialien zur Geschichte der deutschen Arbeiterbewegung* (Berlin, 1957), vol.II/1, pp. 198–200. The first day's interrogation is not printed in this collection.

54. FES/ASD Bonn, NL Henke 1/43: Zetkin to Henke (22 April 1915).

55. Whether this reflected a genuine belief, or was designed merely to placate the authorities, is uncertain. It is clear, however, that the great majority of Social Democrats believed at least in Bethmann Hollweg's desire for peace. Cf. Susanne Miller, *Burgfrieden und Klassenkampf. Die deutsche Sozialdemokratie im Ersten Weltkrieg* (Düsseldorf, 1974), pp. 254–67.

56. See J.P. Nettl, *Rosa Luxemburg* (Oxford, 1966), for Luxemburg's opposition to the war; Luxemburg had nothing to do with the women's movement or the Bern conference.

57. Zetkin to Grimm (9 August 1915), in Lademacher (ed.), *op. cit.*, vol.II, pp. 290–2.

58. Ernst Haase (ed.), *Hugo Haase. Sein Leben und Wirken. Mit einer Auswahl von Briefen, Reden und Aufsätzen* (Berlin, 1929), pp. 110f. (Haase to Gottschalk, 7 October 1915.).

59. Dornemann, *op. cit.*, p. 284.

60. Haase to Zetkin (21 October 1915), in Ernst Haase (ed.), *op. cit.*, pp. 111f.

61. Haase to Zetkin (13 November 1915), printed in Richard J. Evans, 'Ein Brief Hugo Haases an Clara Zetkin aus dem Jahre 1915', *Internationale Wissenschaftliche Korrespondenz zur Geschichte der deutschen*

Arbeiterbewegung, 11/1 (March 1975), pp. 139–41.
62. Dornemann, *op. cit.*, pp. 284f.; Lademacher (ed.), *op. cit.*, pp. 314, 319, 326
63. Haase to Zetkin (21 October 1915), in Haase (ed.), *op. cit.*, pp. 111f.; cf. Miller, *op. cit.*, pp. 242f.
64. *Das Kriegstagebuch* (*op. cit.*), p. 181.
65. *ibid.*, and Lademacher (ed.), *op. cit.*, p. 43n.12.
66. StA Hbg, PP, S5883: *VW* (4 and 12 December 1915).
67. StA Hbg, PP, S5883: *HE* (19 November 1915), Polizeibericht 'Zu 264. VII. 4. 1917'.
68. PTP 1919, p. 36; StA Hbg, PP, S8897/IV: *VW* (17 July 1915), *HE* (8 December 1916), *LVZ* (5 October 1915); *ibid.*, S5883: *LVZ* (24 April 1917).
69. StA Hbg, PP, S5883: *LVZ* (26 February 1917), Miller, *op. cit.*, pp. 148–58.
70. *ibid.*, pp. 158–66.
71. See PTP (USPD) 1917, p. 50.
72. *ibid.*, Teilnehmerliste; StA Hbg, PP, S8897/IV: *LVZ* (10 August 1917), *HE* (10 July 1917).
73. StA Hbg, PP S8897/IV: *LVZ* (18 May 1917).
74. Clara Zetkin, *Ausgewählte Reden und Schriften,* vol.I (East Berlin, 1953), (article in *LVZ,* 19 June 1917).
75. StA Hbg, PP, S8897/IV: *LVZ* (5 October 1915).
76. StA Hbg, PP, S8897/IV: *VW* (4 December 1915). Zietz won 408 new members, including 123 in Düsseldorf, 60 in Solingen, 40 in Iserlohn, 40 in Elberfeld, 35 in Barmen, 32 in Krefeld, 25 in Mönchengladbach and 23 in Hagen. Neverthless, total female membership in the Lower Rhine fell from 7,490 in 1915 to 6,454 in 1916.
77. Born 15 March 1879, died 28 January 1956.
78. StA Hbg, PP, S8897/V: *LVZ* (10 August 1917).
79. Figures in Dieter Fricke, *Die deutsche Arbeiterbewegung 1869–1914. Ein Handbuch über ihre Organisation und ihre Tätigkeit im Klassenkampf* (Berlin, 1976), analysed fully in my *Sozialdemokratie und Frauenemanzipation.*
80. See my *Sozialdemokratie und Frauenemanzipation,* ch.3.
81. Fricke, *op. cit.*
82. Sowerwine, *Sisters or Citizens?*, p. 143.
83. *ibid.*, pp. 143–59.
84. *ibid.*
85. cf. Klaus-Dieter Schwarz, *Weltkrieg und Revolution in Nürnberg* (Stuttgart, 1971), pp. 133–45.
86. For food riots, see HStA Hannover, Hann. 122a, XXXIV, 365, Bd.I. Bl. 2–9, 121, 152, 162–5, 177–8, 192, 217; F.L. Carsten, *War against War: British and German Radical Movements in the First World War* (London, 1982), pp. 42–3, 50, 76, 79, 89, 165; Schwarz, *op. cit.*, pp. 146–54; Volker Ullrich, *Kriegsalltag: Hamburg im ersten Weltkrieg* (Cologne, 1982), pp. 39–72, 85–92; Willi Albrecht, *Landtag und Regierung in Bayern am Vorabend der Revolution von 1918* (Berlin, 1968), pp. 148–9, 327–9, 344–6; Wilhelm Deist (ed.), *Militär und*

Innenpolitik im Weltkrieg 1914–1918 (Düsseldorf, 1970–1), vol.I, p. 295; Erhard Lucas, *Arbeiterradikalismus: Zwei Formen von Radikalismus in der deutschen Arbeiterbewegung* (Frankfurt-am-Main, 1976), p. 148; Karl-Ludwig Ay, *Die Entstehung einer Revolution. Die Volksstimmung in Bayern während des Ersten Weltkriegs* (Berlin, 1981), p. 184, and for the broader context Wolfgang J. Mommsen, 'The German Revolution 1918–1920: political revolution and social protest movement', in Richard Bessel and E.J. Feuchtwanger (eds), *Social Change and Political Development in Weimar Germany* (London, 1981), pp. 21–54.

87. Carsten, *op. cit.*, p. 43.
88. See Chapter 3, above.
89. Sowerwine, *Sisters or Citizens?*, p. 150.
90. Stites, *op. cit.*, pp. 301–6.
91. Alfred G. Meyer, *The Feminism and Socialism of Lily Braun* (Bloomington, Indiana, 1985), pp. 171–84.
92. Evans, *The Feminist Movement in Germany*, pp. 207–14, 235–6.
93. Hause and Kenney, *op. cit.*, pp. 192, 195.
94. Stites, *op. cit.*, pp. 30–5; Evans, *The Feminists*, pp. 91–143.

6 Feminism and Fascism

I

'Women', said Hitler in 1933, 'have always been among my staunchest supporters. They feel my victory is their victory.'[1] Others agreed with this view. 'It was the women's vote', observed the disillusioned ex-Nazi Hermann Rauschning in 1939, 'that brought Hitler to triumph.'[2] Rauschning and conservatives like him made such comments not least because German women had only obtained the vote in 1918. Female suffrage, they implied, was one of the reasons for the Weimar Republic's fall. Of course, Hitler was not brought to power by votes alone. The Nazis never in fact won more than 37 per cent of the vote in a free election, that of July 1932. Hitler became German Chancellor in January 1933 as the result of a political intrigue hatched in the circles surrounding the aged President Hindenburg, in whose hands the power of rule by decree had lain since the effective breakdown of parliamentary government not long after the onset of the Depression, in 1930. Following his appointment, Hitler succeeded within a few months in establishing a dictatorship by a combination of murder, violence, intimidation and terror to beat down his opponents on the left, and the skilful use of political blackmail to secure the (by no means wholly unwilling) complicity of his allies on the right. It is indeed the centrality of mass violence to the Nazis' success that justifies the use of the term 'seizure of power'.[3]

Still, without that 37 per cent of the vote, without the fact that they were the largest party in the Reichstag, the Nazis would never have got anywhere, and Papen and his cronies around Hindenburg would never have considered trying to use them to back up their own schemes for a conservative restoration in January 1933. So the women's vote was important after all. In July 1932 a total of 13,734,000 people voted for the Nazis, so if half of these were women, that would mean the NSDAP received some 6,867,000 female votes. However, because of their greater longevity in an ageing population and because of the massive loss of adult males on the front in the First World War, women actually predominated in the electorate. Altogether there were about 2,150,000 more female than male electors in Germany in July 1932, so if the same proportion of each had voted, the Nazis would have received about 7,207,000 votes from women and 6,539,000 votes from men.[4] So there does seem some *prima facie* justification for the belief that the female vote was an important element in the Nazis' success.

This was, on the face of it, a very surprising fact. For the Nazis were undoubtedly a very strongly anti-feminist movement. In many ways they represented, indeed, the ultimate in male chauvinism. 'The message of women's emancipation', wrote Hitler in *Mein Kampf*, 'is a message discovered solely by the Jewish intellect and its content is stamped by the same spirit.'[5] By this he meant to imply that it was subversive and anti-German. On another occasion, referring to the Social Democrats, he wrote:

The so-called granting of equal rights, which Marxism demands, in reality does not grant equal rights but constitutes a deprivation of rights, since it draws the woman into an area in which she will necessarily be inferior. It places the woman in situations that cannot strengthen her position *vis-à-vis* both men and society—but only weakens it.[6]

The Nazis never tired of proclaiming that the rough-and-tumble of the political world would alienate women from their true character by making them aggressive, or be too much for their gentle, homely nature altogether. 'The mission of women', as Hitler's Minister of Propaganda Josef Goebbels declared, 'is to be beautiful and to bring children into the world. This is not', he added, 'at all as rude and unmodern as it sounds. The female bird pretties herself for her mate and hatches the eggs for him. In exchange, the mate takes care of gathering the food, and stands guard and wards off the enemy.'[7] This curious analogy demonstrated among other things Goebbels' extreme ignorance of ornithology. There are many species of birds where the male hatches the eggs and the female gathers the food: for example, the emu, the kiwi and the emperor penguin, and others where the male is prettier, such as the peacock, or the pheasant. That aside, however, Goebbels' analogy gave a fair indication of how the Nazis regarded the role of women in society. Men were to fight wars and earn the family's keep: women were to stay at home and look after the children.

Nazi thought on women was governed in the first place by political considerations. The regeneration of Germany was to be achieved by the *Männerbund*, by the male group united in comradely feelings and trained in the 'virtues' of 'hardness', aggressiveness, and ruthlessness.[8] These qualities Hitler described as 'masculine' in contrast to the 'feminine' qualities he thought were shown in the masses.[9] Ideas such as this went back to thinkers such as Otto Weininger, who erected this masculine/feminine, strong/weak dichotomy into a cosmic principle.[10] The word *Feminismus* in German referred to these supposed qualities of the female sex. Thus when the extreme right-wing *Hammer Bund* attacked Imperial Chancellor Bülow for his 'feminism' in 1909, it was not referring to the sympathetic attitude he adopted towards female emancipation,[11] but rather to what it regarded as his policies of compromise and appeasement and his failure to emulate the 'Iron Chancellor' Bismarck.[12] And *Antifeminismus,* for the *völkisch* writer Hans Blüher, historian of the youth movement, meant an assertion of the 'masculine' values of 'hardness', comradeship and so on, which, he believed, were only to be found in all-male societies such as the youth movement.[13]

The Nazi political system did not rest on representation, or on constitutionalism, but on 'leadership'. Leadership, it was believed, was an exclusively masculine quality. Women were not admitted to positions of responsibility in the NSDAP before 1933. There were no women among the party's hundreds of elected parliamentary deputies in the Reich, the provinces and the towns and rural districts. In the Third Reich, women were excluded from all positions of political power. Moreover, all those organizations and political movements in the Weimar Republic which either claimed that women were capable of leadership or aimed to give even a small number of them a part in the running of the country were singled out by the Nazis for especial condemnation. Most prominent of these objects of Hitler's scorn was perhaps the women's movement, led by the Federation of German Women's Associations (*Bund Deutscher Frauenvereine,* or BDF, founded in 1894). Here the Nazis once more took up ideas that had gained currency before the First World War. The origin of these ideas was to be found in the German League for the Prevention of the Emancipation of Women *(Deutscher Bund zur Bekämpfung der Frauenemanzipation)*, a 'national opposition' organization founded in 1912 by a group of right-wing extremists who included General August Keim, the organizer of the Navy League, and Professor Dietrich Schäfer, a leading Pan-German.[14] The 'Anti-League', as it was known, and its ally the German-national Commercial Assistants' Union *(Deutschnationaler Handlungsgehilfenverband,* DHV), an anti-Semitic white-collar union,[15] believed that the women's movement was part of an international Jewish conspiracy to subvert the German family and thus destroy the German race.[16] The movement, it claimed, was encouraging women to assert their economic independence and to neglect their proper task of producing children.[17] It was spreading the 'feminine' doctrines of pacifism, democracy and 'materialism'. If the movement's demands for female suffrage were granted, the Jewish race would have Germany at its mercy.[18] These ideas were repeated almost without amendment by the Nazis. The Nazis regarded the women's movement as an attempt to subvert the qualities of 'leadership' in German men, to convince them that aggression and war were evils instead of necessities for the survival of the German race. The area in which the German woman was 'necessarily inferior' was of course politics. By introducing a 'feminine' influence into politics, the women's movement was subverting the will and the survival capability of the German race. It was undermining the 'leadership' on which Germany's future rested. By encouraging contraception and abortion and so lowering the birth rate it was attacking the very existence of the German people. Its claim to represent all German women was an outrage, since in Nazi eyes there was only one organization that could legitimately do this, and that was the Nazi party itself. Thus the feminist movement incorporated in the BDF, was defamed as a tool of the 'Jewish world conspiracy' to destroy the unit and existence of the German people.[19].

Secondly, the Nazi view of women was also framed by the party's racist and biological ideology. After seizing power, the Nazis introduced a variety of 'eugenic' measures including medals, tax concessions and other privileges for fecund mothers and large families, and strong efforts to confer equality of status on unmarried mothers, who were offically called '*Frau*'. Special marriage loans were made available for working women on condition they gave up work. In addition, the 'racially unfit' or 'hereditarily diseased' were to be compulsorily sterilized. Abortion was allowed in such cases. There were indeed 320,000 sterilizations and 5,000 'eugenic abortions' from 1933 to 1939. Divorce was made easier for the infertile, just as it had been for similar reasons in the days of Frederick the Great's Prussian Civil Code, replaced in 1900 by laws making it more difficult to obtain a divorce. Later on in the Third Reich, Himmler founded special maternity homes, the so-called *Lebensborn* scheme, for unmarried mothers whose children had been conceived by 'racially valuable' men, particularly by members of the SS. Such conceptions were also actively encouraged. In addition, towards the end of the war, Hitler was even thinking of introducing selective polygamy for the purpose of making up the loss of men in the war, 'improving the race' and rewarding the all-male élite of the Thousand-Year-Reich. Women appeared in the Nazi world-view primarily as mothers—either as Aryan mothers, to be encouraged to have more children and to be made fit to do so by the new emphasis on physical training which the Nazis introduced into schools, workplaces and organizations such as the League of German Girls; or as 'inferior' mothers, as Jewish, gypsy, handicapped or other 'degenerate' mothers and potential mothers, to be discouraged or prevented from having children and to be rigidly separated from the favoured majority of the population. The Nazis thus offered to women an extreme separation of spheres, public life for men, home life for women, and an extreme version of the sexual division of labour, in which women would be largely excluded from areas (such as politics, administration and the professions) into which they had begun to intrude during the Weimar Republic.[20] And they offered a world run by men, with the shutting down of autonomous women's organizations, above all if they were feminist, and the drafting of their members into Nazi women's organizations which were ultimately under the control of the male party leadership.[21] It was not surprising, therefore, that the American writer and historian Mary Beard already felt impelled to ask of the German woman in 1931, 'Why does she vote for a group that intends to take the ballot from her? Why does she support antifeminism?'[22]

II

Of the few attempts that have been made to explain why German women voted for Hitler in 1932–3, undoubtedly the most popular, the most widely repeated and (probably) the most generally accepted is that which explains it in terms of their supposedly inherent irrationality. In supporting the anti-feminism of the Nazis, it has often been claimed, women were letting their hearts rule their heads in a characteristically female way. The first major commentator to advance this interpretation was the disillusioned Nazi sympathizer Hermann Rauschning. Rauschning's remarks about the emotional effect which Hitler had on women—'one must have seen from above, from the speaker's rostrum, the rapturously rolling, moist, veiled eyes of the female listeners in order to be in no further doubt as to the character of this enthusiasm'[23]—have been echoed by many commentators. According to Joachim Fest, for example, the 'over-excited, distinctly hysterical tone' of Hitler's meetings 'sprang in the first place from the excessive emotionalism of a particular kind of elderly woman who sought to activate the unsatisfied impulses within her in the tumult of mighty political demonstrations before the ecstatic figure of Hitler'.[24] 'Hitler's monkish persona', Richard Grunberger has written, 'engendered a great deal of sexual hysteria among women . . . not least among spinsters, who transmuted their repressed yearnings into lachrymose adoration.'[25] And William L. Shirer, attending his first Nuremberg rally as a foreign journalist working in Germany in 1934, 'was a little shocked at the faces, especially those of the women, when Hitler finally appeared on the balcony for a moment . . . If he had remained in sight for more than a few moments', he concluded, 'I think many of the women would have swooned from excitement.'[26]

Nor, according to these writers, was the sexual sublimation which, they argue, provided the driving-force of popular, and above all, of female enthusiasm for Hitler, merely one-sided. For Hitler, too, it is suggested, found an outlet for his frustrated sexuality, a compensation for his lack of a 'normal sexual relationship', in whipping up hysteria among his female listeners. Thus Nazi rallies became a 'collective debauch', resembling 'the public sexual acts of primitive tribes'.[27] Moreover, whatever personal gratifications Hitler may have derived from the way in which, as he is reported to have said, he 'systematically adapted himself to the taste of women',[28] there were also considerable political dividends to be gained. According to his most recent biographer, Hitler exploited and manipulated 'specific female qualities, such as capacity for self-surrender or demand for authority and order'[29] to the advantage of his party as well as himself; and much, though not all, of 'the secret of Hitler's success as an orator lay in this use of speech as a sexual surrogate'.[30]

Hitler himself regarded the root of his success as an orator as lying in the reduction of the whole of his audience, both male and female, to a condition of 'femininity', in which he could play on their emotions and abandon any attempt to appeal to their reason. He thought that the masses were already in a 'feminine' state. 'The people', he wrote in *Mein Kampf*, 'in their overwhelming majority are so feminine by nature and attitude that sober reasoning determines their thoughts and actions far less than emotion and feelings.'[31] There is, it seems then, if we are to take him at his word, just as much likelihood that the emotional appeal which Hitler is said to have held for women derived more from the general oratorical and propagandistic techniques that he employed than from any attempt to elaborate techniques specifically directed at women. Nevertheless, if Hitler did in fact exert the kind of appeal he is claimed to have exerted, then it would most probably have evoked its strongest response in women.

However, there are many problems with these arguments. They seem to have gained currency by commentators on Nazism taking Hitler's own comments on his mob oratory at their face value, giving them a Freudian twist, and presenting them as a serious attempt to penetrate the secret of Hitler's appeal. In this respect, as in many others, it is Hermann Rauschning's interpretation which has proved most influential. It had the incidental, and by no means unintentional effect of passing the blame for Hitler's rise to power from the class to which Rauschning himself belonged on to the mass of the people, and more particularly on to the women of Germany, without whose enfranchisement in 1918, Rauschning implied, the Third Reich would never have happened. It was Rauschning who first injected the psychological element into the theory, already implicit in *Mein Kampf*, that the relations between Hitler the speaker and those who listened to him could be likened to the relations between a dominant male and his submissive female partner. In recent years, this theme has been taken up and elaborated, though not substantially modified, by Joachim Fest, whose biography of Hitler has received high praise for its 'psychological acumen' even from those reviewers who have strongly criticized its historical judgement.[32] Yet there is little scientific basis for such a psychological view. It was not Freud who was ultimately responsible for the interpretations we have been discussing, nor was it even the French theorist of crowd psychology, Gustave LeBon, whose ideas Hitler's writings on propaganda closely resembled,[33] for, as the latest commentator of LeBon has pointed out, these theories 'were the *lingua franca* of nearly all European collective psychologists by 1905'.[34] The stereotype of women as emotional and submissive was so general in European society before the First World War that to ascribe it to any one theorist would be absurd. The figure of speech by which certain qualities in a crowd, a people or even in the universe could be described as 'feminine' came naturally to a generation which took this stereotype for granted. It still lies at the root of interpretations, such as Joachim Fest's, which ascribe much of Hitler's oratorical success to the way in which he catered for 'specific female qualities' such as 'self-surrender' and a 'demand for authority'.[35] The sexism of such comments should be obvious. There is nothing specifically female about these qualities, nor are they common to all women. The stereotype of the submissive and emotional woman is best regarded as part of the conservative social ideology of the politically dominant classes in early twentieth-century Europe; it should be seen as an aspect of political and social conservatism, not as a self-evident fact of life or a conclusively proven theory of modern psychology. In conformity with the conservative ideological background of this stereotype, the writers who have supported the view that Hitler won over the women of Germany to his cause by an appeal that was essentially emotional have either been German conservatives, like Rauschning, or conservative journalists like Shirer and Fest.

Freudian psychologists such as J.A.C. Brown have argued that 'the potency of Hilter's propaganda . . . has been grossly exaggerated',[36] a view shared by Hitler's earliest biographer, Konrad Heiden, who considered that Hitler's own description of his relationship with the masses was a distortion, if not a reversal, of the truth.[37] Our image of Hitler's oratory has been indelibly fixed by films like Leni Riefensthal's *Triumph of the Will,* and by newsreel shots of Hitler speaking to massed and hysterical audiences at the Nuremberg rallies. But these were carefully stage-managed occasions, designed with the aim of generating emotional enthusiasm, mounted with all the resources of the state at the disposal of the Third Reich, and packed with hand-picked fanatical Nazi supporters. The same goes for the crowd scenes such as those taken during Hitler's motorcade through Nuremberg at the start of Riefensthal's film: the crowds were partly self-selecting, partly hand-picked, and the shots were carefully edited to produce the maximum impression of public support for Hitler. Before 1933, when the Nazis were not in power, when they were often short of money, and when they were not always able to select their audiences, Nazi meetings were generally much less grandiose affairs. They were often quite small, and only a tiny fraction of the millions of women who voted for Hitler can ever have gone to them. Hitler's speeches often had little impact, and the common notion of a perfectly orchestrated propaganda machine manipulating the German people into voting for the Nazis against their better judgement, of emotion overriding the dictates of reason, is, as Richard Bessel has pointed out, something of a myth.[38]

III

A large part of the implausibility of psycho-historical explanations of why women voted for Hitler lies in their sexist assumption that women must have been emotionally swayed, while for men it was a matter of rational choice. Feminist historians naturally reject this view and look instead for rational considerations behind women's choices. Thus Renate Bridenthal, writing in 1973, argued that women in the Weimar Republic were not as emancipated as previous commentators had tended to assume. Women in Germany in the 1920s, despite gaining the vote and other rights, and despite the image portrayed on film, in literature, and (not least) in historical writing, 'lost status and relative independence and, quite probably, a corresponding sense of competence and self-worth'. Industrialization was transferring women from agricultural and domestic employment to jobs in shops, factories and offices, and it was bringing an increasing number of married women into the labour market. This process, according to Bridenthal, had two contradictory effects. Firstly, the new jobs were more conspicuous than the old, and the increase in the numbers of shopgirls, women factory operatives, secretaries, shorthand typists and clerks gave men the impression that women were becoming economically emancipated. This led to a rise in anti-feminism among men, which culminated in the Nazis' call for women to leave the labour market and return to the home. Secondly, the new jobs were less rewarding than the old, not least because they involved a trivialization of the female image, in the process of which 'German women came to approximate the helpless, clinging and coy sex object projected onto the movie screens and encouraged by the *Kitsch* of the Weimar period.'

Condemned for her abandonment of the family, suffering consequently from a sense of failure at home as well as at work where her socially induced feeling of inferiority was reinforced by low pay and lack of advancement, it would not be surprising if the woman of the Weimar Republic failed to embrace her supposed emancipation and even actively rejected it in politics'.[39]

This, then, is the reason why German women voted for the Nazis in the elections of 1930–33: and Bridenthal's view has been taken up more recently by feminist historians in West Germany who argue that women were right to retreat into the home in the early 1930s, and even assert that this was a valid form of resistance to the Nazis' attempted politicization of the whole of everyday life.[40]

Yet there are serious problems with this view. While it is certainly true that the promises of equal rights for women that were enshrined in the Weimar Constitution remained for all practical purposes a dead letter, both in the economic sense and in other spheres, such as the Civil Law, education and the professions,[41] there was nevertheless a sense in which it could be said that some groups of women at least were becoming more emancipated, though this—like all the economic and social trends discussed in Bridenthal's article—was a gradual, long-term development which was taking place irrespective of short-term changes in the political structure. The decline in the birth rate, the increasing expectancy of life, the decreasing size of the average family—these and other demographic effects of improving standards of living and the spread in the use of contraceptives were all having a profound effect on the life-pattern of the female sex.[42] Among the working classes, the power of the family over its grown-up, unmarried daughters was beginning to decrease. Those women who made up the bulk of the workforce—unmarried women in their teens and twenties—were becoming financially independent, especially with the feminization of white-collar work. Their financial situation may have been precarious, and their social image may well have been trivialized, but it was not, after all, a state in which they expected to remain for long, and it was probably preferable to the authoritarian atmosphere of the family home in which they had grown up. The notion that German women were trivialized as 'sex objects' may have been true of unmarried working women in their twenties, but those were only a minority of the female population. The dominant social ideology of the era concentrated on women as mothers and housewives, and sentimentalized them in terms of self-sacrifice and family commitment. For the many women widowed or unmarried in the older age-groups, society had a more negative image, expressed in the opinions quoted earlier in this chapter by Richard Grunberger and Joachim Fest, with their contemptuous references to 'elderly spinsters'. Women predominated in the electorate in the upper age brackets, and even if younger women had voted disproportionately for the Nazis, they would have been unlikely to have made up more than a relatively small proportion of the Nazis' female voting support.

Bridenthal's arguments may have some validity for certain younger groups of women. In the Depression of 1929–32, nearly seven million people, the majority of them men, lost their jobs, and it is not surprising that political parties like the Nazis urged that married women workers should go back to the home to make way for jobless men. But most women workers were in jobs that men were not willing to take because they were identified as 'women's work'. Men did not want to become secretaries, shop assistants selling women's lingerie, domestic servants, textile workers, laundry operatives or most of the other things that women were, in their working lives outside the home. So the possibilities for women to vacate the labour market in favour of men were severely restricted by the sex-segmented nature of the labour force. Moreover, many housewives who had previously not had a job—effectively, women in the middle and lower middle classes—were now forced to go out and look for one to keep up the family income after their husbands had been made idle. So thousands of women actually entered the labour market during the Depression; and employers were more than willing to take them on because they were cheap—they were not paid equal wages for equal work—they were often employed on a part-time basis so that the employer did not have to pay insurance contributions for them, they were adaptable because of their previous working experience before marriage, and they could easily be dismissed if the need arose. These women may well have resented having to work, and provided a ready audience for Nazi promises to subsidize a return to the home. Similarly, many younger women had been deferring getting married because they had to carry on working during the Depression since their prospective husbands were not able to earn a family wage by themselves. These women must have made up the bulk of those who took advantage of the Nazis' marriage loan scheme in 1933.[43] Most of them probably came from the urban petty bourgeoisie, and it is not surprising that a feminist observer attending a Hitler meeting in October 1932 found in the audience 'housewives of the lower middle class, predominating among others of all classes'.[44]

Nevertheless, these arguments can only apply to a small fraction of the millions of women who voted for the Nazis. And in any case they pass over the problem that many other groups apart from the Nazis themselves were advocating a return of women to the home in the early 1930s. Bridenthal's own article of 1973, indeed, noted that the thesis it advanced was intended to apply not just to the NSDAP but to the Catholic Centre Party as well.[45] This party too—as can be imagined—laid a strong emphasis on women as mothers and guardians of the home. Social Catholicism stressed the integrity of the family, frowned on emancipated womanhood, and had a clear bearing on the measure introduced by the government of Chancellor Brüning—himself a Catholic—in 1930 to dismiss married women from the civil service. That measure passed with the backing of the liberal and conservative parties too; the campaign against the 'double earner' had a wide measure of support on the German political scene at this time. Yet it was to the Nazis that the voters flocked: the Catholic vote held reasonably firm, but certainly did not increase—if anything it declined slightly from 1928 on, and the liberal and conservative parties collapsed, losing most of their votes to the NSDAP by 1932.[46]

Moreover, despite the Nazis' attacks on the feminist movement, it too had become socially and politically conservative. Largely left-liberal (Progressive) before 1914, by 1930 BDF had opened up to the right, and divided its support evenly between the DDP, DVP and DNVP.[47] It opposed contraception, sexual libertarianism and abortion on demand, defended the family as an institution, and held that woman's proper destiny lay in marriage and childbearing.[48] In 1910 it banned from membership the *Bund für Mutterschutz,* which campaigned for free love, legal abortion and equal rights for unmarried mothers.[49] During the war, it expelled all its pacifist members; it rejected the Treaty of Versailles, and in the early 1920s it refused to co-operate with the International Council of Women.[50] Its programme of 1919, which was binding on the 750,000 or more women who belonged to it,[51] emphasized the differences between the sexes and said that the real task of the women's movement lay in bringing a 'motherly' influence to bear on society. It declared marriage, childbearing and housekeeping to be women's major aims in life, and announced its intention of trying to improve the status of the housewife and mother.[52] The BDF thought that political parties were divisive and supported the idea of an organic national community (*Volksgemeinschaft*).[53] It claimed to 'unite German women of every party and world view, in order to express their national solidarity and to effect the common idea of the cultural mission of woman'.[54] This was not to be taken literally, of course: the BDF had nothing whatever to do with socialist or communist women; its membership was exclusively middle-class, and it never seriously tried to win over the women of the proletariat.[55] It is hard to escape the suspicion that the BDF shared the general view of the right that the SPD and KPD were not 'German' but 'international'. Moreover, the very use of the words 'German' (*deutsch*) and 'national' (*national*) in the BDF programme indicated the movement's nationalistic character and its affinities with the Protestant right.[56]

By 1932, indeed, the BDF was joining in the general attack launched by the right on the parliamentary system and urging the establishment of a fascist-style corporate state in which one of the 'corporations' would consist of women. When the BDF was about to be dissolved in the spring of 1933, its President, Agnes von Zahn-Harnack, protested that its aims were thoroughly compatible with those of the National Socialists, and pointed as confirmation of this claim to the movement's support for 'eugenic' policies and the sterilization of 'anti-social elements', its condemnation of the Revolution of 1918 and the Treaty of Versailles, and its denial of the equality of men and women. Gertrud Bäumer, the BDF's most influential figure, believed that the replacement of the movement by a Nazi women's organization merely signified that the women's movement was 'moving into a new phase'. This was evidence of a considerable overlap between the ideas of the BDF and those of the NSDAP. The BDF had believed since before the First World War that only a minority of women had either the ability or the need to enter politics or pursue a career—which it portrayed in terms of 'self-sacrifice' or 'service' analogous to those in which it portrayed the childbearing and housekeeping that were the lot of the majority of women. It was taken for granted that women who pursued a career would remain unmarried. Marriage and childbearing were thought by the women's movement to be incompatible with a career in politics, education or administration. Thus the BDF supported the legal requirement for women school-teachers to resign when they married, and refrained from opposing a measure introduced in 1930 providing for the dismissal of married women from public service. This measure, it is important to realize, was supported by *all* political parties in Germany except the KPD. All political parties save the socialists had opposed female suffrage up to the Revolution of November 1918. No-one campaigned with sufficient vigour for a revision of the Civil Code (1900), which gave the German husband and father wide powers over his wife, her property and their children, to secure even a proper debate in the *Reichstag*, let alone the actual approval of a Bill to this effect.[57]

Feminist historians, particularly in Germany, have been reluctant to accept that the feminist movement in the late Wilhelmine and Weimar periods moved to the right until it became, like other bourgeois liberal associations, vulnerable to the lure of Nazi ideology. In the first place, they have argued that this argument represents an inappropriate assimilation of feminism to 'male' political categories (such as 'liberal', 'Nazi', 'middle class' etc.). They suggest that feminism should be seen, rather, in its relation to women's daily life and experience.[58] Yet the feminist movement did not remain aloof from factional struggles in the political movements to which it was allied, nor—as we have seen—did it shirk from pronouncing on national and international problems like the justice (or otherwise) of the Treaty of Versailles. Even in feminist terms, it would seem justifiable to argue that the BDF moved to the right before 1914, as it rejected legalized abortion and began to claim that motherhood was the essence of the female experience, thus condemning millions of women to second-class status, above all after the war.

Recently, however, Irene Stoehr, a German feminist, has alleged that it is a 'male point of view' to criticize the German feminist movement for failing to offer any serious opposition to Nazism. By insisting that it was 'unpolitical', and by concentrating increasingly exclusively on 'women's issues' in the last years of the Weimar Republic, she argues, the feminist movement was actually becoming more radical, not less so, because it was opposing a consistent model of 'women's politics' to the 'men's politics' with which the Nazis and the Weimar parties were concerned. In any case, she goes on, why should the movement have stopped 'a certain men's group' (*Männerfraktion*) – the Nazis – from coming to power, when all of them were as bad as each other on women's issues? Parliamentary democracy had brought mass unemployment, hunger and violence and had pushed women's interests into the background. Why should they trouble to rescue it?

Stoehr defends the attitude of the leading feminist of the time, Gertrud Bäumer, in praising women who resigned their legislative positions because engagement in political struggle in such an atmosphere was forcing them to participate in activities that were foreign to women's nature (*'wesensfremde Formen der politischen Arbeit'*). Women's politics were not just about women's issues, they were about political style as well, and here too, argues Stoehr, the feminist movement was becoming more radical by withdrawing from the Weimar system when the style of politics became more 'masculine'. Bäumer argued that women should stop using their votes altogether because to continue doing so would be to accept part of the guilt for the failure of 'men's politics'. Stoehr sees this as a form of 'resistance against the integration of women into male society through the means of political rights'. When, in 1931, feminists urged a retreat into the home because the struggle for jobs was leading to the 'spiritual impoverishment' of women, this is seen by Stoehr as part of the same process.

The Nazi seizure of power, she concludes, made little difference to the situation of women. 'Everything went on as before.' Things were already so bad for women that 'the women's movement could not imagine they could get worse, whatever changes of regime took place'. Women's 'indifference' to the fact of whether the state was organized on 'parliamentary, democratic or fascist' lines was 'one of the most serious forms of resistance to Nazism' because for the Nazis themselves the overthrow of democracy was a political question of paramount importance.[59]

Not surprisingly, perhaps, Stoehr's arguments, put forward on the occasion of the fiftieth anniversary of the Nazi seizure of power, met with a good deal of criticism from within the German feminist movement. In particular, Regula Venske, writing in another feminist periodical, asked:

Is it for example a 'male point of view' to ascribe a part of the responsibility for the course of German history to the organized women's movement and to ask what concrete mistakes allowed a whole movement and an organization of millions like the BDF to be swallowed up in 1933 without discernible resistance?

Was it, she continued, a 'male point of view' to ask whether the feminist movement was successful or unsuccessful, and to conclude that the record of women's politics before 1933 did not exactly deserve to be inscribed on the roll of honour of women's history? For German women to wash their hands of responsibility for Nazism because it was men who led the Nazi Party and devised its policies is 'virtually criminal', says Venske, in view of the degradation and murder which millions of women suffered under the Third Reich. Indeed as the feminist historian Gisela Bock has argued, Nazi policies on other issues besides the place of women in society had a profound effect on women almost from the very beginning of the Third Reich. Minority women bore the brunt of the 320,000 compulsory sterilizations carried out on racial and 'eugenic' grounds in Germany between 1933 and 1939, while the majority—those deemed racially pure and eugenically satisfactory—were increasingly forced by the regime to have children they did not want. The militarism of the Nazis caused the deaths of millions of civilian women in the Second World

War, while the culmination of the Third Reich in the mass murder of Jews and other racially and socially stigmatized groups once more subjected millions of women to an appalling process of humiliation and death, often—as in the case of female patients in mental hospitals—because they deviated from some norm of female behaviour, or—as in the case of medical experimentation on female inmates of Auschwitz—in ways that were specifically related to the fact that they were women.[60]

Because the German feminist movement refused to recognize the relevance of the Nazi threat to women, Venske argues, it can be reasonably accused of 'ignorance and political blindness'. She denies that it is arrogant to voice such criticisms: on the contrary, she asserts, it is important for feminists to learn from past mistakes. Using biological sex as the starting-point for political judgements, which Stoehr regards as a form of resistance, says Venske, 'has been part of the male repertoire since time immemorial', and it is no more plausible when women use it. Women's withdrawal, or rather, forced retreat, into a 'female' political sphere of welfare and social work may well have been a factor in allowing the male political world to become so violent. Equating biological sex with social values, the German feminists found themselves on the slippery slope that led directly to acceptance of the same equation when it was implemented by the Nazis.[61]

All in all, therefore, it is far from inappropriate to speak of a rightward move on the part of German feminism in the years after 1908. It was a move that paralleled a similar shift in German liberalism as a whole, and encompassed attitudes to other political questions besides those which directly affected women. Much feminist ideology involved taking liberal ideas and applying them to women—though often with consequences that liberals at large were unwilling to accept. Similarly, as German liberal ideology moved rightwards, under the influence of Friedrich Naumann, so too did the ideology of mainstream German feminism, under the influence of Gertrud Bäumer, who was—not accidentally—a close associate of Naumann and collaborated on his magazine, *Die Hilfe*. Most of the leading moderate German feminists were also active in the liberal

Progressive Party and its successor the German Democratic Party, and to an increasing degree after 1918 in the German People's Party, which represented the right wing of the German liberal tradition, and it seems reasonable to argue, therefore, that liberalism and feminism were closely linked. Finally, the consequences of this rightward shift were evident not only in the feminists' policies on issues like abortion and contraception but also in the eventual vulnerability of the feminist movement and its supporters to the appeal of National Socialism, with the fatal consequences this entailed. To understand these political developments, they have to be seen in relation to the overall political context of the times, and not simply in relation to German women and their everyday experience of being women, though it is of course equally important to study this aspect of feminism too.

It remains to ask whether or not it is appropriate to classify German feminists as middle-class. It is not true that this class assignment has been made purely on the basis of the class position of these women's husbands or fathers. Records available for the German Union for Women's Suffrage, Hamburg branch, for 1904 show that 48 out of the 82 members were unmarried, and of the 38 whose profession was known, thirteen were school-teachers, four were accounts clerks, two were described as ladies of private means, two were shopkeepers, and there was also a nurse, a painter, a receptionist, a dressmaker, a commercial student and a factory inspector's assistant. If we accept a definition of class based on income and property then it would seem reasonable to describe these women as a mixture of middle-class and petty bourgeois. In fact most of the leading activists in German feminism were unmarried; some of them like Lida Gustava Heymann, were women of substantial inherited wealth, while others, like Gertrud Bäumer, worked in a variety of quite well-paid jobs. Those who were married generally enjoyed a high standard of living. In their education, their social consciousness, their dress, their manners and their whole lifestyle they were unmistakably middle-class and were universally regarded as such by the society they lived in. Their wealth, status, appearance and deportment gave them access to a whole range of goods, benefits and institutions from which the women of the proletariat were barred. Women of course had a different socialization from men and played different social roles in the bourgeois world, but this does not mean to say they were not middle class, and in fact there is a whole range of sources, especially relating to bourgeois and aristocratic marriage and marriageability, to suggest that the social position of most middle-class women was indeed largely determined by that of their husbands and fathers. That, surely, is one of the things we mean when we describe Victorian England or Imperial Germany as a 'patriarchal society'.

The development of political debate on the place of women in German society was thus inseparable from the development of political debate on other issues, and closely related to changing class alliances and alignments. There was a broad area of agreement between the Nazis and their opponents, including the women's movement, on many matters concerning the social position of women. All were agreed that policies should be introduced to try and boost Germany's declining birth rate. Here too the Nazis looked to the *Kaiserreich* for ideas. Since the publication in 1912 of a Prussian government report, drawing attention to the 'dangerous' implications of the decline in the German birth rate since the 1870s, had sparked off a national crisis of confidence in the Darwinian capabilities of the German race,[62] there had been an almost uninterrupted debate raging on the means by which the falling trend in the birth rate could be reversed.[63] Scarcely anyone challenged the basic assumptions behind this debate; the question was merely one of methods. Here also there was a broad area of overlap between the Nazis and their opponents, including the women's movement. The Nazis' insistence on the raising of birth rate, their 'eugenic' policy of weeding out 'unfit elements' from the reproductive process, their attempts to raise the status of the mother, their belief in encouraging abortion in the case where the foetus or father was thought to be 'racially inferior', their attack on contraception, their enthusiasm for 'racial hygiene' and 'population policy' *(Rassenhygiene and Bevölkerungspolitik)*—all these were shared to a significant degree by the women's movement and by all parties to the right of the SPD. They had been made familiar to the public at large in countless conferences, debates, articles and books since before the war.[64] Even the attack on syphilis which occupies such a prominent place in Hitler's *Mein Kampf* that it has led some commentators to think that there were personal reasons behind it, would not have appeared at all remarkable to a readership that had followed the pre-war publicity of the Society for the Suppression of Veneral Diseases,[65] the wartime debate on population policy or the political discussions culminating in the Law Against Veneral Diseases passed in 1927.[66]

Just to confuse matters further, the Nazi Party was not uniform or consistent in its anti-feminist attitudes before 1933. Some Nazis, for example, gave considerable support to ideas of female equality and emancipation. Gregor Strasser declared early in 1932 that 'the working woman has equality of status in the National Socialist State, and has the same right to security as the married woman and mother.'[67] And Alfred Rosenberg wrote in his *Myth of the Twentieth Century:* 'The woman belongs deeply to the total life of the people. All educational opportunities must remain open to her. . . . Nor should any difficulties be created for her in the vocational world under present-day social conditions.'[68] 'Of course', said the party in an official statement issued in March 1933, 'we unconditionally recognize women as the completely equal companions of men in political life.'[69] In July 1933, Frau Goebbels, wife of the Propaganda Minister, told an English woman journalist 'that the accounts printed in England about the expulsion of women from their jobs are highly exaggerated. The German woman has been excluded from only three professions: the military (as is the case all over the world), government, and the practice of law.'[70] In 1936 Hitler himself claimed that 'an unlimited range of work opportunities exists for women. . . . I am often told: You want to drive women out of the professions. Not at all.'[71]

Of course, these statements were made for reasons of expediency as well as, or perhaps even rather than, reasons of doctrine or ideology. The party's claim that it regarded women as the equal companions of men in political life was made in response to a questionnaire issued by the BDF for the 'orientation' of its members in the spring elections of 1933, so it is hardly surprising that the party's response was a positive one.[72] Frau Goebbels' statement to the English woman journalist was obviously designed to reassure a segment of foreign opinion that was clearly thought by the Nazis to be particularly concerned about the status of women. And the concern voiced by Hitler and Rosenberg about the 'work opportunities' open to women stems from a period, in the mid-to-late 1930s, when an acute and rapidly worsening labour shortage in the German economy was forcing the authorities of the Third Reich actively to encourage women to enter the labour force, to train as skilled workers, and to take university degrees as a preparation for professional and managerial work.[73] Such statements, particularly those, like Strasser's, issued before the seizure of power, must have made it even more difficult for female electors to distinguish Nazi policies on women from those of other parties and movements.

What the Nazis did offer, above all, was the prospect of actually putting such policies into effect. The dynamism and extremism of the NSDAP, its emphasis on 'smashing the system', backed up by constant marches, parades and demonstrations in the streets, created a popular image of a movement that was seriously bent on making an end to the tame compromises on which Weimar politics so often depended. Moreover, in the early 1930s the party increasingly identified potentially receptive groups in the population and 'targeted' them for a special propaganda effort.[74] In 1932 this technique was extended by the party organizer Gregor Strasser to include women. The Nazi women's organization (NS-*Frauenschaft)* was given greater prominence, leading members were given a more important role in propaganda, and pro-Nazi leaders of far-right women's organizations, such as Elsbeth Zander and Guida Diehl, who claimed the allegiance of hundreds of thousands of women, were co-opted in the party's drive to get female support.[75] The views of such women were certainly rather unorthodox from a Nazi point of view; as Claudia Koonz has shown, they could even be described as 'feminist', to the extent that they claimed women's right to control their own sphere of activity, although this was to be rigidly separated from that of men. Indeed, on the fall of Gregor Strasser and in the following months of the Nazi seizure of power they were quickly brought to order, disciplined or removed from positions of power.[76] Nevertheless, there is no doubt that the Nazis put a big effort into winning the female vote in 1932, and were aware, of course, that the female electorate included millions of working women who did not want to lose their jobs. Unmarried working women made up 19 per cent of the electorate, and were worth cultivating. But 71 per cent of the female voters conceived of themselves primarily as housewives;[77] and it is this majority which, doubtless, provided the bulk of the Nazis' female votes. They did not vote for the Nazis because they promised a return to the home: they were already there. It is time, therefore, to turn back to the majority of the female electorate and to ask precisely how far they supported the Nazis, and why.

IV

Fortunately for the historian, the statisticians of the Weimar Republic were driven to satisfy their intellectual curiosity about the effects of the female suffrage introduced in 1918 by persuading the responsible officials to count men's votes and women's votes separately, so that the differences between them could be satisfactorily ascertained. Unfortunately for the historian, this was done only in a limited number of districts and localities, so that the picture is incomplete. But usable results did emerge from the exercise. They can be grouped together roughly under five headings: percentage poll, support for Hitler, support for the NSDAP, support for other parties, and voting patterns among different groups of female voters.[78]

First, as far as the percentage poll is concerned, in comparison with men, a relatively high percentage of women voted in the 1919 elections. Because political tension was running high, all the parties made a special effort to get women to the polls, women were keen to use their newly acquired rights, and many younger men were still under arms or outside Germany as prisoners of war. In subsequent elections women's participation fell sharply. In Catholic areas such as Cologne it could be as much as 10–14 per cent lower than men's, and among older women the percentage poll fell even more sharply, being about 20 per cent behind men's in the over-seventy age group. In Protestant areas such as Leipzig, Magdeburg or Nuremberg the difference was less marked, at around 4 or 5 per cent in the late 1920s. In the crucial period of the Nazis' success, in 1930–2, as the overall percentage poll climbed, the difference narrowed; although in July 1932 it was still 14 per cent in Cologne, in Protestant areas it had diminished substantially. Overall, the available samples show that the 14 per cent difference between the male and female percentage poll in the first Reichstag election of 1924 had narrowed to 6 per cent by 1930. By 1930–2 women formed not merely a majority in the electorate, but assuming the differences continued to narrow, a majority of voters as well.[79]

The idea that Hitler had some special personal attraction for women is revealed, secondly, as a myth by the figures for the elections in which he stood as an individual candidate for the Reich Presidency. Women voters preferred the venerable Hindenburg, and it was not least thanks to them that he came out as victor both in 1925 and in 1932, with, respectively, 58 per cent and 56 per cent of the female vote in the run-off. In the first ballot of the presidential election in 1932, in fact, Hindenburg got 52 per cent of the female vote and 44 per cent of the male, compared to 27 per cent of the female and 28 per cent of the male voters who supported Hitler, so had it been left up to women to decide, Hitler would have been defeated on the first ballot.[80] Indeed Hitler proved less popular with women than his party did, for, to move on to the third point, although the Nazi Party too was less popular with women than with men for most of the Weimar elections, the gap narrowed in the crucial years 1930–2. In Bavaria the Nazi vote increased by 199 per cent among men and 231 per cent among women from 1928 to 1930, and from 1930 to July 1932 the difference between male and female support for the Nazis fell from 4.3 per cent to 3.6 per cent in Cologne, continuing to drop till it was only 1 per cent in the March election of 1933. In the 1930 Reichstag election 52 per cent of Nazi voters in Berlin were women, 51 per cent in Leipzig, 42 per cent in Cologne, and 58 per cent in Frankfurt-am-Main—figures which indicated the varying sex-ratio of the population of these cities as well as varying voter preferences. According to Jürgen Falter, some 42 per cent of Nazi voters in the 1928 elections were women; by 1930 the proportion had increased to 49 per cent overall. By the July elections of 1932, the Nazis were gaining a higher percentage of the female vote in Protestant areas than the male—2.6 per cent more in Magdeburg, 1.0 per cent more in Bremen, 0.7 per cent more in Wiesbaden.[81]

The most striking difference between men's and women's votes lay in the differing support they gave to other parties, most notably to the Catholic Centre Party, which invariably got a high proportion of the female vote: 35 per cent in Cologne in the first Reichstag election of 1932 as compared to 21 per cent of the male vote. 64 per cent of Centre Party voters in Cologne and Berlin were women in the 1930 Reichstag election, and 60 per cent in Leipzig. Women were also inclined to support other parties with a religious orientation, such as the Protestant DNVP, 61 per cent of whose voters in Leipzig in 1930 were women. The Catholic preference in particular affected the Nazi party, which before the early 1930s had an anti-religious image; and one political scientist has calculated that while the Centre Party gained 12 seats in the Reichstag from the women's vote in 1928, and the DNVP 9, the Nazis lost 4 (and the Communists 8). Religious factors were clearly very important in influencing the female vote, in Protestant as well as the Catholic areas, though it was noticeable that while the Catholic vote held up well in 1932, the Protestant vote—for the DNVP and DVP in particular—mostly went over to the Nazis. So the NSDAP was gaining not only first-time, or long-dormant, women voters, it was also gaining women voters from other parties, although not, it seems likely, to any greater extent than they were gaining men, since there is some evidence that female voting choice was a little more stable than male.[82]

Balancing out all these factors is made even more complicated by other divisions within the female electorate which had a powerful influence, is particular, on whether or not women actually voted. The fragmentary nature of the evidence makes it difficult to do more than advance a few tentative hypotheses, but one important factor must have been the markedly low turnout of women voters in small towns and country districts, where—at least in Protestant areas—the Nazi vote was often especially strong, and where women were potentially important in electoral terms by sheer weight of numbers. In Hesse, in the Reichstag elections of 1928, 30 per cent more men than women electors in communities of under 2,000 inhabitants went to the polls; in communities of 2,000 to 5,000 the difference shrunk to 15 per cent in communities of over 5,000 it was only 11 per cent. In Saxony in 1922, indeed, 79 per cent of women in towns voted (5 per cent fewer than men), but only 58 per cent of women in the countryside (22 per cent fewer than men). Even if, as seems likely, the gap narrowed in 1930–3, some difference almost certainly remained. By contrast the percentage poll of all female occupational groups (including housewives, widows and living-in daughters) seems to have been about the same—except for domestic servants, who were about 12 per cent less inclined to vote than the norm, and prostitutes, who apparently hardly bothered to vote at all.[83]

In sum, four conclusions seem to emerge from the available figures. First, women's numerical preponderance in the electorate was to some extent diminished by their reluctance to vote. Even though this reluctance declined, both absolutely and in relation to men, in 1928–32 it still remained, and was made more important by being more marked in the kind of rural and small-town districts where the Nazis often had their greatest electoral successes. Secondly, women were less inclined to vote for the Nazis than men were, and here too, though the gap narrowed in 1928–32, it does not seem in general to have been overcome, certainly not in Catholic areas. Thirdly, women voters were more inclined to vote for the Nazi Party than they were for Hitler (e.g. in the Presidential election of 1932), thus suggesting that the appeal of the NSDAP to women voters was not principally exerted through the person of its leader. Fourthly, the Nazis did make proportionately greater gains among women, especially Protestant women, from 1928–32. Protestants made up two-thirds of the population of Weimar Germany, so since the Nazis got more support from women than from men in Protestant areas by 1932, and since women constituted a substantial majority of the electorate, it seems reasonable to suppose that women formed a small majority of Nazi voters in the crucial elections of July and November 1932. If, to make an educated guess, perhaps 51 per cent of Nazi voters were women, that would mean that just over 7 million voted for the NSDAP in July 1932, or half a million more than some historians have estimated.[84]. This is hardly enough to have made a really major difference to the party's fortunes under a system of proportional representation.

The relatively minor differences that existed between male and female voting patterns suggest that the great majority of women voted along the same lines as men, and for much the same reasons. German women were believed to have little interest in the world outside the home. Those few women who did take an active part in politics, in the Reichstag, in provincial diets and in local councils, almost invariably concerned themselves exclusively with 'women's questions'. and took no part in the discussion of more general political issues.[85] Similarly, it was assumed that when they voted, what concerned them most were the same narrow issues—above all, perhaps, the problem of food prices in the shops. Yet we should be wary of making a similar assumption ourselves in discussing women's attitudes towards the Nazis. Implicit in the argument that women voted for Hitler because he promised to lead them back to the security of the nursery and the kitchen sink is the assumption that women did not take any other issues into consideration when they voted. Men might vote on the great issues of the day—foreign policy, economic revival, constitutional change, social stabilization—but women (it is implied) were blind to all this, perhaps incapable of understanding it. Instead, they voted purely on the kind of future which the various parties offered them as women.[86] Yet in the elections of 1930–3, the female vote behaved, in general, in roughly the same way as the male vote. The DVP, DNVP, DDP (*Staatspartei*) and splinter groups lost almost all their female support, just as they lost almost all their male support. The female support of the Centre held more or less firm, as did the party's male support; the SPD lost a little, the KPD gained quite considerably, the respective decline and increase being (proportionately) roughly the same in both sexes; and the Nazi Party increased by leaps and bounds up to the first Reichstag election of 1932, drawing its new voters in approximately though not precisely equal proportions from both sexes. The obvious inference to make, therefore, is that the same factors were responsible for the change in voting patterns in both sexes. A great many of those women who voted Nazi in 1932–3 very probably did so because the male head of their household voted Nazi. This was particularly likely in the urban and rural petty bourgeoisie, where support for the Nazis was strongest, where female members of the family were least likely to have gained economic independence from the male head of the household, and were most likely still to be 'family assistants', accustomed to obeying the dictates of the *Familienvater* in the family workshop, farm or retailing business.[87] The characteristic belief of the Nazis that women knew nothing of politics further indicated that when it came to voting, male Nazi supporters would tend to insist that the female members of the household would put the crosses in the same boxes as they did. Millions of women voters were of course unmarried, divorced, or—especially—widowed, but they too voted more along class lines and by relgous, regional, town or country domicile, and so on, than along lines laid down by the parties' policies on women's issues.

Class, sex and religious divisions were not separate in Weimar Germany, but intersected in a number of ways. As we have seen, lower-middle-class housewives were quite likely to have been prominent among those women compelled to go out to work because their husbands were unemployed or their businesses were in difficulties. Most working-class women were probably working outside the home already, expected to do so, and were correspondingly less inclined to seek a return to the home. Women were prominent among a number of groups who gave disproportionate support to the Nazis, for example, older people on small pensions who feared a loss of income if the Depression continued. Many middle-class housewives, too, must have been desperate at the thought of making ends meet as family income fell. Conversely, Catholic women owed their allegiance to the church not least because of the network of social institutions with which it provided the basis for female sociability outside the home, and this network in turn supported the Catholic vote in its tendency to go to the Centre Party; this was true even in industrial districts where their menfolk voted Social Democrat or Communist, although here the rival cultural milieu of the labour movement offered many working-class women an alternative which led them towards the SPD and KPD.[88] These complex cross-currents of different social factors are only just beginning to be explored, but already it is clear that to assign the women's vote purely to parties' policies on women's issues is an over-simplification. The Nazis won support fundamentally because they were able to appeal to the many different sectors of the population who for varying reasons wanted the Republic and its guarantors, the Social Democrats, destroyed, but in a way that would not open the situtation up to a Communist revolution. It was for such reasons that women voted Nazi, rather than because they were seeking a return to the home, even though for a minority of them such a desire was most probably one of the factors they took into consideration when making their choice.

V

The Nazis may have owed at least some of their electoral success among men, and more generally in rural and small-town districts, to their anti-feminist image and their unceasing attacks on the feminist movement and the 'modern woman'. It is doubtful whether, as Bridenthal has claimed, the new jobs being created for women in the Weimar Republic were any more publicly conspicuous than those of the Imperial period, when thousands of women factory workers, domestic servants and other employees were seen daily on the streets of Germany's great cities. The new developments of the 1920s had a more direct effect; the growth of female white-collar employment, the spreading practice and effectiveness of family limitation, and the increasing financial and social independence of unmarried girls in their late teens and twenties from their parents and families, were all concentrated in the big cities, most of all in Berlin. Rapid social changes such as these threatened the male-dominated structure of the family in peasant farming, handicrafts and small-scale family businesses, where the male head of the household relied on the help of the female members of his family to keep the business going. In the case of peasant agriculture, too, the widespread survival and even predominance of old-established social structures, customs and attitudes in peasant areas into the Weimar Republic must have made new social developments in the great cities seem even more strange and reprehensible to the small-scale peasant farmer and the pious peasant woman of the older generation. Here were further inducements to people in these categories to pay especial attention to the anti-feminist propaganda of the Nazis and to give their support—as we know they did in Protestant areas at least—in especially large numbers to Hitler at the ballot box.[89]

Yet the Nazis did not merely offer a conservative blend of family and sexual policies in which they wanted women to return to their 'traditional' role in the family. Although it was by no means clear to those middle-class conservatives and liberals—including the feminists—who continued to stress the sanctity of the family, to frown on abortion and contraception, to insist on the sacred character of marriage, and to stigmatize illegitimacy and unmarried motherhood, the Nazi movement did not share the conventional view of the family as a vitally important instrument of education and socialization. Indeed, the Third Reich reduced its function in this respect to almost negligible proportions by its insistence on the male group or *Männerbund* as the primary influence on the character of the male child, and its creation of institutions, such as the Hitler Youth, designed to put this belief into practice. The Nazis' hostility to the 'bourgeois family' was expressed in theoretical works such as Horst Becker's *Die Familie,* where it was attacked because it created and furthered 'private' values and allegiances. Becker looked instead to an idealized peasant family of the past, a 'working community' led by the father and taking a full part (through him) in the work life of the people. The value-orientation of the 'peasant family', it was argued, was public and national, rather than private and personal.[90] It was probably within this institutional, 'tribal' framework that Hitler later thought of introducing practices such as polygamy. Here too his ideas looked back to those of pre-war right-wing extremists such as the militarist Colonel Max Bauer and the *völkisch* utopian Willibald Hentschel,[91] both of whom attacked the conventional bourgeois marriage and advocated polygamy. But others of the Nazis' policies, notably the equalization of the status of the unmarried mother and the establishment of eugenic rather than Christian or moral criteria for reaching decisions in matters such as abortion, contraception, motherhood and marriage, can be traced to groups such as Helene Stöcker's *Bund für Mutterschutz* which stood to the left of the women's movement and were rejected by it as too radical.[92] They certainly were in no sense 'traditional'.

The Third Reich laid bare a real contradiction between the Nazis' sentimental idealization of the family on the one hand, and their ruthless pursuit of eugenic success and masculinization of the process of education and socialization on the other. The more the Nazis stressed the virtues of a stable family life, the more they took away from the family all its most important functions, including even (towards the end of the Third Reich) the production of children. Nor was this simply a case of attempting to cover up the undermining of the family as a public institution by a cynical propaganda campaign designed to persuade people that the party still considered the family to be important. The very real nature of the contradiction between the familial and eugenic aims of the Third Reich was shown by the fact that the Nazi government poured considerable amounts of money into family allowances as well as (during the war) investing funds in schemes such as Himmler's *Lebensborn* project. Similarly, the attempt to equalize the status of unmarried mothers took place at the same time as a massive effort to persuade more women to marry.[93] Even more serious for the Third Reich as a whole were the contradictions implicit in the Nazis' attempt to provide social stability at home as an essential prerequisite of successful war abroad. Fear of 'another' 'stab in the back' prompted from the regime a whole series of practical relief measures and cash allowances to non-working married women designed to reassure the men at the front that their families at home were not suffering in any way because of the war. These measures had the effect of taking women out of the labour market at a time when the labour shortage was already threatening to cripple Germany's war effort before it had really begun.[94] The attempts by the Nazis to mobilize women *voluntarily* by means of propaganda—which was, however, much less vigorous than its US counterpart—merely served to introduce yet further contradictions into the picture.[95]

It is this inherently contradictory and irrational character of

Nazi policies towards women that makes it difficult, if not impossible, to ascribe these policies and ideas to any one single cause. Tim Mason, for example, is undoubtedly right when he points out that the protective attitude of the Nazis towards women, the generous allowances to the wives of soldiers fighting at the front, and the persistent reluctance of the Nazis at all levels to order the full mobilization of women for the war effort, were due to a large extent to the fear of creating discontent among male heads of households and so possibly arousing their opposition to the regime. Yet it is rather more doubtful whether—as he asserts—the Nazis' policies towards women can be explained by the fact that the more brutally competitive 'public' life becomes, at work and in society and the state, the more importance the family gains as 'both the refuge from the compulsions of work and the unquestionable good for the sake of which the public sphere is endured'.[96] One of the features of the Nazi state was its 'totalitarian' tendency to wipe out the boundaries between public and private life, and to politicize every aspect of the individual's existence.[97] Thus the family, for the Nazis, became as public an institution as the state, and as such tended further to lose its unique significance and become simply one institution among many. It was this attitude which enabled the Nazis to bypass the family to an ever-increasing extent in the pursuit of their eugenic and educational aims. Even women were organized to a greater and greater extent outside the family. The great mass of women were organized in the huge official women's organization, the *Deutsches Frauenwerk,* while specific groups were gathered together in specialist societies such as the *Bund deutscher Mädel,* for young girls, the *Mutterschule* for pregnant women, and so on.[98] This was in marked contrast to the ideas of conservative anti-feminists, who considered that women had no place in organizations of any sort outside the home. The Nazis certainly followed this line as far as abolishing all separate women's organizations with professional, social or political aims concerned with problems which arose outside the home. But they also went further and tried to take away from the female members of the family their previous functions of teaching young women the ABC of household management, pregnancy and childbirth. As time went on, women came to resist this politicization of the family. The stage was set for the 'retreat into the home' and the cult of domesticity which was such a central feature of German social and political life in the two decades following the collapse of the Third Reich in 1945.

NOTES

This chapter is based on my article 'German women and the triumph of Hitler', *Journal of Modern History*, vol. 48, no. 1 (March, 1976).

1. Quoted in Helen Boak, 'Women in Weimar Germany: the "Frauenfrage" and the female vote', in Richard Bessel and E. J. Feuchtwanger (eds), *Social Change and Political Development in Weimar Germany* (London, 1981), p. 155.
2. Hermann Rauschning, *Hitler Speaks. A Series of Political Conversations with Adolf Hitler on his Real Aims* (London, 1939), p. 259.
3. The best basic narratives are still Karl Dietrich Bracher, *Die Auflösung der Weimarer Republik* (Cologne, 1954) and Karl Dietrich Bracher, Wolfgang Sauer, Gerhard Schulz, *Die nationalsozialistische Machtergreifung* (3 vols, Cologne, 1954–6).
4. These rough-and-ready estimates are based on *Statistisches Jahrbuch für das deutsche Reich*, 51 (1932), p. 541, and *ibid.*, 54 (1935), p. 11. Curiously, no serious attempt seems to have been made to calculate the absolute number of women who voted for the Nazis in July 1932. The figure of 6.5 million given by Jill Stephenson's very useful survey of the current state of knowledge in 'National Socialism and women before 1933', in Peter D. Stachura (ed.), *The Nazi Machtergreifung* (London, 1983), pp. 33–48 (here p. 38), appears to be based on halving the total Nazi vote, which itself is underestimated by Stephenson at 13.0 instead of the true figure of 13.75 million. Recent works on the Nazi vote by Thomas Childers, *The Nazi Voter. The Social Foundations of Fascism in Germany 1919–1933* (Chapel Hill, 1983) and Richard Hamilton, *Who Voted for Hitler?* (Princeton, 1983), pay little attention to sex as an independent variable, perhaps because the fragmentary nature of the evidence for the female vote does not allow it to be built into their statistical analysis. The absence of any real discussion of female voting preference seriously limits the value of their work as a contribution to our understanding of the rise of the Nazi Party. Jürgen Falter, 'Die Wähler der NSDAP 1928–1933: Sozialstruktur und parteipolitische Herkunft', in Wolfgang Michalka (ed.), *Die nationalsozialistische Machtergreifung* (Paderborn, 1984), pp. 47–59, has a brief, though very general discussion of the question.
5. Quoted in Clifford Kirkpatrick, *Nazi Germany: its Women and Family Life* (New York, 1938), p. 110.
6. Quoted in George L. Mosse, *Nazi Culture: Intellectual, Cultural and*

Social Life in the Third Reich (New York, 1966), pp. 30–47.
7. Josef Goebbels, *Michael: Ein Deutsches Schicksal in Tagebuchlättern* (Munich, 1934), p. 41, quoted in Richard Grunberger, *A Social History of the Third Reich* (Harmondsworth, 1974), p. 322.
8. Ingeborg Weber-Kellermann, *Die deutsche Familie. Versuch einer Sozialgeschichte* (Frankfurt-am-Main, 1974), pp. 178–85.
9. Adolf Hitler, *Mein Kampf* (trans. Ralph Manheim, ed. D. C. Watt, London, 1969), p. 167.
10. Mosse, *op. cit.*, p. 215.
11. StA Hbg, PP, S9001/I: cutting of *Die Post* (20 March 1902), for Bülow's claim that he supported the emancipation of women.
12. *Hammer*, no. 158 (15 January 1909).
13. Hans Blüher, *Der bürgerliche und der geistige Antifeminismus* (3rd edn, 1920). For Blüher, see G. L. Mosse, *The Crisis of German Ideology. Intellectual Origins of the Third Reich* (London, 1966), pp. 172–8.
14. Michael H. Kater, in his article 'Krisis des Frauenstudiums in der Weimarer Republik', *Vierteljahrschrift für Sozial und Wirtschaftsgeschichte*, 59 (1972), 2, pp. 207–55 (here pp. 247–8) suggests that Hitler's anti-feminism (in the sense of opposition to women's engagement in politics) derived from Lanz von Liebenfels (cf. Wilfried Daim, *Der Mann, der Hitler die Ideen gab*, Munich, 1958). This, however, is rather doubtful. For the 'national opposition', see Dirk Stegmann, *Die Erben Bismarcks. Parteien und Verbände in der Spätphase des wilhelminischen Deutschlands* (Cologne Berlin, 1970). For the connections between the 'national opposition' and the emergent Nazi movement, see Dirk Stegmann, 'Zwischen Repression und Manipulation: Konservative Machteliten und Arbeiter- und Angestelltenbewegung 1910–1918. Ein Beitrag zur Vorgeschichte der DAP/NSDAP', *Archiv für Sozialgeschichte*, XII (1972), pp. 351–432. For a fully documented analysis of the 'Anti-League', see my *The Feminist Movement in Germany 1894–1933* (London, 1976), pp. 175–87.
15. The DHV provided bouncers and stewards for the Anti-League's meeting.
16. P.J.P. Pulzer, *The Rise of Political Anti-Semitism in Germany and Austria* (New York/London, 1964), ch.23.
17. Ludwig Langemann, *Frauenstimmrecht und Frauenemanzipation* (Berlin, 1916).
18. W. Heinemann, *Die radikale Frauenbewegung als nationale Gefahr!* (Berlin, 1913).
19. There is now a substantial literature on Nazi attitudes to women, and on German women in the Third Reich. For useful introductions in English, see Jill R. Stephenson, *Women in Nazi Germany* (London, 1975); Jill R. Stephenson, *The Nazi Organization of Women* (London, 1981); Renate Bridenthal, Atina Grossmann and Marion Kaplan (eds), *When Biology Became Destiny: Women in Weimar and Nazi Germany* (New York, 1984). In German, see Annette Kuhn and Valentine Rothe, *Frauen im dritten Reich* (2 vols, Düsseldorf, 1982); Dorothea Klinksiek, *Die Frau*

im NS-Staat (Munich, 1982); Frauengruppe Faschismus, (ed.), *Mutterkreuz und Arbeitsbuch. Zur Geschichte der Frauen in der Weimar Republik und im Nationalsozialismus* (Frankfurt, 1981).

20. Richard Grunberger, *A Social History of the Third Reich* (Harmondsworth, 1974), chs. 16–17; Joachim C. Fest, *The Face of the Third Reich* (Harmondsworth, 1972), pp. 397–414.

21. See Stephenson, *The Nazi Organisation of Women,* and Claudia Koonz, 'The competition for women's *Lebensraum, 1928–1934',* in Bridenthal *et al.* (eds), *When Biology Became Destiny,* pp. 199–236.

22. Quoted in Boak, *op. cit.,* p. 155.

23. Rauschning, *op. cit.,* p. 250.

24. Fest, *op. cit.,* p. 401.

25. Grunberger, *op. cit.,* p. 117.

26. William L. Shirer, *Berlin Diary* (London, 1970), pp. 22–3.

27. Fest, *loc. cit.*

28. Albert Zoller, *Hitler privat* (Düsseldorf, 1949), quoted in Fest, *loc. cit.*

29. Fest, *op. cit.,* p. 402.

30. Joachim C. Fest, *Hitler* (London, 1974), pp. 323–4.

31. Adolf Hitler, *Mein Kampf,* trans. Ralph Manheim, ed. D.C. Watt (London, 1969), p. 167.

32. Hermann Graml, 'Zur neuen Hitler-Biographie von Joachim C. Fest', *Vierteljahreshefte fur Zeitgeschichte* (1974), no.1.

33. Alfred Stein, 'Adolf Hitler and Gustave le Bon', *Geschichte in Wissenschaft und Unterricht,* 6 (1955), pp. 362–8. The point that Hitler's ideas on propaganda were no more original than the other ideas outlined in *Mein Kampf* still stands, however.

34. Robert A. Nye, *The Origins of Crowd Psychology: Gustave le Bon and the Crisis of Mass Democracy in the Third Republic,* SAGE Studies in 20th century History, vol.2 (London, 1975), p. 179.

35. Fest, *Face of the Third Reich,* pp. 323–4.

36. J.A.C. Brown, *Techniques of Persuasion. From Propaganda to Brainwashing* (Harmondsworth, 1963), p. 111, note. Dr Brown's analysis leans heavily on Rauschning's work.

37. Konrad Heiden, *Adolf Hitler. Eine Biographie,* vol.I, *Das Zeitalter der Verantwortungslosigkeit* (Zurich, 1936), pp. 324 ff.

38. Richard Bessel, 'The rise of the NSDAP and the myth of Nazi propaganda', *Wiener Library Bulletin,* 33 (1980), pp. 20–9.

39. Renate Bridenthal, 'Beyond *Kinder, Küche, Kirche:* Weimar women at work', *Central European History* (1973), pp. 148–66. This essay has since been republished in a revised form on more than one occasion: the latest version is Renate Bridenthal and Claudia Koonz, 'Beyond *Kinder, Küche, Kirche*: Weimar women in politics and work', in Bridenthal *et al.* (eds), *op. cit.,* pp. 33–65.

40. Irene Stoehr, 'Machtergriffen? Deutsche Frauenbewegung 1933', *Courage: Aktuelle Frauenzeitung* 8 (February 1983), pp. 24–32.

41. The Civil Law, with clauses giving the German husband ownership of his wife's property, control over the children, and so on, remained in force in West Germany at least until the passage of the *Gleichberechtigungsgesetz*

in 1956. Even this law did not establish a real situation of legal equality. See J.R. McIntyre, 'Women and the professions in Germany 1930–1940', in Anthony Nicholls and Erich Matthias (eds), *German Democracy and the Triumph of Hitler,* St Antony's Publications no.3 (London,1971), esp. pp. 175–88; Werner Thönnessen, *The Emancipation of Women. The Rise and Decline of the Women's Movement in German Social Democracy 1863–1933* (London, 1973), pp. 75–147; Jürgen Kuczynski, *Die Geschichte der Lage der Arbeiter unter dem Kapitalismus,* Bd. 18: *Studien zur Geschichte der Lage der Arbeiterin in Deutschland von 1700 bis zur Gegenwart* (East Berlin, 1963), pp. 201–68; Kater, *op. cit.*; the literature cited in notes 19 and 39 above; and Stefan Bajohr, *Die Hälfte der Fabrik. Geschichte der Frauenarbeit in Deutschland 1914–1945* (Marburg, 1979).

42. Ulrich Linse, 'Arbeiterschaft und Geburtenentwicklung im Deutschen Kaiserreich von 1871', *Archiv für Sozialgeschichte,* XII (1972), pp. 205–71; John E. Knodel, *The Decline of Fertility in Germany 1871–1939* (Princeton, 1974); Tim Mason, 'Women in Germany 1925–1940: family, welfare and work', *History Workshop: A Journal of Socialist Historians,* 1–2 (March-September 1976).

43. Helgard Kramer, 'Frankfurt's working women: scapegoats or winners of the Great Depression?' in Richard J. Evans and Dick Geary (eds), *The German Unemployed: Experiences and Consequences of Mass Unemployment in the Weimar Republic and the Third Reich* (London, 1976), chapter 5.

44. Katherine Thomas, *Women in Nazi Germany* (London, 1943), p. 20.

45. Bridenthal, *op. cit.* (1973).

46. Evans, *The Feminist Movement in Germany 1894–1933,* pp. 252–3.

47. *ibid.,* pp. 235–81.

48. *ibid.* The suggestion, in Ulrich Linse, 'Arbeiterschaft und Geburtenentwicklung im Deutschen Kaiserreich von 1871', *Archiv für Sozialgeschichte,* XII (1972), that the opposite was true, is based on a failure to consult the unpublished sources, and on a false equation of the policy of the BDF's radical Legal Commission with the policy of the BDF itself, which in fact rejected the Legal Commission's report in 1908.

49. Deutsches Zentralinstitut für Soziale Fragen, Berlin-Dahlem; Archiv des Bundes Deutscher Frauenvereine (ABDF), 5/XIII/5: Bensheimer to Stritt (18 August 1909, 11 September 1909); Bensheimer to von Forster (11 September 1909); *ibid.,* 16/II/I: Protokoll der Sitzung des Gesamtvorstandes (11 March, 13 March 1910).

50. Irmgard Remme, 'Die Internationalen Beziehungen der deutschen Frauenbewegung vom Ausgang des 19. Jahrhunderts bis 1933' (Phil. Diss., West Berlin, 1955), *passim.*

51. This estimate is based on the membership figure for the year 1930. For the problems of computing the number of women in the BDF—problems which remained essentially the same from the turn of the century until its dissolution in 1933—see Deutsches Zentralinstitut für Soziale Fragen, Berlin-Dahlem; ABDF, 4/2: cutting of *Schleswiger Nachrichten* (2 January 1914).

52. *Jahrbuch des Bundes Deutscher Frauenvereine* 1919: 'Programm'.
53. For this argument, see Evans, *op. cit.*, chapter 8.
54. *Jahrbuch des Bundes Deutscher Frauenvereine* 1919: 'Programm'.
55. For comments on the social composition of the women's movement and its leadership, see Katherine Thomas, *op. cit.*
56. *Jahrbuch . . ., loc. cit.* For comments on the significance of these words, see Pulzer, *op. cit.*, p. 219 and note.
57. Agnes von Zahn-Harnack, 'Schlussberichte über die Arbeit des Bundes Deutscher Frauenvereine', *Die Frau* (June 1933); ABDF: BDF 'Erklärung' (14 March 1933); Emmy Beckmann (ed.), *Des Lebens wie der Leibe Band. Briefe von Gertrud Bäumer* (Tübingen, 1956), pp. 50–1, 65; McIntyre, *op. cit.*, p. 186; Evans, *The Feminist Movement in Germany*, pp. 223–30.
58. Ute Gerhard, 'A hidden and complex heritage: reflections on the history of Germany's women's movements', *Women's Studies International Quarterly*, vol. 5 (1982), 6, pp. 561–7. In 'Mothers of the new generation: Adele Schreiber, Helen Stöcker, and the evolution of a German idea of motherhood, 1900–1914'. *Signs*, 10 (1985), pp. 418–38, Ann Taylor Allen attempts to criticize the argument that German feminism drifted to the right by alleging (without foundation) that it has been applied to *all* German feminists, including 'radicals' such as Helene Stöcker, who were in fact well-known pacifists; by abstracting one issue (motherhood) from the ideas of feminism as a whole (including ideas on war and peace): and by confusing different periods of time (before and after 1908).
59. Irene Stoehr, 'Machtergriffen? Deutsche Frauenbewegung 1933', pp. 24–32.
60. Regula Venske, 'Der "andere Blick"?—Frauen, Faschismus, "weiblicher Widerstand"', *Hamburger Frauenzeitung* (summer 1983). See also Gisela Bock, 'Racism and sexism in Nazi Germany: motherhood, compulsory sterilization and the state', in Renate Bridenthal, Atina Grossmann and Marion Kaplan (eds), *When Biology Became Destiny: Women in Weimar and Nazi Germany* (New York, 1984), pp. 271–96.
61. Venske, *op. cit.*
62. *Der Geburtenrückgang in Deutschland. Seine Bewertung and Bekämpfung* (Berlin, 1912).
63. Cf. Linse, *op. cit.*; and *Jahrbuch der Frauenbewegung 1916* (Leipzig/Berlin, 1916). The progress of the debate may be observed in subsequent issues of the *Jahrbuch*, and in the various periodicals devoted to *Rassenhygiene* and *Bevölkerungspolitik*. There were also a large number of societies devoted to solving this problem, e.g. *Bund der Kinderreichen, Deutsche Gesellschaft für Bevölkerungspolitik*, which frequently had their own periodicals. For various levels of government interest in the problem, see Zentrales Staatsarchiv I, Potsdam, Reichsamt des Innern 9342–6 (Massregelen gegen den Geburtenrückgang); Niedersächsisches Hauptstaatsarchiv Hannover, Hann. 122a XXXVIII Nr. 14 (Rückgang der Geburten); Stadtarchiv Frankfurt-am-Main, Magistratsakten, 531/2011 (Deutsche Gesellschaft

für Bevölkerungspolitik).

64. For full bibliographical references, see Agnes von Zahn-Harnack and Hans Sveistrup, *Die Frauenfrage in Deutschland. Strömungen und Gegenströmungen 1790–1930. Sachlich geordnete und erläuterte Quellenkunde* (2nd edn., Tübingen, 1961) and Supplements.

65. *Deutsche Gesellschaft zur Bekämpfung der Geschlechtskrankheiten.* The society published a *Zeitschrift.*

66. W. Adler (ed.), *Reichsgesetz zur Bekämpfung der Geschlechtskrankheiten* (Munich, 1929). See the *Stenographische Berichte über die Verhandlungen des Deutsche Reichstags* at various sittings over the decade 1917–27 for debates on the subject.

67. Quoted in David Schoenbaum, *Hitler's Social Revolution* (London, 1967), pp. 188–9. See Kater, *art. cit.*, for details of the Nazi left's politics towards women.

68. 1938 edition, quoted in George L. Mosse, *Nazi Culture: Intellectual, Cultural and Social Life in the Third Reich* (New York, 1966), p. 40.

69. ABDF 1/A/2: Mitteilung an die dem Bund Deutscher Frauenvereine angeschlossenen Verbände (29 March 1933), Anlage 1.

70. Quoted in Mosse, *op. cit.*, p. 42.

71. Quoted in *ibid.*, p. 39.

72. The documents are reprinted in Stoehr, *op. cit.*

73. Jill R. Stephenson, 'Women in German Society 1930–1940' (unpublished Ph.D. thesis, Edinburgh University, 1974), pp. 150 ff.; see also Jill R. Stephenson, 'Girls' higher education in Germany, 1930–1940', *Journal of Contemporary History,* January 1975.

74. Ian Kershaw, 'Ideology, propaganda and the Nazi Party', in Stachura (ed.), *op. cit.*, pp. 162–81.

75. J. Stephenson, in *ibid.*, pp. 33–48.

76. C. Koonz, in Bridenthal *et al.* (eds), *op. cit.*, pp. 199–236.

77. Hans Beyer, *Die Frau in der politischen Entscheidung. Eine Untersuchung über das Frauenwahlrecht in Deutschland* (Stuttgart, 1932), pp. 4–10 and 78–84.

78. For the fullest available analysis, see Joachim Hofmann-Götig, *Emanzipation mit dem Stimmzettel. 70 Jahre Frauenwahlrecht in Deutschland* (Bonn, 1986), pp. 27–35.

79. Gabrielle Bremme, *Die politische Rolle der Frau in Deutschland* (Göttingen, 1956), pp. 41, 231–5; Hofmann-Götig, *op. cit.*

80. *ibid.*, and Karl Dietrich Bracher, *Deutschland zwischen Demokratie und Diktatur* (Munich, 1964), pp. 50–82, here p. 67.

81. Falter, *op. cit.*; Hofmann-Götig, *op. cit.*; Boak, 'Women in Weimar Germany', in Bessel and Feuchtwanger (eds), *op. cit.*, p. 158. See also W. Philips Shively, 'Party identification, party choice, and voting stability. The Weimar case', *American Political Science Review,* lxvi (1972), 4, pp. 1203–25.

82. Bremme, *loc. cit.*; Beyer, *loc. cit.*; Hofmann-Götig, *op. cit.*

83. Bremme, *op. cit.*, pp. 45, 63; Beyer, *loc. cit.*; Hofmann-Götig, *op. cit.*

84. Cf. note 4, above.

85. Bremme, *op. cit.*

86. Feminist historians have recently taken up this view, but without offering any evidence to substantiate it. See for example the contribution by Atina Grossmann in Ernst Bornemann (ed.), *Arbeiterbewegung und Feminismus. Berichte aus vierzehn Ländern* (Frankfurt, 1982–4, 2 vols).
87. Cf. Mason, 'Women in Germany'.
88. Brian Peterson, 'The politics of working-class women in the Weimar Republic', *Central European History*, X (June 1977), 2, pp. 87–111.
89. Cf. Mason, *op. cit.*
90. Horst Becker, *Die Familie* (Leipzig, 1935), quoted in Weber-Kellermann, *op. cit.*, p. 181.
91. Bundesarchiv Koblenz, NL Bauer, 1c, 1d; Mosse, *Crisis of German Ideology*, pp. 112–16.
92. Agnes von Zahn-Harnack, *Die Frauenbewegung-Geschichte, Probleme, Ziele* (Leipzig/Berlin, 1928), pp. 35–6. This official account of the women's movement by the President of the BDF in the last years of the Weimar Republic also contains interesting indications of the BDF's attitude on other problems mentioned in this chapter.
93. Stephenson, *Women in Nazi Society*, for details. More generally, see Gisela Bock, 'Racism and sexism in Nazi Germany: motherhood, compulsory sterlization and the state', in Bridenthal *et al.* (eds), *op. cit.*, pp. 271–96.
94. T.W. Mason, 'Zur Funktion des Angriffskriegs 1939', in Gilbert Ziebura (ed.), *Grundfragen deutscher Aussenpolitik seit 1871* (Darmstadt, 1975).
95. Leila G. Rupp, *Mobilizing Women for War. German and American Propaganda 1939–1945* (Princeton, 1978).
96. Mason, 'Women in Germany'.
97. W.S. Allen, *The Nazi Seizure of Power. The Experience of a Single German Town* (2nd edn, New York, 1984).
98. Stephenson, *The Nazi Organization of Women*.

Index